Hitler
& Geli

Hitler &Geli

Ronald Hayman

BLOOMSBURY

First published in Great Britain 1997
Bloomsbury Publishing Plc, 38 Soho Square, London W1V 5DF

Copyright © 1997 by Ronald Hayman

The moral right of the author has been asserted

PICTURE SOURCES
Bildarchiv Preussischer Kulturbesitz: page 4 *top*
Bundesarchiv: pages 6, 7
David Gainsborough Roberts: pages 1, 9 *top*, 10, 11, 12, 15 *bottom*
Ronald Hayman: page 13 *top*
Süddeutscher Verlag Bilderdienst: pages 3 *top*, 14 *top*
Ullstein Bilderdienst: pages 2, 3 *bottom*, 4 *bottom*, 5, 8, 13 *bottom*, 14 *bottom*,
15 *top*, 16

A CIP catalogue record for this book
is available from the British Library

ISBN 0 7475 2723 7

10 9 8 7 6 5 4 3 2 1

Typeset by Hewer Text Composition Services, Edinburgh
Printed by Clays Ltd, St Ives Plc

CONTENTS

Credits

Perhaps this sounds less casual than 'Acknowledgements'. In movies there are always too many credits – we don't want to know who drove the trucks or cooked the food or wielded the clapper-board. But a book rarely offers any indication of the work done by the editor, the copy-editor, the designer and the dozens of other people who have made substantial contributions.

While writing *Hitler and Geli* I became indebted to many friends, acquaintances, strangers, historians, biographers, screenwriters, editors, librarians, archivists, researchers, television producers and other people who were more generous with their time (and their photocopying equipment) than I could possibly have hoped. I can't thank them all adequately.

First, I don't know how to define or delimit my indebtedness to Jan Etheredge. For about six months in 1994–5, conversations about Hitler and Geli were integral to our everyday life.

I am immensely grateful to Professor Ian Kershaw, who was kind enough to read the book twice in draft, and to make comments which were helpful; and to Dr William Dorrell and Mrs Jane Dorrell, who read it and discussed it with me. This is not to accuse them of agreeing with me.

My editor, David Reynolds, has done much more than can reasonably be expected of an editor, and I would like to thank (in chronological order of helping) Dr Dennis Friedman, Dr Ashley Grossmann, Brett Kahr, Monica Macdonald, Dr Gerhard Hirschfeld, Professor Guido Knopp, Lutz Becker, Professor Niall Ferguson, Professor Michael Burleigh, Deirdre Headon, Andrea Lowe, Elsa Kormann, Klaus A. Lankheit and Hermann Weiss of the Institut für Zeitgeschichte, Munich, Dr Kruse and Dr Weber of the Bayerisches Hauptstaatsarchiv, Ciaran Headon, David Irving, Wolfgang Wippermann, Michael Schäfer, Ernst-Ludwig Wagner, my New York editor, Scott Moyers, my London copy-editor, Esther Jagger, the New York graphologist Arlyn Imberman, and Elsie Donald.

I am grateful to D. Gainsborough Roberts for allowing me to use photographs of Geli from his collection, and to the Munich auctioneers Hermann Historica for sending a photocopy of Geli's letter to Emil Maurice and letting me quote it.

Chronology

1837: *7 June* Alois Schicklgruber born, the illegitimate son of Maria Anna Schicklgruber

1842: Maria Anna marries Johann Georg Hiedler

1847: Maria Anna dies

1860: Klara Pölzl born

1873: Alois Schicklgruber marries Anna Glassl

1876: Klara Pölzl comes to work for Alois

1877: *6 January* Alois changes his name to Alois Hitler

1880: Alois and Anna divorce

1882: Franziska Matzelsberger bears Alois an illegitimate son, Alois

1883: Anna Hitler dies; *22 May* Alois marries Franziska; *28 July* Their daughter, Angela, is born

1884: Franziska dies

1885: *7 January* Alois marries Klara Pölzl

1889: *20 April* Adolf Hitler born in Braunau, Austria

1892: *August* Family moves to Passau, Bavaria

1895: Adolf goes to school; *April* Family returns to Austria and settles in Hafeld; *25 June* Alois retires because of ill-health; *12 October* Angela moves to Vienna

1896: *21 January* Hitler's sister, Paula, is born

1897: *July* The Hitlers settle into lodgings in Lambach

1898: *January* They move into a house

1899: *February* They move to Leonding

1903: *3 January* Alois Hitler dies; *Spring* Adolf start at secondary school in Steyr, sleeping in school's boarding house; *September* During term time, Adolf lives in lodgings; *14 September* Angela marries twenty-four-year-old Leo Raubal

1905: Adolf Hitler leaves school; *June* The family move into a house in Linz

1906: *October* Adolf has piano lessons; *2 October* Angela's first child, Leo, is born

1907: *January* Klara Hitler has operation for breast cancer; *May–June* Hitler goes to Vienna; *September* He fails entrance to art academy there; *21 December* Klara Hitler dies

1908: *4 June* Angela (Geli) Raubal born in Linz; *8 August* Hitler breaks off his relationship with Angela and family

1910: *10 January* Elfriede Raubal born; *8 February* Hitler moves into men's hostel in Meldemannstrasse; *2126 June* He has five nights in a hotel; *10 August* Angela's husband, Leo, dies

1913: *25 May* Hitler moves out of hostel and, having failed to register for military service as he should have done in 1911 and 1912, leaves Vienna illegally to settle in Munich; *13 August* Polica Department of Linz magistracy starts looking for him

1914: *18 January* He is arrested for evading military service; *5 February* He fails Austrian army medical; *16 August* Enlists as a volunteer in a Bavarian reserve infantry regiment; *December* Awarded Iron Cross, second class

1918: *August* He is awarded Iron Cross, first class; *9 November* Kurt Eisner proclaims republic in Bavaria

1919: *February* Hitler chosen for army training course in agitation and public speaking; *15 April* Hitler elected as spokesman for soldiers in Bavaria's red army; *May* Bavaria's soviet government overthrown; Hitler arrested; *June* Hitler attends army political course at Munich University; Angela takes job in kitchen of Jewish students' hostel in Vienna; *August* Hitler attends course in Lechfeld; *September* He joins German Workers' Party; *November* He becomes one of its speakers

1920: *February* German Workers' Party changes its name to National Socialist German Workers' Party (*National Sozialistische Deutsche Arbeiter Partei* NSDAP); *31 March* Hitler discharged from army; *1 May* He rents a room at 43 Thierschstrasse; NSDAP acquires the *Münchener Beobachter*, which becomes *Völkischer Beobachter*

1921: *29 July* Hitler elected first president of NSDAP

1923: *January* French and Belgian troops occupy the Ruhr; Chancellor, Wilhelm Cuno, calls for passive resistance; NSDAP holds first rally in Munich; *89 November* Unsuccessful putsch; *9 November* NSDAP and *Völkischer Beobachter* banned; *11 November* Hitler arrested

1924: *26 February–1 April* Trial; *1 April* Hitler sentenced to five years' imprisonment; *June* He starts work on *Mein Kampf*; *17 June* Angela, her son Leo and her daughter Geli visit him in prison; *20 December* His sentence is remitted

1925: *26 February* NSDAP refounded and *Völkischer Beobachter* revived; *27 February* Hitler speaks at a meeting; *9 March* He is banned from public speaking in Bavaria and Prussia; *26 April* Hindenburg elected President of the Republic; *Summer* Hitler goes to Bayreuth Festival as guest of the Bechsteins

1926: *Summer* Hitler's liaison with Maria Reiter; *October* Angela leaves the girls' hostel

1927: *3 March* Angela starts working as housekeeper for her half-brother in Haus Wachenfeld, Obersalzberg; *5 March* Ban lifted in Bavaria Hitler can make speeches; *9 March* He addresses a meeting in Munich; *Summer* Hitler fetches Geli from Vienna; *19–21 August* Party rally in Nuremberg; *October* Geli settles into the Pension Klein, Königinstrasse 43, Munich; *7 November* She registers as a medical student at Munich University; *Winter* She breaks off her studies

1928: *28 May* In Reichstag elections NSDAP gets 2.6 per cent of the votes, gaining twelve seats; *5 August* Geli moves into house belonging to Hitler's neighbour in Thierschstrasse, Adolf Vogl

1929: *10 September* Hitler rents a nine-room flat in Prinzregentenplatz; *Early October* He meets Eva Braun; *October* He meets Brüning; *29 October* Wall Street Crash; *5 November* Geli moves into Hitler's flat

1930: *1 March* Horst Wessel's funeral

1931: *18 September* Geli found dead in Prinzregentenplatz flat with a bullet wound near her heart; *19 or 20 September* Geli's body taken to East Cemetery, Munich; *21 September* Body released for burial; articles in newspaper prompt police to order a further investigation; *23 September* Geli buried in Central Cemetery, Vienna; *24 September* Hitler makes a speech in Hamburg; *28 September* Police report presented to Ministry of the Interior; *10 October* Hitler's first meeting with Hindenburg

1932: *February* Hitler becomes a German citizen and is appointed attaché to Brunswick Legation in Berlin; *March* As candidate for presidency he wins over 30 per cent of vote; *June* Ban on SA and SS is lifted; *July* NSDAP becomes strongest party in Reichstag, with 230 of 608 seats; *August* Hitler rejects and invitation to become Vice-Chancellor; *2 December* Schleicher appointed Chancellor

1933: *January* Hitler, Hess and Himmler meet Papen to plan future; *28 January* Schleicher's government resigns; *30 January* Hindenburg invites Hitler to be Chancellor

Hitler's Family Tree

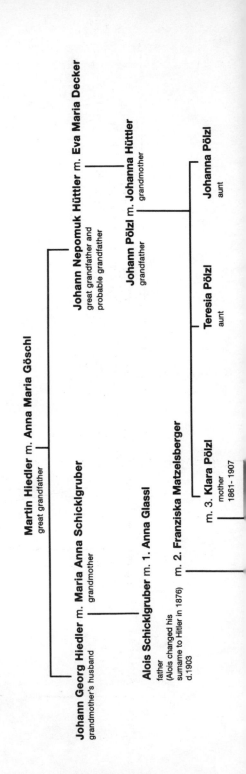

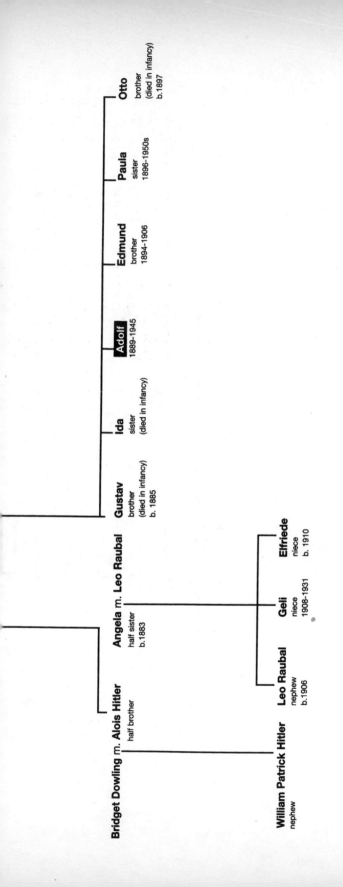

Prologue: Hitler in Love

In 1927, when Hitler rented a house for the first time, he was nearly thirty-eight. Previously, he had never even had his own flat. Since July 1921 he had been leader of a political party, the National Socialist German Workers' Party (NSDAP), but had cared more about having an impressive car than a comfortable room. During boyhood he had seven homes – one in Germany, the rest in Austria – as his father, a customs officer, got promoted and posted to different places, sometimes settling his family into lodgings, sometimes buying a house.

Only thirteen when his father died in 1903, Hitler had a brief spell of living in a school boarding house, and one in a house with his mother and sister. He spent seven years in Vienna (1907–13), four of them in a furnished room and three in a hostel for men. His six years in the army (1914–20) were divided between France, where he was at the front, and Munich, where he was living in barracks. In 1913, when he tried to settle in Munich, his first home was above a tailor's shop in Schleissheimerstrasse, and after being discharged from the army he lived as sub-tenant of a small, shabby one-room flat in Thierschstrasse. He kept it on for about nine years. No one could have been in less of a hurry to achieve domestic stability.

Nor had he kept in touch with the surviving members of his family. He had nothing to do with his half-brother, Alois, who was seven years older, and little to do with his widowed half-sister, Angela, or even with his younger sister, Paula, who never married. But now, having found himself a house, he invited Angela to be his housekeeper. On 3 March 1927, at the age of forty-three, she started working for him.

Of her three children, the eldest, her son, stayed in Austria, but her two daughters were coming to Germany, so Hitler, though anything but a family man, would once again have members of the family around him.

Ernst Hanfstaengl, one of the few friends allowed to see the inside of Hitler's room in Thierschstrasse, said he had been living there 'like a down-at-heels clerk'. The room had a fair-sized entrance hall, but

> it was all modest in the extreme and he remained there for years, although it became part of an act to show how he identified himself with the workers and have-nots of the world. The room itself was tiny. I doubt if it was nine feet wide. The bed was too wide for its corner and the head of it projected over the single narrow window. The floor was covered with cheap, worn linoleum with a couple of threadbare rugs, and on the wall opposite the bed there was a makeshift bookshelf, apart from a chair and a rough table the only other piece of furniture in the room . . . Hitler used to walk around in carpet slippers, frequently with no collar to his shirt and wearing braces.[1]

Friends rarely came for tea, but when they did, he produced 'a blue and white teapot and cups from certainly long-since-broken sets. Everything was very primitive.'[2]

The house he rented in 1927 was in Obersalzberg, a small Alpine village not far from the Austrian border. Angela had been widowed only a few months after the birth of her younger daughter. The elder, who was now almost nineteen, had been named after her mother, but 'Angela' was later shortened to 'Geli'. Her sister, Elfriede, was seventeen.

From now on, Hitler's meals would be prepared for him, and he was waited on at home as if he were in a restaurant. When Angela arrived, Geli was still at school in Vienna, but Hitler collected her at the end of the school year after she had taken her school leaving certificate (*Abitur*). For a few months at least, she would share with her mother and sister the tasks of looking after his clothes, tidying up after him, cooking, washing crockery and cutlery, preparing hot drinks, fetching his slippers, making his bed, doing his shopping, running the water for his bath, opening the door for visitors, carrying messages and performing errands.

The diffident Elfriede rarely asserted herself, but once the high-spirited Geli arrived there was a constant flow of animated talk with frequent bursts of full-throated laughter. If he had been told to expect something not unlike family life, Hitler would have been apprehensive, but later on, when he had to do without Geli's company, he missed it.

> Women play a bigger role in men's lives than men are inclined to acknowledge, unless they are deprived of female company . . . The greatest gap I find – a yawning chasm – is when I sit down to breakfast in the morning and when I come home at lunchtime or in the evening to find that I'm alone, quite alone. Her cheerful laughter was always a joy to me and her innocent chatter was a pleasure. Even when she sat next to me in silence, doing crossword puzzles, I felt surrounded by good health and wellbeing.[3]

Her presence was enough to change his mood.

> I can sit next to young women who leave me completely cold. I feel nothing, or they actually irritate me. But a girl like the little Hoffman [the daughter of his photographer] or Geli – with them I become cheerful and bright, and if I have listened for an hour to their perhaps silly chatter – or I have only to sit next to them – then I am free of all weariness and listlessness. I can go back to work refreshed.[4]

Geli was the crucial woman in Hitler's life, more important than Eva Braun. Reminiscing many years later, the little Hoffmann wrote: 'Geli was opera; Eva was operetta.'[5] According to Alan Bullock, whose 1952 biography of Hitler is still one of the best, Geli's death dealt him 'a greater blow than any other event in his life. For days he was inconsolable and his friends feared he would take his own life. . . . For the rest of his life he never spoke of Geli without tears coming to his eyes; according to his own statement to a number of witnesses, she was the only woman he ever loved.'[6]

This is confirmed in the best of the German biographies – the one by Joachim Fest. 'The affection Hitler felt for this pretty, superficial niece soon developed into a passionate relationship hopelessly burdened by his intolerance, his romantic ideal of womanhood and avuncular scruples.' Though Fest thought she might have been driven to suicide by his friendship with Eva Braun, he saw the uncle–niece relationship as having a strongly 'erotic element', unlike the liaison with the insipid blonde who was 'merely his mistress'.

Assessing Geli's importance to Hitler, Fest went further, pronouncing their relationship to be

> one of the key events in his personal life. It seems to have fixed forever his relationship to the opposite sex, which was curious enough in any case. . . . His fear of all undignified attitudes included, according to a remark by a member of his entourage, constant anxiety about 'having his name linked with a woman'. His complexes appear to loosen up only after Geli Raubal appeared with her sentimental and at first, evidently, half-childish fondness for 'Uncle Alf'.

Many women became superficially involved with Hitler, but 'none meant as much as to him as Geli Raubal. She was, oddly inappropriate though the phrase sounds, his great love, a tabooed love of Tristan moods and tragic sentimentality.'[7]

Ernst Hanfstaengl, who often saw them together, took a similar view of her importance.

> I am sure that the death of Geli Raubal marked a turning point in the development of Hitler's character. This relationship, whatever form it took in their intimacy, had provided him for the first time in his life with a release to his nervous energy which only too soon was to find its final expression in ruthlessness and savagery. His long connexion with Eva Braun never produced the moon-calf interludes he had enjoyed with Geli and which might in due course, perhaps, have made a normal man out of him. With her death the way was clear

for his final development into a demon, with his sex life deteriorating again into a sort of bisexual narcissus-like vanity, with Eva Braun little more than a vague domestic adjunct.[8]

For over four years Geli was living either in Hitler's home or in a room he chose for her close to his, but Bullock's narrative gives us no information about their relationship till it arrives at Hitler's first meeting with the Reich President, Paul von Hindenburg, on 10 October 1931. 'Hitler was nervous and ill-at-ease; his niece, Geli Raubal, with whom he was in love, had committed suicide three weeks before.' We now get a terse summary of what had happened. She was

> simple and attractive, with a pleasant voice which she wanted to have trained for singing. During the next six years [actually four] she became Hitler's constant companion, and when her uncle acquired his flat on the Prinz-Regentenstrasse [actually Prinzregentenplatz] she spent much time with him in Munich as well as up at the Obersalzberg. This period in Munich Hitler later described as the happiest in his life; he idolised this girl, who was twenty years younger than himself, took her with him whenever he could – in short, he fell in love with her. Whether Geli was ever in love with him is uncertain. She was flattered and impressed by her now famous uncle, she enjoyed going about with him, but she suffered from his hypersensitive jealousy. Hitler refused to let her have any life of her own; he refused to let her go to Vienna to have her voice trained; he was beside himself with fury when he discovered that she had allowed Emil Maurice, his chauffeur, to make love to her, and forbade her to have anything to do with any other man. Geli resented and was made unhappy by Hitler's possessiveness and domestic tyranny.

Bullock tells the rest of the story in three paragraphs. On 17 September 1931 she was found dead in Hitler's flat. According to some accounts, his refusal to touch meat dates from his disorientation at this time. Her room in the Obersalzberg house was kept exactly as she had left it. 'Her photograph was hung in his room in Munich and Berlin, and flowers were always placed before it on the anniversary of her birth and death.'[9]

In his 1973 biography Joachim Fest provides more information, but not much. He tells a different story about Emil Maurice. During the early summer of 1928 Hitler was in Geli's room when the chauffeur came in. Hitler 'raised his riding whip in such threatening fury that Maurice saved himself only by leaping out of the window'.

In 1929 Hitler changed his lifestyle, taking a nine-room flat in Munich, and within two months Geli moved in, though her presence in his life had already caused a certain amount of gossip. According to Fest, this 'bothered him somewhat, but he also rather enjoyed the aura of bohemian freedom and the suggestion of a grand and fateful passion in this liaison between uncle and niece'.

What actually went on? Like Bullock, Fest does not tell the story of how the relationship developed. Coming to Geli's death, he says that news of her suicide reached Hitler when he was setting out on an election campaign visit to Hamburg.

> Hitler, stunned and horrified, abruptly turned about; and, unless all the indications are deceptive, no other event in his personal life affected him as strongly as did this one. For weeks he seemed close to a nervous breakdown and repeatedly swore to give up politics. In his fits of gloom he spoke of suicide.... According to his intimates, tears would come to his eyes whenever he spoke of his niece in later years; it was an unwritten rule that no one but he might mention her name.[10]

But why did her death bring Hitler close to a nervous breakdown? And if memories brought tears to his eyes, what was he remembering?

1

The Boy Who Shot Rats

Ashamed of his background, his family and his childhood, Hitler was secretive about all three. 'People must not know who I am. They must not know where I come from, or from what family.'[1] In *Mein Kampf* he appears to be telling the story of his life, but the book is the first fanfare in a long programme of personal propaganda. Wanting to be worshipped like a hero, he gave his past a mythical dimension.

The family came from the Waldviertel, an impoverished area on the northern edge of Austria between the Danube and the Bohemian border. When he was born in 1889, Czechoslovakia did not yet exist, but the name Hitler, with its variants Hiedler and Hüttler, is probably of Czech origin. Bohemia and Austria belonged to the Dual Monarchy, the enormous empire created in 1867 by the compromise that united Austria with Hungary under Habsburg rule, its territory extending into Poland, Romania, the Ukraine, the Balkans and Italy. The capital, Vienna, attracted tourists, but few ventured into the Waldviertel, an inhospitable region with steep hills, dark forests and a harsh, windy climate. Shallow soil on granite yielded only a meagre living for the predominantly peasant population, and from the mid-nineteenth century onwards younger people trekked out to settle in Vienna or Linz.

Rife among the peasants, inbreeding damaged many of the families, including Hitler's, which was afflicted with deformity and insanity. His mother's hunchbacked sister, Johanna Pölzl, may have been schizophrenic; his first cousin, Edward, son of his other maternal aunt, Theresia, was another hunchback, and had a speech defect. (See family tree on pp. xiv–xv.) When

Hitler denounced 'thousands of years of inbreeding' among the Jews, this was almost certainly a disguised reference to his own family.

But what worried him most was the mystery surrounding his paternal grandfather. In Munich, during the early twenties, Hitler was rumoured to be of Jewish descent, and the rumours had not died out by the beginning of the thirties. After briefing a lawyer, Hans Frank, to find out the facts, Hitler was told that his grandmother, Maria Anna Schicklgruber, who became pregnant in 1836 when she was forty-one and still unmarried, had been working as maid or cook for a Jewish family in Graz, the old capital of Styria and the second largest town in Austria. The Jewish family, said Frank, was called Frankenberger, and, believing his nineteen-year-old son to be responsible for the pregnancy, Herr Frankenberger went on paying Maria Anna a paternity allowance till her son was fourteen.[2]

Subsequent research has revealed that there were no Jewish families in Graz, but Hitler did not know this, and never found out who his grandfather was. According to Rittmeister von Schuh, a physician who had known him since 1917, he 'suffered all his life from painful doubts: did he or did he not have Jewish blood? And he told us this.'[3]

Blood featured prominently in Hitler's muddled thinking about race. The superiority of the Aryans, he maintained, depended on the purity of their blood. The Jews were conspiring to take control of the world by polluting Aryan blood and poisoning public life. Germany was the main bastion of Western civilisation because the proportion of Aryan blood was so high, but Germanic purity was in danger from prostitution, syphilis, Marxism, decadent art, feminism, liberalism, land speculation and the Jewish influence on the press.

In a book on Hitler's psychopathology, Robert Waite has analysed his response to the idea that his blood might be contaminated. Compulsively, he had blood drained from his body by leeches, and later, after Theodor Morell became his doctor, with syringes. The image of blood-poisoning is recurrent in his speeches. 'Alone the loss of purity of the blood destroys the inner happiness for ever; it eternally lowers man, and never again can its consequence be removed from body and mind.'

Christ was an Aryan, according to Hitler, though his mother may well have been Jewish.[4] Humanity's original sin was the poisoning of German blood. 'All of us are suffering from the ailment of mixed, corrupted blood. How can we purify ourselves and make atonement?'

Before giving birth to her baby, Maria Anna, now forty-two, went to the house of a peasant named Johann Trummelschlager in another Waldviertel village, Strones; here, on 7 June 1837, she produced a boy. Strones was too small to have a parish, and the baby's illegitimate birth was registered in a neighbouring village, Döllersheim. Since she refused to name the father, the boy, Alois, was given her surname – Schicklgruber.

Maria Anna spent the next five years in Strones, where her father, who was in his seventies, helped to look after his grandson. When, at the age of forty-seven, she married an unemployed millworker, Johann Georg Hiedler, they moved to a nearby village named Spital but did not settle. Alois spent the rest of his boyhood in the village, though not with his mother and stepfather. Hiedler moved about from place to place, and Maria Anna gave the boy to his brother, Johann Nepomuk Hüttler, a farmer. They were both sons of a man called Martin Hiedler: the three spellings, Hiedler, Hüttler and Hitler, were interchangeable. The father of the baby may have been Trummelschlager, who acted as godfather, but his wife was the godmother,[5] and it seems likelier that the father was Johann Nepomuk Hüttler.

Alois would probably have been worse off with Maria Anna and Hiedler, who, according to Fest, became so poor that they had to sell their bed and sleep in a cattle trough.[6] But another of Hitler's biographers, Werner Maser, says Maria Anna had inherited substantial funds from her peasant parents. This would make it harder to explain why she gave her son away to a foster-father, unless Hüttler was the boy's real father. He had a wife, Eva Maria, fifteen years older than he was, and three daughters. As Maser argues, they may all have accepted Alois's presence in the house on the assumption that they were giving a home to the son of Johann Georg Hiedler.[7]

Alois was eleven when his mother died, and two years later (according to Adolf Hitler's unreliable autobiography) he ran away from his foster-parents' home. Hardships that he suffered in boyhood may have helped to make him tough and aggressively competitive. After becoming a customs official, he rose rapidly through the ranks. He remained single until, at the age of thirty-seven, he married a woman fourteen years older, Anna Glassl, possibly for her money. She bore him no children, but his second and third wives produced a total of eight.

Soon after he married, Alois acquired a teenage mistress, Franziska Matzelsberger, who was working as waitress or kitchen maid in the inn at Braunau, a village on the river Inn, which formed the border between Austria and Germany. Nor was he content with just a wife and one mistress. A sixteen-year-old relative, Klara Pölzl, came to work as his servant. She had large staring eyes, pleasant regular features and short brown hair. Her father, Johann Pölzl, was a farmer in Spital, and her mother, whose maiden name was Johanna Hüttler, was one of Johann Nepomuk Hüttler's daughters.

In January 1877, soon after Klara had moved in – and soon after his wife, Eva Maria, died – Johann Nepomuk Hüttler suddenly made efforts to legitimise the birth of Alois, who was now thirty-nine and had not been handicapped in his career by illegitimacy. (In Lower Austria, the province that included the Waldviertel, 40 per cent of the population was illegitimate.) Maria Anna had been dead for thirty years, and Hiedler for twenty, but Hüttler affirmed that his dead brother accepted paternity of the baby and wanted his name to be entered in the parish register. If Hiedler had been the father, and had really expressed this wish, why had Hüttler done nothing about it sooner? It seems more likely that he was the father and that, wanting to take the boy into his home, he had persuaded (or possibly paid) his good-for-nothing brother to marry Maria Anna. But if Alois had acquired the surname Hitler or Hiedler or Hüttler while Eva Maria was still alive, she might have become suspicious.

Taking three 'witnesses' with him, Hüttler went to see the elderly priest in the parish of Döllersheim, Josef Zahnschirm, who seems to have accepted the story about Hiedler's wishes. Agreeing to change the parish register, he substituted 'legitimate' for 'illegitimate', and in the blank space opposite 'Father' wrote

'George Hitler'. Confirming what Johann Nepomuk had told the priest, the witnesses, who were all illiterate, signed with a cross. Deliberately or by mistake, Zahnschirm failed to add his own signature. In any case, the emendation of the register would have had no legal validity in the absence of written proof that the dead man wanted to recognise Alois as his son. But the church and state authorities agreed to let him sign his name as Alois Hitler from now on.[8] It was lucky for the future Führer that the change was made. As William Shirer pointed out in his history of the Third Reich, it is hard to imagine excited crowds yelling: '*Heil Schicklgruber!*'[9]

Before his wife died, Alois's young mistress, Franziska, became pregnant. He wanted to marry her as soon as Anna died, but Franziska refused to move until his even younger mistress, Klara, moved out. Left in sole possession of Alois, Franziska gave birth to a boy, who was named after him, and then a girl, Angela. But when she became too ill to look after them Franziska could not stop Alois bringing Klara back into the house as maidservant, cook, nursemaid and mistress.

She soon became pregnant. Franziska was dying, but, according to rumour, she was still alive when Alois ordered her coffin. Wanting Klara to be his third wife, he needed dispensation from the Vatican, which would not have been granted if she had not been pregnant. When they married in 1883, nine years after she had started working for him, she was twenty-five and he was forty-eight. She was meek and pious, a subservient wife and a regular churchgoer. Uncomplainingly, she did the housework, shopping and cooking as well as looking after the children – young Alois and Angela as well as the new babies. She went on calling her husband 'Uncle Alois', and if he was the son of Johann Nepomuk Hüttler, Adolf Hitler's mother was the granddaughter of her husband's father. In other words, Hitler's paternal grandfather was also his maternal great-grandfather.

It was fortunate for them that Hüttler had no other male heir. Most of his assets were converted into cash and transferred to Alois, who in 1888, the year Hüttler died, bought a valuable house in Wörnharts, a village near Spital. But instead of moving into it, he went on living in rented accommodation. He sold the house in 1892, making a profit of over 50 per cent.[10] By 1889, when Adolf was born, the family had moved into a comfortable boarding house in Braunau.

Mein Kampf gives a false impression of Hitler's boyhood, making his parents out to be less prosperous than they were, and some of the most important revelations in the book are accidental. This passage, for instance, was not meant to seem autobiographical:

> In a basement apartment, consisting of two stuffy rooms, dwells a worker's family of seven. Among the five children there is a boy of, let us assume, three years. This is the age in which the first impressions are made on the consciousness of the child. Talented persons retain traces of memory from this period down to advanced old age. The very narrowness and overcrowding of the room does not lead to favourable conditions. Quarrelling and wrangling will very frequently arise as a result. In these circumstances, people do not live with one another, they press against one another. Every argument ... here leads to loathsome wrangling without end. Among the children, of course, this is still bearable ... But if this battle is carried on between the parents themselves, and almost every day in forms which for vulgarity often leave nothing to be desired, then, if only very gradually, the results of such visual education must ultimately become apparent in the children. The character they will inevitably assume if this mutual quarrel takes the form of brutal attacks of the father against the mother, of drunken beatings, is hard for anyone who does not know this milieu to imagine. At the age of six the pitiable little boy suspects the existence of things which can inspire even an adult with nothing but horror. Morally poisoned, physically undernourished, his poor little head full of lice, the young 'citizen' goes off to public school [i.e. state-run].[11]

There were five children in the house when Hitler's sister, Paula, was born in January 1896. Born on 24 March 1894, his brother Edmund was still alive. His half-sister, Angela, was twelve, and her brother, Alois, thirteen. Adolf, who was six, was the oldest of Klara's children still living, but the fourth to be born. She had previously given birth to two boys and a girl, but one died in infancy and the other two before reaching the age of two. Also living in the house was the hunchbacked aunt, Johanna Pölzl.

In early childhood Adolf had been sickly and Klara had been over-protective, wanting nothing less than to lose another child. 'I have never seen a closer attachment between mother and son,' said her Jewish doctor, Edward Bloch. In the surviving photographs of Hitler as a baby he looks over-fed, and according to his half-brother, Alois, Adolf was spoilt. In a book about the family Helm Stierlin has suggested that Hitler's lifelong addiction to sweet things may have developed out of his mother's over-indulgence in feeding him sugary treats.[12] In adult life his partiality to cakes and puddings was prodigious. His breakfast regularly consisted of hot milk, sweet biscuits and a slab of chocolate. Among his favourite desserts were macaroni pudding and plums and cream sauce, and pancakes with either jam or orange.[13]

Though Adolf did not find it easy to love, he claimed to have been deeply fond of his mother, and said that one of his happiest memories was of sleeping alone with her in the big bed when his father was away. Temperamentally, he bore more resemblance to his father: both were ambitious, headstrong, impatient, intolerant, dogmatic and manipulative. But the only resemblance that Hitler acknowledged was to Klara: 'A mother's characteristics', he said, 'are usually to be found in her son.'[14] After her death he had pictures of her on the walls of the Chancellery in Berlin and of his homes in Obersalzberg and Munich. There were none of his father, and Adolf Hitler's small moustache could not have been less like that of Alois, who followed the example of his emperor and grew a lot of facial hair.

In August 1892 Alois Hitler was promoted to the rank of Customs Officer, Grade I (Acting), which entailed a move across the border to Passau in Bavaria. The family stayed there when, at the end of March 1894, Alois was transferred to Linz only a week after Klara had given birth to another son, Edmund. For about a year the young Adolf saw little of his father, but in April 1895 the family rejoined Alois, first in Linz and then in Hafeld, near Lambach, not quite thirty miles south-west of Linz, where he bought a house with nine acres of land, and Adolf started going to school in the nearby village of Fischlam, escorted there by Angela.

Alois's health was deteriorating rapidly, and in June 1895, at the age of fifty-eight, he retired after forty years in the customs service. Suddenly the six-year-old Adolf was seeing a lot of him. Alois had to farm his nine acres, and he kept bees, but though he spent a lot of time drinking with friends, he was at home more than ever before, and this was the main period of what Hitler called 'brutal attacks of the father against the mother, of drunken beatings'.

Klara was not the only victim. The young Alois was beaten regularly, and in 1896, at the age of fourteen, he left home never to return. Angela was thirteen, Adolf seven, and though the age-gap was too big for them to be playmates they became allies now that her brother was no longer there. Since their father now had only one son he could beat – at two, Edmund was too young – Adolf had to put up with even more punishment than before. One of the beatings was so violent that Alois thought he had killed the boy.[15]

But Hitler may have been exaggerating when he boasted about emulating the heroes in adventure stories by Karl May, Germany's most popular writer of boys' books.

> After reading one day in Karl May that the brave man gives no sign of being in pain, I made up my mind not to let out any sound next time I was beaten. And when the moment came – I counted every blow. My mother thought I'd gone mad when I proudly told her 'Father hit me thirty-two times'.[16]

It looked as though Adolf was going to do well at school. He was awarded high marks at both Fischlam and the school he attended in a Lambach Benedictine foundation between 1896 and 1898. But his passion was for playing war games. This was apparent at the next primary school he attended – in Leonding, near Linz, where his father bought a house in November 1898; the family moved in during February 1899. Eight months later, war broke out in South Africa between the British and the Boers. Hitler was the ringleader who organised games in which the Leonding boys were Boers, with him in command, and the boys from the neighbouring village of Untergaumberg were the British.[17]

The house at Leonding was close to the churchyard, and here he discovered the pleasure of killing. Not even a teenager yet, he should not have been allowed to use any kind of rifle, but when his father was away, neither his mother nor Angela could control him, and, reminiscing in later life about Angela, he called her a 'silly goose' for refusing to join in his favourite game – taking pot shots at rats with an airgun.[18] With the church and the tombstones in the background, he could use the gun to assert godlike superiority over animals that moved about freely, exerting their own willpower, till he finished them off. With his finger on the trigger, he was in command. The little legs on the dark inhuman bodies waved frantically in the air, and never moved again. The boy could not have explained why the game excited him.

2

Sit Down, Hitler

War games and rat-shooting assorted oddly with Adolf's passion for Wagner, but this had developed by the age of sixteen. Between 1905 and 1907 the son of the baker in Leonding, Hagmüller, had lunch four times a week at the Hitlers' house. Recalling this in 1938, he said: 'I can still see the weakly lad pacing up and down the room singing "Now swan, farewell!" '[1]

When the weakly lad was fifteen, he started to attend a secondary school in Linz. After finding it easy to outshine his peasant classmates in the village schoolroom, he was now surrounded by brighter boys, and refused to compete. At the end of his first year, his teachers reported that his work in maths and natural history had been so poor that he could not move up into the next class.

Throughout the school, boys were divided into two factions – one loyal to the Austro-Hungarian Empire, the other to Germany. Germany had not existed – as a state – until the nineteenth century, and German nationalism gained no momentum till 1848. In 1815 the Holy Roman Empire, which had been dissolved in 1806, was replaced by the German Confederation, incorporating Austria and Prussia, together with four kingdoms (Bavaria, Saxony, Württemberg, Hanover) and thirty-two smaller states, some of them only city-states. The two great powers, Austria and Prussia, were careful not to let a nation-state emerge in the centre of Europe.

The first German Reich was created by the revolution of 1848, but survived for less than a year. It was replaced in 1849 by a smaller confederation, including neither Bavaria nor Württemberg. In the 1850s, as Bismarck became territorially acquisitive, he tried to align German nationalism with Prussia. In June 1886 Prussia dissolved the confederation, invaded Saxony, Hanover and Hesse, and at the beginning of July ended the 'Seven Weeks' War' by defeating the Austrians at Sadowa. Austria was then excluded from Bismarck's new Reich which emerged at the end of the Franco-Prussian War in 1871, when German nationalism was encouraged by a victory that seemed to compensate for defeats suffered at the hands of Napoleon.

Together with Württemberg, Baden and Hesse-Darmstadt, Bavaria was now linked to Prussia by military agreements and a customs union, though in 1866, talking about the need to consolidate the confederation, Bismarck had said: 'I consider it impossible to draw the South German Catholic element into it. The latter will not willingly let itself be governed from Berlin for a long time yet.'[2] Bavaria kept its independent system of taxation, its postal services, its railway system and even its own army, which was subject to the Kaiser only in wartime.

Austria, now separated from the other German-speaking territories for the first time in a thousand years, was forced into the alliance that created the Austro-Hungarian Empire. In 1924 Hitler wrote: 'Only he who has felt in his own skin what it means to be a German, deprived of the right to belong to his cherished fatherland, can measure the deep longing which burns at all times in the hearts of children separated from their mother country.'[3] He was often undecided about which parent to identify with Germany.

Some boys collected photographs of the Habsburgs and insignia coloured in the imperial black and yellow; others treasured pictures of Bismarck, beer mugs inscribed with mottoes from the Germanic past, and objects in the colours that represented the status quo before Prussia had united Germany without Austria – red, black and gold. 'We emphasised our convictions by wearing cornflowers and red, black and gold colours; "*Heil*" was our greeting, and instead of the imperial anthem we sang "*Deutschland über Alles*" despite warnings and punishments.'[4] The cornflower was the emblem of Germans loyal to the House of Hohenzollern; *Heil!* was the ancient German equivalent to the imperial *Hoch!*

In *Mein Kampf* Hitler attributed his political awakening to Dr Leopold Poetsch, who taught him geography throughout his three years at the school and history during the last two. 'He had more understanding than anyone else for all the daily problems which then held us breathless. He used our budding nationalistic fanaticism as a means of educating us.'[5] But Poetsch, who was regarded as loyal to the Austro-Hungarian throne, later gave away the two copies of *Mein Kampf* he received from his grateful pupil. Hitler's incipient Pan-Germanism may have derived less from Poetsch than from the polemical paper *Linzer Fliegende*, which took a vigorously anti-Semitic, anti-clerical and anti-imperialist line.[6]

Once, during a scripture lesson, Hitler infuriated the teacher with a desk-top display of red, black and gold crayons.

'You will immediately get rid of those pencils with those abominable colours.'

'Huh!' said the whole class. 'They represent the national principle.'

'What you should have in your hearts isn't a national principle but a single principle, and that's our fatherland and the imperial House of Habsburg. If you're against the House of Habsburg, you're against the Church, and if you're against the Church, you're against God. Sit down, Hitler.'[7]

If his parents had been trying to make him into a sado-masochist, they could hardly have done a better job. He never forgot the thrashings he had received, and a casual remark he made in August 1942 suggests that his relish for inflicting pain was rooted in these memories. Recommending that his Minister of Justice, Franz Gürtner, should 'allow the Gestapo to try their hand' on a man accused of thirty-six murders, Hitler explained 'that at the most he would get a good hiding, that had I myself received in one fell swoop all the thrashings I deserved (and had had) in my life, I should be dead! The net result was that the blackguard confessed to one hundred and seven murders.'[8] It did not occur to Hitler that the man might have confessed under torture to murders he had not committed.

Hitler's experience of being thrashed gave him something in

common with Stalin. Erich Fromm has diagnosed a strain of narcissism in both personalities: both dictators grew up without learning the sort of human interaction that involves both giving and taking. Feeling isolated in a hostile world, they cared only about their own feelings, needs and experiences. Other people, like slaves or animals or objects, were interesting in so far as they were useful.

Even if Hitler loved his mother, she could play only a passive role in power games, and he did not want to resemble her. Her pious self-abnegation seemed to compound her suffering. Believing in the divinity that hedges the master of the house, Alois used her like a slave, and when she wanted to issue an order in his absence, she used to point to his pipe-rack as if invoking his authority. While she loved, honoured and obeyed, the young Adolf learned that bullying produces results. Pitying her, he hated, feared and admired his father, but also loved him enough to weep at his funeral. Watching the daily interaction between victimiser and victim, he could see which role was more enjoyable.

He often watched his father in action, imposing his will on other people, and once, when he took his son to a law court at Ried in Upper Austria, Alois showed him a collection of weapons confiscated from criminals and brawling peasants – revolvers, knives, blackjacks and clubs. The weapons made the boy feel high-spirited.[9]

This was natural, from the viewpoint that was developing. If masculine power was connected with weapons, death, beating and pain, there was something inferior and contemptible about females who could neither stop him shooting rats nor join in the fun. At an age when other Linz schoolboys were becoming interested in the female body, he shrank from any form of physical contact. Seven years his junior, his sister Paula never forgot his boyhood aversion to being kissed. It was even stronger than his reluctance to wake up. 'When mother wanted him to get up in the morning, she had only to say to me, "Go and give him a kiss." She said it not very loud but enough for him to hear; as soon as he heard the word "kiss" and that he was to get one from me, he was out of bed in a flash because he just couldn't stand that."[10]

In later life he made out that he had always got on well with
girls. He told a story about seducing a milkmaid in Leonding
when he was no more than fifteen. Before his family moved to
Linz, he said, he made love to a peasant girl who had been
milking cows in a shed. Disturbed by a noise, they knocked
over a lantern, almost setting fire to the shed.[11] But earlier, in
Vienna, he had told a less boastful version of the same story.
Still milking one of the cows, the girl started behaving in a 'very
foolish way', and Hitler, remembering what the consequences
might be, ran away in such confusion that he knocked over a
pail of milk.[12]

He may also have been scared of a feminine component in
his own nature. Franz Jetzinger, an ex-priest who wrote about
Hitler's early life, held a series of interviews with one of his
classmates at the secondary school, a boy called Keplinger, who
was friendly enough with the young Adolf to be remembered
and presented with one of his drawings after the annexation
of Austria in 1938. Asked whether Hitler had done badly at
school because he was distracted by girls, Keplinger answered:
'Out of the question. Adolf was never interested in girls.'[13]

On 3 January 1903, while the boy was in his third year at
the Linz school, his father collapsed and died. Adolf stayed on
but made little effort. He usually passed muster in drawing and
gymnastics, but not in history, geography, maths or German. It
took him five years to cover the ground that other boys covered
in three, and he became insecure. Now that he could no longer
be ringleader, he held back from joining groups led by other
boys. In a boarding house with five of his own age, he failed to
make friends with any of them, and went on addressing them
in the formal plural, *Sie*, while they talked to each other in the
singular, *du*. When he was fifteen, Klara was asked to take him
away from the school.

Just over nine months after their father died, Angela got married. She was twenty, and her twenty-four-year-old bridegroom
was Leo Raubal, an assistant tax collector who came from Ried
and was working in Linz. For Klara it was more like losing a
daughter than a step-daughter. After being brought up more
by Klara than by Franziska, Angela had done more than any of
Klara's children to help her with the cooking, housework and

looking after the younger children. After Edmund's death, the only survivor was the mentally defective Paula, and it was on her companionship, such as it was, that Klara had to depend after Angela left.

Klara still doted on Adolf, but got little in return. Though he did not spend much time with boys of his own age – he was aloof and unassertive with them – he liked being with younger boys who did what he told them when they played war games. He was fifteen when he was confirmed, and at the party given after the ceremony, he rudely left early to play with boys who had been waiting for him. Fantasies of himself as a military hero survived in his enjoyment of Karl May's adventure stories, which he went on reading as an adult.[14]

Resentful about having to leave the secondary school in Linz and to attend one in a smaller town to the south, Steyr, he made even less effort than before, doing so badly during his first term that when he was given his report he got drunk and wiped his bottom on it. After being equally idle for another twelve months, he left school at the age of sixteen.

He had inherited some of his father's willpower, but none of his self-discipline and capacity for hard work. Hitler now maintained his self-esteem by taking trouble over his appearance. Carrying a black, ivory-tipped cane, he wore a broad-brimmed, round-topped black hat, a white shirt, black kid gloves and a silk-lined black overcoat. In these dandyish clothes he indulged in such pleasures as a daily stroll and regular visits to the theatre. Klara, who had not wanted him to leave school, disapproved of his lazy life. But the habit of subservience was deeply ingrained in her, and she stood no chance of regaining the upper hand.

He had a genuine talent for sketching – he was better at buildings than people – and his ambition was to study at the art academy in Vienna. But he was in no hurry to give up the life that gave him so much time for daydreaming about his future greatness. He had no intention of working unless work consisted of what he enjoyed doing – drawing architectural designs. He made detailed plans for rebuilding Linz; he would give the city 'a bridge unequalled anywhere in the world'. Other people were underrating him, he thought, but they would realise their mistake soon enough when he inaugurated sweeping social changes.

His fantasies were so vivid that he could convince himself it was possible to have anything he wanted, simply by desiring it. Even when he thought he had fallen in love, he expected to possess the girl without taking any trouble to woo her. In fact his 'love' never went beyond idealisation and fantasy, and the only human interaction it involved was with a boy, August Kubizek, his one close friend. Son of a Linz upholsterer, Kubizek was his senior by nine months, but after having completing only an elementary education he worked as assistant to his father. Willingly dominated by the younger boy, Kubizek became Hitler's first audience. Much of their conversation consisted of making plans based on fantasy, and once, when Hitler presented him with a sketch of a villa, they both talked as if it were a real building.

The Landstrasse was where the citizens of Linz promenaded, and one evening when the two boys were strolling together, Hitler pointed out a slim, blonde girl walking arm-in-arm with her mother. 'You must know, I'm in love with her.'[15] This was in the spring of 1905, and, according to Kubizek, Hitler's passion for her lasted four years, though he never met her. Her name was Stefanie, and she was eighteen when the non-relationship started.

In no doubt that she would fall into his arms as soon as they spoke to each other, Hitler decided to marry her. He wrote poems for her, and spent hours making architectural drawings for their marital home. Kubizek suggested he should introduce himself to her and her mother by raising his hat, telling them his name and asking for permission to walk along the Landstrasse with them. Was this not the obvious thing to do? Hitler explained that 'Between such exceptional beings as himself and Stefanie there was absolutely no need for the usual form of spoken communication. He told me that exceptional people arrive at mutual understanding through intuition.'[16]

In the Landstrasse, when Stefanie and her mother passed Hitler, there was no sign of mutual understanding, but she smiled at some of the young officers. Hearing that she danced with them at balls, Hitler was so upset that he threatened to drown himself in the Danube. He made the threat not to her but to Kubizek, who offered another suggestion. Why not take dancing lessons? This idea was dismissed as absurd. As soon as they were married, Stefanie would lose all interest in such frivolities.

Suicide was not the only idea that involved violence: Hitler thought of kidnapping her. After working out a detailed plan he explained it to Kubizek, who was to distract the mother's attention while he grabbed the girl. But he had no answer to the question: 'What are you both going to live on?'[17]

Before leaving for Vienna Hitler wrote to her, promising to come back and marry her when he had established himself as a painter. Deciding that it was more prudent not to reveal his identity, he left the letter unsigned. She read it, but thought one of her girlfriends was playing a joke.[18]

Hitler's behaviour was even more eccentric than Kubizek makes it out to be. Though his book *Young Hitler* was not published till 1953, it was based on memories written when he could not tell the truth. During the thirties he was a municipal official, and after joining the Nazi party in 1942 he was given a propaganda job in the organisation Strength through Joy. Hitler's private secretary, Martin Bormann, commissioned him to write memoirs of his boyhood friendship with Hitler for the party's archives.

Deviating from the facts, Kubizek makes out that Stefanie, aware of Hitler's passion, encouraged it by smiling at him and throwing him a flower from her bouquet during the parade in the flower festival, when, together with her mother, she was sitting in a flower-decked carriage. In reality, as Jetzinger found out after tracking her down, she had been unaware of Hitler's existence. He would not have been obsessed with her so long if he had not been exceptionally reluctant to risk being rebuffed. She had given no sign of interest in him, but so long as there was no proof of her indifference he could go on daydreaming, talking about her, writing poetry and making architectural drawings based on the assumption that they were going to be married.

But even in fantasy the affair could not have lasted as long as Kubizek claims. Stefanie was studying in Munich and Geneva. Though she returned to Linz during holidays, she did not settle down to live there again till November 1906, and in 1908 she was engaged to the army officer whom she afterwards married.

In 1913 Hitler was still talking about her, and just before
Christmas, a friend, Rudolf Häusler, found it extraordinary
that the twenty-four-year-old Hitler should send an anonymous
greeting in a Linz newspaper to the 'girlfriend' he had not seen
since he was eighteen. By now, in fact, she was married.[19]

Nor was it only over Stefanie that the teenage Hitler confused
fantasy with reality. When he was eighteen, he persuaded
Kubizek to share the cost of a ten kronen lottery ticket.
Assuming they would win the first prize, Hitler made detailed
plans for spending the money on a flat that they would share.
He drew a groundplan and made scale drawings for each piece
of furniture. They discussed curtains and draperies. He designed
decorations for the walls of each room, and decided that they
should employ a refined lady as housekeeper. 'She must be a
lady of advanced age, so that there should be no expectations
or intentions that would distract us from our artistic calling.'

All this was pure fantasy, with no sexual components. In the
summer they would go to Bayreuth and travel all over Germany,
but without female companions. Logically, of course, the idea
of chaste devotion to art conflicts with the idea of marrying
Stefanie, but in the hothouse of fantasy discrepancies are
admissible.

Hitler was furious when he heard they had not won a prize in
the lottery. It was typical of the Dual Monarchy, this patchwork
of nations created by Habsburg marriages, that two poor devils
should be cheated out of their last few kronen.[20]

3

Doss House

Headed by tanks and field guns, the procession made its way into Vienna on 14 March 1938. Standing in an open Mercedes and giving the Nazi salute to an enormous cheering crowd, the forty-eight-year-old Adolf Hitler was dressed, like his stormtroopers, in brown uniform. Church bells rang out, and girls in national costume threw flowers into his car. The previous day, Austria had lost its independence. Shop windows were smashed, and Jews had to clean pavements with toothbrushes as Hitler took his revenge on the city where he had twice been rejected by the academy of arts and where he had lived like a pauper for three years in a hostel for men.

He first went there in May or June 1907, wanting to see the city before he presented himself at the academy in September 1907 for the entrance examination. It was a bad time to abandon his mother, who was suffering from breast cancer and had gone into hospital for an operation during January. In the past, Angela had always looked after Klara when she was ill, but Angela had given birth to her son, Leo, in October 1906, and she was soon pregnant again. She did what she could, though, for the eleven-year-old Paula. Twenty-three years earlier, when the dying Franziska could not take care of Alois and Angela, Klara had helped her out; now that Klara was dying, Angela did her best to reciprocate.

For Klara the whole year was miserable. She was only forty-six, but illness and anxiety about Adolf were joining forces to age her. In his absence, nothing interested her. All she could do was discuss him with Kubizek, and by the autumn she was saying that Adolf would just carry on living ruthlessly and pig-headedly as if he were alone in the world.[1]

Believing in his future as an artist, he felt full of confidence when he appeared at the academy in September. After finding that he had failed, he demanded an interview with the director, who said he might do better to study architecture. But Adolf made no efforts to enrol at one of the architectural colleges that would have accepted him even with an incomplete school education.

Staying on in Vienna, he kept his mother in ignorance of his failure. When he finally went home, he behaved, according to Kubizek, like a model son, nursing Klara, staying up all night at her bedside, never contradicting her, fetching whatever she needed, cooking food for her and scrubbing the kitchen floor. Dr Bloch, who started giving her morphia at the beginning of November, reported that all her thoughts centred on her son.

Klara still believed he was an art student when she died at two in the morning of 21 December 1907. Sitting next to her, he stayed awake all night. He also made a sketch of her corpse.[2] He spent Christmas Eve sitting with his head in his hands, alone with the body, refusing to open the front door when neighbours knocked.

Before Alois Hitler died he had appointed his friend Josef Mayrhofer, a former mayor of Leonding, as guardian of the two children. But Adolf, who was now eighteen, safeguarded his idle life by keeping Mayrhofer and the family ignorant of what had happened in Vienna. Believing him to be an art student, they did not expect him to give up his studies to earn money and provide for his sister, who was not quite twelve when their mother died.

As a junior tax official Leo Raubal did not earn much, but this did not stop him and Angela from offering to take Paula into their family. Otherwise, Mayrhofer would have sent her to an orphanage. Now that both parents were dead, Adolf and Paula were jointly entitled to a monthly sum of fifty kronen – about two pounds. It was for their guardian to decide how this should be divided, and he gave them half each. Adolf had no scruples about leaving the Raubals with only twenty-five kronen to subsidise the cost of bringing up Paula.

Young Leo was now two years old, and in June 1908, less than six months after Paula moved in, Angela gave birth to a girl. Since her brother had been named after their father, Leo, she was named after their mother – Angela Maria. It was not until thirteen years later that Hitler, whom she called 'Uncle Alf', started calling her Geli, and everyone else followed suit.

Returning to Vienna after his mother's funeral, Hitler stayed for six years, indulging in most of the pleasures that the city had to offer and gradually sinking to the bottom of society. Apparently, as Thomas Mann said, he wanted only to drift about lazily in a moral and mental bohemia. He seemed to be a good-for-nothing, incapable of steady work, unable to ride a horse, drive a car or beget a child.[3]

In Vienna he took only an observer's interest in sexual opportunities. Stefan Zweig describes the pavements as

> speckled so richly with women for sale that it was harder to keep out of their way than to find them. . . . At all prices and all times of day, female human merchandise was openly for sale, and it really took a man no more time or trouble to buy himself a woman for fifteen minutes, an hour or a night than it did to buy a packet of cigarettes or a newspaper.[4]

In 1912, when young Viennese doctors answered a newspaper questionnaire about their first sexual experience, 75 per cent said it was with a prostitute, and 17 per cent with a servant or waitress. Only 4 per cent had lost their virginity to a girl whom they might later marry.[5] Respectable bourgeois parents showed off their daughters' waistlines by dressing them in whalebone corsets, but kept them uninformed about the facts of sexuality.

At the beginning of 1908 Leo Raubal still did not see why Hitler should be allowed to shrug off responsibility for his mentally defective sister. Angela was doing all the hard work of bringing her up. Why could Hitler not at least get a job, earn some money and contribute to the cost of feeding her and buying her clothes?

Pitying himself for having to tolerate such insensitive criticism, Hitler complained in a letter to Kubizek. Missing him, Hitler urged him to settle in Vienna and study music. Did he not want to be a musician? Was there anywhere better to study it? Besides, Hitler did not like being alone, and could not put up with any more interference from Philistine relations who did not understand his artistic nature. He was going to prove that he was right and they were wrong.[6] There was a violent quarrel in August 1908 when he, Angela and Paula were in Spital. He told them he wanted nothing further to do with them.

Hitler's intervention helped Kubizek to put pressure on his parents, and he arrived in Vienna during the autumn of 1908. Seeing that Hitler was holding aloof from Vienna's pulsating sex life, Kubizek thought – or said he thought – the main reasons were febrile puritanism and fear of venereal disease. He lived, said Kubizek, in 'strict monklike asceticism', having

> too high an opinion of himself for a superficial flirtation or a merely physical relationship with a girl. . . . He was afraid of infection, as he often said. Now I understand that he meant not only venereal infection, but a much more general infection – the danger of being dragged down into the prevailing conditions and ultimately into the whirlpool of corruption.[7]

Briefed to idealise him, Kubizek is at pains to show how attractive the young Hitler was. In the foyer of the opera house women would give him more than a casual glance, and once, when a liveried servant handed him a message, his nonchalant reaction was: 'Yet another.' During his years in Vienna, says Kubizek, he had no affairs and lived with exemplary self-control.

But his isolation may have been due mainly to shyness. In the shop where he bought frames for his paintings, Adele, daughter of the proprietor, Jakob Altenberg, sometimes worked as an assistant. Though she was only fourteen he never looked her in the eye. She remembered his 'unkempt outward appearance . . . but also the way he kept his gaze constantly on the ground when he spoke to you'.[8]

In Kubizek's view, nothing that Hitler did or said was

compulsive or neurotic. Describing his friend's confrontation with a predatory homosexual, Kubizek comments: 'It seemed to me quite natural that he should feel horror and disgust at this and other sexual aberrations encountered in the capital, and that unlike most adolescents he did not indulge in frequent masturbation – adhering, indeed, in all sexual matters to the rigid code which he prescribed both for himself and for the future state.'[9]

Not that Hitler was uncurious about prostitution. After seeing Frank Wedekind's play about adolescent sexuality, *Spring Awakening*, he wanted to visit Vienna's red-light district, the Spittelberggasse. He and Kubizek walked past low houses that had illuminated windows at street level, like shops. The lights were turned out or the curtains drawn when the prostitute had a client with her. Some of the soldiers and citizens were merely window-shopping; others were looking the girls over to make a choice. Never realistic about other people's reactions to Hitler, Kubizek says at least two of the girls had suspected there was something special about him. One 'seized just the moment when we were passing her window to take off her chemise, whilst another busied herself with her stockings, showing her naked legs . . . Adolf grew angry at the prostitutes' tricks of seduction.'[10]

Throughout the tour of inspection he showed more self-righteous disgust than erotic interest, and back in their lodgings he delivered a homily about the shamelessness of prostitution.

> The origin lay in the fact that men felt the necessity for sexual satisfaction, whilst the girls in question thought only of their earnings with which, possibly, they kept one man they really loved, always assuming that these girls were capable of love. In practice, the 'Flame of Life' in these poor creatures was long since extinct.

Kubizek admitted – though not in his book – that Hitler liked to chat 'by the hour' about depraved sexual practices. It was characteristic that the prurience existed alongside the pretension to moral seriousness.

After Kubizek arrived, Hitler helped him to find digs. Seeing a 'Room to let' sign in the Zollergasse, they rang the doorbell; a maid fetched her mistress, who was wearing a silk dressing-gown and fur-trimmed slippers. According to Kubizek, the woman could not hide her disappointment when she found out he was the only one looking for a room. Suggesting that Hitler should move into her flat and give his present room to his friend, she briefly undid the belt around her dressing-gown, revealing that underneath she was wearing only a scanty pair of knickers. Hitler blushed and, gripping Kubizek's arm, led him out into the street, muttering balefully about Potiphar and his wife.

Though Hitler's life was nothing if not leisurely, and though this was the Vienna of Freud, Mahler, Schoenberg, Klimt, Schiele, Hofmannsthal and Otto Wagner, Hitler remained unaware of their work. The architecture that excited him was not the innovative work associated with the Secession but the neo-Classical façades of the Ringstrasse. 'From morning till late at night, I ran from one object of interest to another, but it was always the buildings that interested me most. I could stand for hours in front of the opera, for hours I could stare at the Parliament. The whole Ringstrasse was for me like an enchantment out of the Arabian Nights.'[11]

Mostly built between 1861 and 1888 on the site of the medieval fortifications that had separated the inner city from the suburbs, the street consisted of ministries, museums, theatres, blocks of offices and flats, all designed to look like classical monuments. It was the Ringstrasse that inspired the pretentious buildings he later erected in Munich. With its long row of pseudo-classical columns, the Haus der Deutschen Kunst, which was built between 1933 and 1937, has been called the Athens Railway Station or the Munich Art Terminal. He would have been making a mistake, he boasted, if he had started with housing estates and workers' tenements. Any Marxist or bourgeois government could do that. 'We are the first, since the time of the medieval cathedrals, to provide the artist with important and imposing tasks. Not homes and little private buildings, but the most tremendous architecture that has been seen since the gigantic buildings of Egypt and Babylon.'[12]

*   *   *

Angela's third baby, another daughter, was born on 10 January 1910. They named her Elfriede, and she grew up to be quieter than her sister. While Geli seems to have made a strong and favourable impression on almost everyone she met, Elfriede remained in the background both as a child and later. Few references to her are to be found in any of the statements recorded by people who knew both sisters: Geli went on attracting more attention and more comment.

In spite of saying in 1908 that he wanted nothing further to do with the Raubals, Hitler went on turning up from time to time at their home in Linz, expecting to be fed, and rebuffing Leo's efforts to make him contribute towards the cost of bringing up his mentally defective sister.[13] Feeling no obligation to earn more money, than he needed for himself, Hitler refused to do any other work than drawing and painting. When he ran out of money, he is said to have begged for the cash he needed, but this may be untrue, though it is possible that he spent nights on park benches and in cafés before he took refuge at a hostel for men in the suburb of Meidling, an area where 20 per cent of the population was Jewish.[14]

In the hostel each man was given an iron bed, a horsehair bolster, a double blanket and a chamber pot.[15] On his first night, while queuing for admission Hitler met Reinhold Hanisch, who claims to have shared with him some bread he had been given by peasants. According to Hanisch, Hitler was wearing a long frock coat – a present from a Hungarian Jew. 'Under a greasy black bowler hat, his hair was hanging out over his coat collar and his chin was framed by a thick fluffy beard.'[16] According to another man who met him, Joseph Greiner, his cultivated voice was at odds with his dirty, ragged clothes, his pale, sunken cheeks and his agitated manner.[17]

For seven months he and Hanisch worked as partners: Hitler copied postcards and lithographs; Hanisch, who sold them in streets and bars, got more money when he made himself out to be blind or tubercular. They split the proceeds fifty-fifty. During his three years in the hostel, Hitler spent a lot of time in cafés, reading the papers that were provided free, eating cakes and haranguing anyone who would listen with information gleaned from pamphlets and nationalistic politicians. The squalor of his life was partly compensated by inordinate self-esteem. He saw himself as a misunderstood genius waiting, like the young Richard Wagner, for his greatness to be recognised.

Nothing could have jolted him out of his lethargy, and the only difference it made to him when Leo Raubal died abruptly on 10 August 1910 was that his main persecutor was silenced. Hitler was unconcerned about the effect of the tax collector's death on Angela, on Paula, who was now fourteen and a half, and on the three children. The boy, Leo, was nearly four, Geli two, and the baby, Elfriede, only seven months old. From now on, Angela had to feed and clothe four children, one of them not her own, on her widow's pension plus twenty-five kronen, while Hitler went on pretending to be an art student and pocketing the other twenty-five kronen.

It was not until the spring of 1911, when his hunchbacked aunt, Johanna Pölzl, died, that the truth was exposed. From 1907 until the end of 1909 he had been living mainly on his inheritance from his father, but when this money was running out he had managed to convince his aunt that he needed her savings more than she did. After the death of her sister, Klara, Johanna had been doing domestic work for her younger married sister, Theresia Schmidt. On 1 December 1910 Johanna withdrew all her money – about 3800 kronen – from the local savings bank, and when Angela discovered it had all gone to Hitler, who had kept quiet about receiving it, she consulted Mayrhofer, who advised her to brief a lawyer. Summoned to give an account of his financial position in the court of Leopoldstadt in Linz, Hitler admitted he had received substantial sums from his aunt 'for the purpose of advancing his career as an artist', and on 4 May 1911 he 'voluntarily' turned over his orphan's pension of twenty-five kronen to his sister, who was now fifteen.[18] Now twenty-seven, the hard-pressed Angela had already been looking after her for four years, but apparently bore Hitler no grudge.

Hitler claimed in *Mein Kampf* that his understanding of the racial problem and his anti-Semitism dated from his seven years in Vienna. But he had several Jewish friends there, including the Hungarian Josef Neumann. Throughout the first half of 1910 they spent a lot of time together in the men's hostel, and for five nights in June, when Hitler was in funds, they moved out together into a hotel.[19]

On the other hand, Hitler did become resentful about the variety of races to be seen and languages to be heard in Vienna. At the turn of the century in the Austro-Hungarian Empire, about 36 per cent of the population was German, 24 per cent Czech, 21 per cent Ruthenian or Slovenian or Serbo-Croat and 17 per cent Polish.[20] There were also Italians, Romanians and Hungarians. Vienna contained more of a racial conglomeration than any other city in the empire, and Hitler came to hate the fact that the Germans were in a minority.

Without becoming anti-Semitic yet, he learnt how useful anti-Semitism could be in politics, though he never admitted how much he was influenced by two local politicians, Georg von Schönerer and Karl Lueger. It was from Schönerer that he took the phrase: 'A Jew can't be a real German.'[21]

The son of a railway engineer who had received a patent of nobility, Georg von Schönerer attended agricultural college and worked for a prince as a farm manager before embarking on a parliamentary career and becoming a nationalist demagogue. He made his first onslaught on the Jews in 1879 – ten years before Hitler was born, and a year before the Society for the Defence of the Handworker, the first Viennese anti-Semitic society, was founded. In the mid-eighties Schönerer led a campaign for the nationalisation of a railway that the Rothschilds had built. His ideas, as Carl Schorscke puts it, centred on nationalism, but 'he needed a negative element to give coherence to his system. Anti-Semitism was that element, enabling him to be simultaneously anti-socialist, anti-capitalist, anti-Catholic, anti-liberal and anti-Habsburg.'[22]

Like many German Austrians of his generation, Schönerer resented their exclusion from the Germany that Bismarck had created, and, introducing a raucous ferocity into political agitation, he fomented hatred against Jewish refugees from Russian pogroms. With the slogan 'Germany for the Germans' he insistently put pressure on German-speaking Austrians to feel that they were betraying the German people if they did not side against the Jews. *Deutschtum* (Germanism) began to take on a religious tone, as he exploited such old Germanic words as *Heil* and *Führer*. He established himself as the *Führer* of the Pan-Germanist movement, with the right to determine its policy unilaterally.

By 1907, when Hitler arrived in Vienna, Schönerer's most spectacular successes were behind him, but several nationalist groups were active in the district where Hitler settled, the Mariahilf. He learnt from Schönerer's party newspaper his use of songs, youth groups and sporting events, while, as Brigitte Hamann observes, the tone of *Mein Kampf* echoes Schönerer's.[23]

By 1908 the most powerful politician in Vienna was the Burgomaster, Karl Lueger, who had learnt from Schönerer how anti-Semitism could be used to galvanise the more impoverished and disaffected sections of society. Children of a powerful mother, Lueger and his two sisters remained single. It was rumoured that at the age of forty-four he promised his dying mother not to marry and to go on taking care of them. They both kept house for him.

Like Schönerer, he was a skilful demagogue, and his rhetoric was at its best when he was using crude, rabble-rousing methods to promote the idea that Austria should be included in a new German state. But unlike the anti-Catholic Schönerer, Lueger sided with the radical Catholics, helping them to establish their own press, found sporting clubs, develop a schools association and organise disorderly demonstrations.

In 1889 he founded the Christian Socialist party, and the following year, speaking to the Reichsrat (Parliament), he approvingly quoted a friend's suggestion that the Jews should be made to board a ship that would be sunk on the high seas so that none of them would survive. After Lueger was elected Burgomaster in 1895, the Emperor stopped him from taking office until 1897, when he launched a successful series of reforms, improving supplies of water, gas and electricity.

Both politically and as role models, these two Viennese anti-Semites were important to Hitler. Reinforcing the pro-German, anti-imperial feelings that had begun in secondary school, they bolstered his determination to evade compulsory service in the Austrian army. Having failed to register for it in either 1911 or 1912, he illegally crossed the

German border in May 1913, soon after his twenty-fourth birthday.

He settled in Munich, where he registered himself as 'stateless' and rented a room on the third floor of a house in Schleissheimerstrasse. His landlord, tailor Joseph Popp, had a shop on the premises. Hitler's flatlet had a private entrance, which might have been useful had he been sexually active, but Popp and his wife Elisabeth have testified that he never brought women into the house and never had dealings with prostitutes. They could remember neither seeing him with a woman, nor hearing him talk about a girlfriend. He spent his time as he had in Vienna – in cafés and beer halls, reading newspapers and sketching. According to Frau Popp, letters sometimes arrived from Angela.[24]

He was now living in Germany for the first time, apart from his three years in Passau as a child. On 18 January 1914, arrested for evading military service and leaving the country illegally, he was taken to the Austrian consulate. But when he presented himself in Salzburg during February for a medical examination, he was found to be unfit for military service. Returning to Munich, he settled back into his lazy routine. But only until war was declared.

4

Playing on the Black Notes

On May 1945 five Red Army pathologists signed their report 'concerning the forensic examination of a male corpse disfigured by fire'. One hundred and sixty-three centimetres long (five foot four), it was between fifty and sixty years old and it was dressed in a tattered yellow singlet. Lung, liver and intestines were exposed because the right side of the thorax and stomach had been burned away. They could not find the left testicle, though they searched on the spermatic cord inside the inguinal canal and in the small pelvis. The details were not released until 1968, when they appeared in a book by Lev Bezymenski, *The Death of Adolf Hitler: Unknown Documents from Soviet Archives*. A later book, *The Death of Hitler* by Ada Petrova and Peter Watson, revealed that Hitler's organs were removed during the autopsy and sent in jars to the Kremlin.

In the summer of 1992 British newspapers explained what had happened to the bodies of Hitler and Eva Braun. They had been entrusted to a Soviet counter-intelligence unit that reported directly to Stalin, who wanted another autopsy. It confirmed the findings of the first. What remained of the two bodies – apart from Hitler's organs – was buried in a Magdeburg garage or parking lot and covered with asphalt. But in 1970, during the Brezhnev regime, the remains were dug up and destroyed because it looked to the Soviet leadership as if Germany might be reunified under Willy Brandt and a shrine erected to Hitler's memory.

If we accept the autopsy as authentic, we must reject the testimony of Theodor Morell, Hitler's principal doctor throughout the war. Claiming to have examined Hitler's genitalia more than once, he told the United States Commission that 'The sexual organs showed no signs of abnormality or pathology, and the secondary sexual characteristics were normally developed.'[1] This is contradicted by the evidence of a Munich urologist, Professor Kielleuthner, who said Hitler had consulted him about monorchism (having only one testicle) but that it was too late to help him.[2]

Complaining throughout his life about a wide variety of ailments, Hitler consulted innumerable doctors, but few were allowed to examine him. 'Hitler was extremely reticent over showing his body,' said Dr von Hasselbach. 'His former driver and servant Maurice would probably know something about whether he had a physical defect in the genitalia, and in captivity he did make suggestions to this effect.'[3]

From 1936 Hasselbach was working in Munich University's surgical clinic. One of his colleagues there, Dr Karl Brandt, was on Hitler's personal staff, and Hasselbach acted as his locum. His vague summary of what Maurice said about Hitler's genitalia has to be balanced against the evidence of Heinz Linge, Hitler's valet from 1935 onwards. He testified that when, during a picnic, he and Hitler were urinating against the same tree, he saw that there was nothing abnormal about the Führer's penis.[4] Linge kept a diary, writing after Hitler had gone to bed – never before two in the morning.[5] But after the end of the war, giving evidence about events in the bunker before and after Hitler's death, Linge kept changing his story.

It is also striking – we see this in newsreels and Eva Braun's home movies – that both in public and in private Hitler was in the habit of standing with his hands crossed in front of his crotch. In his speeches he gesticulates a great deal, but the hands usually return to this position.

One of the more reliable witnesses was Ernst Hanfstaengl, a Harvard graduate who spent a lot of time with Hitler between 1922 and 1937, especially after he became the Nazi party's foreign press chief. His mother was American, and his father was a well-known Munich art dealer. Known as 'Putzi', Ernst Hanfstaengl was six foot four, with thick hair, twinkling eyes, a big nose and a protruding jaw. At Harvard he had known T. S. Eliot and acquired a reputation as a piano player. He used to

soothe Hitler's nerves by thundering out Wagnerian melodies
on the piano. Unlike most of Hitler's friends, he had a sense
of humour. When the photographer Hoffmann bought one of
Ludwig II's handwritten letters from an antiquarian bookseller
and left it on Hitler's plate in a restaurant, Hanfstaengl asked:
'So the King has been writing to you?'[6]

Hanfstaengl mentions 'a story, probably authentic' which
was 'frequently told' in Munich during the early twenties. It
was said that Hitler's

> old army comrades, who had seen him in the wash-house,
> had noted that his genital organs were almost freakishly
> underdeveloped, and he doubtless had some sense of shame
> about displaying himself. It seemed to me that this must all be
> part of the underlying complex in his physical relations, which
> was compensated for by the terrifying urge for domination
> expressed in the field of politics.[7]

Of course, the absence of one testicle does not stop a man from
functioning adequately as a lover, and does not necessarily cause
psychological problems. But the psychiatrist Dr William Dorrell
has seen several examples of a syndrome in which cryptorchidism
(or having an undescended testicle) contributes to the patient's
conviction

> that his genitals are so small that he could never satisfy a
> woman and [he] may also believe that his general physique
> is underdeveloped. He avoids sex for fear of failure or
> ridicule and dislikes being seen undressed. These patients
> usually show no abnormality and have genitals of average
> size but occasionally something like cryptorchidism can be
> the trigger for this reaction. More often it is in late puberty
> during which the boy was teased (and profoundly humiliated)
> by his more developed peers.[8]

According to the American psychoanalyst Peter Blos, monorchism or cryptorchidism is more likely to cause psychological
problems if the patient's relationship with his parents was
disturbed. In that case, the resultant pattern might involve

feelings of social inadequacy, impatience, hyperactivity, and chronic indecision, together with a tendency to lie, fantasise and exaggerate, while a sense of inferiority may generate a compulsion to rise above other people.[9]

Hanfstaengl took Hitler's problem to centre on impotence.

> From the time I knew him, I do not suppose he had orthodox sexual relations with any woman. He was probably incapable of a normal reaction to their physical proximity.... His eroticism was purely operatic, never operative. An impotent man with tremendous nervous energy, Hitler had to release this tension somehow. He was in turn sadist and masochist, and in the sexual half-light of his life, he never found the physical release which similar unfortunates can sometimes achieve, often due to some trick of circumstance or the attentions of one particular person. In his relations with women Hitler had to dramatise himself, as he had to dramatise himself in his relations with the world as a whole. The barren hero, I suppose you might call him.[10]

Hanfstaengl reformulated this point after the war in a broadcast interview with Lord Bullock, who wrote: 'Sitting at the piano and recalling some of the Wagner transcriptions he used to play for Hitler, he illustrated the latter's sexual condition with inimitable vulgarity. "You see, all he could do was play on the black notes, never the white."'[11]

Between 1919, when Hitler began to make his mark as a speaker, and his death in 1945, he had contact of one sort or another with innumerable ladies, but Hanfstaengl says Geli was 'the one woman in his life who went some way towards curing his impotence and half making a man out of him'. We need, though, to know more about the nature of his impotence and how far she went towards curing it. Hanfstaengl says their relationship constituted 'a psychological turning-point of the most sinister nature'.[12]

Impotence is inability to achieve or maintain penile erection adequate for sexual intercourse. Erection depends on a fairly complex interaction between the brain and the penis, involving not only the nerves but also the flow of blood into and away from the penis. This can be jeopardised by hormonal imbalance, stress or anxiety. It can be difficult to distinguish between psychological and physical causes of erectile failure. Organically the usual cause is a lack of blood or nerve supply to the penis, but this can be caused or increased by insecurity, which may be intensified by ambivalence about the woman or the act of love.

Hitler seems to have suffered only intermittently from impotence, but often enough to be nervous that sexual partners would ridicule him, while nervousness would have exacerbated the impotence. It is possible that in Vienna he had a traumatically humiliating experience with a prostitute, who may have infected him, but the evidence is inconclusive. The rumour spread during the early forties that he had contracted syphilis from a Viennese prostitute, possibly Jewish; when discussing Hitler's sexuality Lord Bullock said two hypotheses should be taken seriously: that he had syphillis, and that he was impotent.

In 1942 the head of the Gestapo, Heinrich Himmler, claimed (according to his physician, Felix Kersten) to be in possession of a twenty-six-page dossier proving that Hitler was suffering from syphilitic disease that could culminate in creeping paralysis.[13] But the doctors interrogated by the US intelligence services were unanimous in saying that Hitler had never suffered from either syphilis or creeping paralysis, while, even if Himmler really possessed documentary evidence – and really used it – it does not follow that he believed it to be authentic.

The best-known champion of the syphilis theory is Simon Wiesenthal, a concentration camp survivor who devoted much of his subsequent life to studying Nazism and tracking down war criminals. In the mid-sixties, a Munich city councillor called Fackler told him that during the First World War, Hitler narrowly escaped being court-martialled in Flanders for 'self-disablement' – the term used for syphilitic infection. He was said to have evaded a trial by claiming that his syphilis had started before the war.

Wiesenthal found supporting evidence when he met Dr Edmund Ronald, a physician living in Portugal with his Viennese wife. In Seattle, during the early fifties, Ronald had met an Austrian doctor from Graz who said his father had treated Hitler for syphilis, which he had caught in Vienna from a Jewish prostitute. In the twenties, according to Ronald, Hitler had consulted a specialist in venereal disease, Professor Spiethof of Jena, near Weimar. Some time after 1938, agents of the Gestapo had arrived at the Graz doctor's surgery and confiscated everything in his files about Hitler.

This would explain why Hitler wanted Theodor Morell, a specialist in skin and venereal disease, to be his personal doctor. This decision, according to Speer, surprised everyone around him, and the brass plate advertising the doctor's areas of specialisation had to be removed from outside his surgery. Wiesenthal thinks Hitler may have infected Geli Raubal with syphilis.[14]

If he had never had a humiliating encounter with a prostitute, it would be hard to explain how he arrived at one of his oddest sayings. 'Politics is like a harlot,' he declared. 'If you love her unsuccessfully, she bites your head off.' Another revealing image appears in his comparison of a girl's first sexual experience with a man's first exposure to gunfire: 'For a young woman her first encounter with her first man is a revelation that can be compared with the revelation that confronts a soldier when he faces war for the first time.'[15] Hitler's view of sexual intercourse as hostile confrontation might have originated from 'loving' a prostitute 'unsuccessfully'. This would also help to explain why there are so many references in *Mein Kampf* to prostitution and venereal disease.

His attacks on the Jews often vibrated with sexual envy. He got morbid satisfaction from his 'nightmare vision of hundreds and thousands of girls being seduced by repulsive, bandy-legged Jew bastards'. He described excitedly how black-haired Jews would pounce on innocent German girls and contaminate their blood, stealing them from their own people. Making the act of love sound obscene, he revealed the sex-starved obscenity in his vision of it. As Herbert Lüthy wrote,

His central political concept is a hackneyed rationalisation of this obsessional idea: an insane world in which history, politics and 'the life struggle of the peoples' are pictured solely in terms of coupling, fornication, pollution of the blood, selective breeding, hybridisation, generation in the primeval slime which will improve or mar the race, violation, rape and harassment of the woman – world history as an orgy of rut in which devilish submen lie in wait for the golden-haired female.[16]

Like Hitler's story about the milkmaid in Leonding, many of his conversational gambits about former girlfriends were intended to mislead. In December 1933, when his secretary Christa Schroeder expressed distaste for the name Emilie, he told her off: 'Don't say that. Emilie is a beautiful name. That's what my first sweetheart was called.' Fräulein Schroeder thought he was talking about a lover, but it was discovered recently that Emilie was the younger sister of his friend Rudolf Häusler. Four years younger than Hitler, he shared his room in Munich for several months in 1913–14. When he started bringing Hitler to his home, Emilie was seventeen. The least extrovert of the five children, she was neither robust nor pretty. She admired Hitler, who painted a postcard for her album, but it is unlikely that they had an affair.[17]

Geli seems to have been the only woman who could make him relax. Combining girlishness with womanliness, she was warm, gentle, affectionate, tactile, straightforward, direct, uninhibited, unpretentious, unprudish, kind, lively, playful, provocative and a member of the family. It was safe to reveal himself fully. No one else was ever allowed to tease him as much as she did, because no one else made him feel so secure. He hated nothing more than being laughed at, but when Geli laughed, she was laughing with him, not at him.

His sexual insecurity had several sources. One was fear of producing a child. Arguing that it would be irresponsible to start a family when he was so busy, he sometimes went on to explain why he would not want to have children. 'I'm aware that the children of a genius usually have a hard time in the world. They're expected to achieve the same stature as their famous father, and they're never forgiven if their achievement is only mediocre. Besides, they're usually cretins.'[18] Though he was sincere in claiming to be a genius, the allusion to cretins is disingenuous. His family background was such a well-kept secret that he could afford to talk like this, but, having so many relations who were deformed or mentally unbalanced, he was naturally worried about the genes he was carrying. Though the danger would have been doubled had he and Geli produced a child, he may have found it reassuring that she came from the same tainted family. With another woman there was always the danger that she might find out the facts. Geli, even if she did not know them, was equally affected by them.

5

The Good Soldier

On 5 February 1914, Austrian military doctors at Salzburg had found Hitler 'not strong enough for combatant and non-combatant duties'. He was rejected as 'unfit for military service'.[1] Had he been rejected again seven months later, when he volunteered for the German army, he might have remained a nonentity for the rest of his life, and history would have taken a different course. It was through being in the army that he found himself, and it was the army that trained him as a speaker.

He was a good soldier. In 1941, when he was fifty-two, he said: 'If I were twenty to twenty-five years younger, I'd be in the front line. I passionately loved soldiering.'[2] When making speeches he was sometimes reminiscent of a corporal shouting orders, and he structured the Nazi party like a fighting machine, recruiting armies of his own in brown and black shirts, and fighting elections as if they were military campaigns. Once in power, he wanted nothing more than to rearm Germany and start another war.

From 1914 to 1918 he mostly worked as a runner between headquarters and advanced positions. When shells knocked telephone lines out of action, runners provided the only means of passing messages between the command posts and the front line. Hitler was reliable, and always willing to work extra shifts of duty. He was so unfrightened by gunfire that fellow-soldiers were only half joking when they said they felt safer while he was around. Temperamentally he was a risk-taker, and he had several narrow escapes from death. His good luck reinforced his superstitious faith that providence was protecting him because it had something special in store for him. In December 1914 he was awarded the Iron Cross, second class.

One reason he liked wearing uniform was that it seemed to solve his problems of identity. As a schoolboy he had always been different from the others. In the peasant schools of the Waldviertel he was brighter and better off than his classmates. A boy from the provinces in Linz, he could not even do justice to his own intelligence; in Steyr he never settled down. In Vienna he lived for a time as if he had been expelled from the art school that had never accepted him, and in the men's hostel he was degraded but different from the other down-and-outs.

In the army he might still be different from the others, but it did not matter. He belonged. They were all soldiers, wearing the same clothes, eating the same food, facing the same discomforts and dangers. Asked where he came from, he said the 16th Regiment was his home.[3]

Front-line experiences were mostly unpleasant. In Flanders, soldiers were living in mud and spending hours at a stretch knee-deep in water. His environment was 'a maze of shelters, trenches with loopholes, communication trenches, barbed wire entanglements, pitfalls and Fladder mines'.[4] He described five days in the middle of October 1914 as the most strenuous he had ever experienced,[5] and later said: 'Marching along the roads was a misery for us poor old infantrymen; again and again we were driven off the road by the bloody gunners, and again and again we had to dive into the swamps to save our skins! All the thanks we got was a torrent of curses – "Bloody So-and-Sos" was the mildest expression hurled at us.'[6]

In October 1916 he was wounded in the left thigh, and, though he asked to stay at the front, he was sent to a field hospital outside Berlin. Paying his first visit to the city, he was bitterly disappointed. He had thought of it as the alternative to Vienna, and had idealised Frederick the Great's Prussia as the alternative to the vast, unwieldy, polyglot empire of the Habsburgs. Ever since going to school in Linz he had hated the messy patchwork of nationalities and languages in the empire and had fantasised about German unity. But there were no signs of unity in Berlin. What he found was hunger, misery, cynicism and impatience for peace among 'scoundrels' with no understanding of war or heroism or nationalism.

After convalescing, he was sent to join a reserve battalion in Munich: 'I thought I could no longer recognise the city.' It was no better than Berlin. He blamed the politicians, the journalists and the Jews, who deserved to be slaughtered, he thought. 'All the implements of military power should have been ruthlessly used for the extermination of this pestilence.'[7] Why should there be so many Jews in civilian clothes here and so few in uniform at the front?

Wearing uniform and being a soldier bolstered Hitler's sense of masculinity. In civilian clothes, as he knew, he seemed effeminate. This continued, even after he became Reich Chancellor. In September 1938, on the day he met the British Prime Minister, Neville Chamberlain, in Bad Godesberg, the American journalist William Shirer watched Hitler come out of his hotel: 'It was a very curious walk indeed . . . very ladylike. Dainty little steps.'[8]

The British diplomat Harold Nicolson records in his diary a conversation with a colleague who regarded Hitler as 'the most profoundly feminine man that he has ever met and there are moments when he becomes almost effeminate'.[9] Goering sometimes referred to him as 'that womanish fool',[10] while the Italian Fascist Curzio Malaparte said Hitler had nothing manly about him, and that 'his feminine side explains Hitler's success, his power over the masses'. This was quoted in an article published under the title 'The Woman Hitler: Psychology around a Leader' in the November 1932 issue of the socialist paper *Das Freie Wort*, which went on to attack his 'prima donna character . . . his rehearsed gestures, his pathological vanity towards himself and his movement'.[11]

When he threw a tantrum, he was in danger of seeming effeminate.

He behaved like a combination of a spoilt child and an hysterical woman. He scolded in high, shrill tones, stamped his feet and banged his fist on tables and walls. He foamed at the mouth, panting and stammering in uncontrolled fury: 'I won't have it! Get rid of all of them! Traitors!' He was an alarming sight, his hair dishevelled, his eyes fixed and his face distorted and purple. I feared that he would collapse or have an apoplectic fit.

Suddenly it was all over. He walked up and down the room, clearing his throat and brushing his hair back. He looked round apprehensively and suspiciously, with searching glances at us. I had the impression that he wanted to see if anyone was laughing. And I must admit that a desire to laugh, perhaps largely as a nervous reaction to the tension, rose within me.[12]

Not that there were any grounds for the rumours of homosexuality that were circulating at the end of the war. In 1952 a homosexual doctor who had once X-rayed Hitler lodged evidence in a Munich court to the effect that he had been fascinated by Hitler's eyes, speech and gait, but knew immediately that he was not 'one of us'.

Discussing the homosexuality of a close associate, Ernst Röhm, Hitler said: 'In a man like Röhm, who has lived so long in the tropics, a disease like this – for it is as a disease that I prefer to regard it – his private life is of no interest to me.'[13]

But Hitler may have had to struggle against latent homo-sexuality. His relationship with his architect, Albert Speer, was emotionally quite complicated. Speer did not understand it till a psychologist, Alexander Mitscherlich, pointed to the erotic element in it. Both men were reticent and emotionally inhibited: they communicated mainly through the passion they shared for architecture and through collaborating on large-scale projects. In a biography of Speer, Gitta Sereny says they were both 'bedevilled from childhood by thwarted, imagined and withheld love, a deficiency which rendered them both virtually incapable of expressing private emotions. . . . Both of them, capable of great charm and courted by women, could barely respond though neither of them was homosexual.'[14]

'In those first years close to Hitler,' wrote Speer, 'I was ready to follow him wherever he led.' In 1937, put in charge of Hitler's architectural planning department with the title *Generalbauinspektor*, he employed a former professor of law, Dr Karl Hettlage, who noticed that 'Speer's relationship with

Hitler was not primarily cerebral – it was very special, spontaneous in a way, for both of them.' In 1938, after watching them together in front of an architectural model, Hettlage abruptly told Speer: 'You know what you are? You are Hitler's unhappy love.'[15]

In 1975, when Speer's *Spandau: The Secret Diaries* was serialised in the *Frankfurter Allgemeine Zeitung*, Mitscherlich wrote: 'In his own way, Adolf Hitler loved Albert Speer and in his own way Albert Speer loves Adolf Hitler.' The attractive, well-born, Nordic-looking Speer was a man Hitler would have liked to resemble, or, ideally, to be. Able to transpose Speer's concepts into reality, Hitler was the all-powerful father, the protector Speer had always needed or believed himself to need. 'Yes,' said Speer, 'Mitscherlich came closest to the truth.'[16]

Never developing the homosexual side of his nature, Hitler was aware of it and sufficiently afraid of it to hit out viciously against homosexuals and homosexuality, fulminating against it as a social evil he would eradicate as soon as he came to power. And he tried to implement this threat. In Germany there were almost 30,000 prosecutions for homosexuality between 1936 and 1939, compared with 3261 between 1931 and 1934.[17]

Some of his most ridiculous behaviour was prompted by the desire to appear robustly masculine and tremendously virile. Showing his library to a young woman and seeing that her attention was wandering, he abruptly stiffened his arm in a Nazi salute and said in a deep voice:

I can hold my arm like that for two solid hours. I never feel tired when my storm troopers and soldiers march past me and I stand at this salute. I never move. My arm is like granite, rigid and unbending. But Goering can't stand it. He has to drop his hand after half an hour at this salute. He's flabby. But I am hard. . . . It's an amazing feat. Sometimes I marvel at my own power.[18]

Talking about the salute as if it were an alternative form of erection – and he made plentiful public use of it to demonstrate his superiority over other men – he may have been trying to compensate for his intermittent impotence. He

Hitler's adjutant Julius Schaub said Geli was full of animal spirits, always ready for a joke, and extraordinarily self-possessed.

Hitler's mother, Klara, had large, staring eyes, regular features and short brown hair. She was meek and pious, a subservient wife and a regular churchgoer.

The illegitimate son of a forty-one-year-old maidservant, Alois Schicklgruber worked as a customs officer. His son talks in *Mein Kampf* about 'drunken beatings' and 'brutal attacks of the father against the mother'.

Family resemblance: Hitler with his half-sister, Angela, and (below) on a North Sea trip with his sister, Paula, in 1930.

Lance-Corporal Hitler at Fournes in April 1915 with two of the other messengers, Ernst Schmidt (left), Anton Bachmann (centre), and the pro-German English terrier Foxl.

Hitler in prison at the Landsberg Fortress in 1924 with four of his supporters. (From left) Emil Maurice, Hermann Kriebel, Rudolf Hess and Friedrich Weber.

Well-groomed convict. Hitler in his cell, 1924.

Hitler campaigning in April 1933 for the election. On the right are adjutant Wilhelm Brückner, Press Chief Otto Dietrich and, in the rear, Emil Maurice. The other adjutant, Julius Schaub, is in the rear on the left.

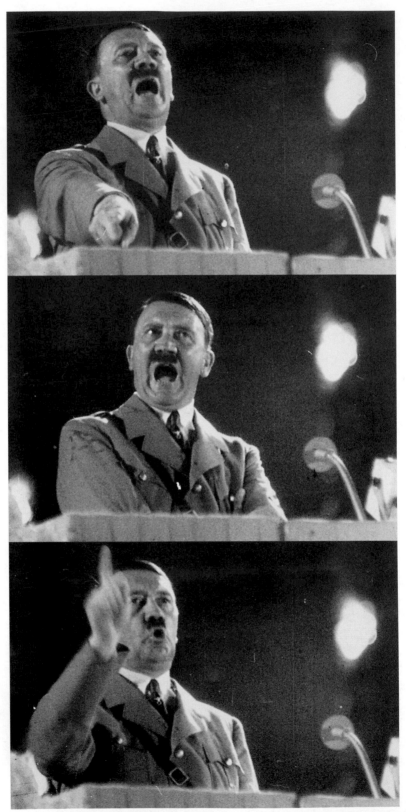

Hitler's oratory was compared to rape and murder. Using rhythm and repetition,

he pushed relentlessly towards a climax that has often been called orgasmic.

Ernst ('Putzi') Hanfstaengl, Foreign Press Chief.

Photographer Heinrich Hoffmann on his fiftieth birthday,
12 September 1935.

could not always satisfy even such an undemanding girlfriend as Eva Braun. Dr Morell told a former patient, Dr Paul Karl Schmidt-Carell, that she had asked him to give Hitler drugs which would boost his sexual appetite. There were also rumours that he was fighting his impotence by having himself injected with pulverised bulls' testicles in grape sugar and with extracts of prostate and seminal vesicles, but the injections probably did not start till the mid-thirties.[19]

As a soldier during the First World War, much as he enjoyed the male solidarity he did not join in conversations about women and did not give fellow-soldiers the impression of sharing their attitude. They took him to be a woman-hater. Relying partly on evidence from Max Amann, the sergeant who served as regimental historian and later edited the Nazi paper, the *Völkischer Beobachter*, Hitler's lieutenant, Oberleutnant Friedrich Wiedemann, said that he 'did not receive any letters; he had no girl friends. I even proposed to various girls that they become his pen friends.'[20] Some soldiers from his unit said he visited a brothel in Brussels during the war, and it has been claimed that a photograph is extant showing him on the way in. But neither the photograph nor any other evidence has been produced.

He may not have lost his virginity by the end of the war, though a story started circulating in the seventies that he had impregnated an eighteen-year-old French girl, Charlotte Lobjoie, in 1917. Told shortly before his mother's death that Hitler was his father, Jean-Marie Loret tried to check the facts by having tests in a Heidelberg institute. But they were inconclusive, and in 1979 he went to see Christa Schroeder, one of Hitler's secretaries, hoping she might recognise a family resemblance. 'It was only by the way he walked, outside in the Blumenau, when Loret was leaving, that I thought I recognised a similarity to Hitler in his gait and his posture, but it's easy to deceive oneself on these matters.'[21] He went on trying to establish whether he was Hitler's son, and the archives of the Hoover Institution in Stanford, California contain certificates, memoranda, military records, notarised statements, photographs and press clippings in German and French; but it looks as if Schroeder was deceiving herself about the similarity. Naturally, German soldiers chatted about French girls, but the consensus of Hitler's former comrades is that it would have been out of character for him to sleep with one.[22]

Reminiscing about the First World War, Hitler rarely mentioned the rats in the Flanders trenches. But they must have recalled his boyhood experiences of shooting in the churchyard at Leonding, and in January 1915, when he adopted a dog, it was after it had chased a rat into his trench. 'Hunting rats was his greatest pleasure.'[23] Naming the dog Foxl belonged to his cult of the predatory, like calling himself 'Herr Wolf'.

He often talked proudly of what warfare had taught him. 'If I weren't myself hardened by this experience, I would have been incapable of undertaking this Cyclopean task which the building of an empire means for a single man.' But he was not uncritical of the German war leaders. It was the British who first used tanks, on the Somme in 1916. No German tanks appeared until 1917, and then only a few. 'With 400 tanks in the summer of 1918 we would have won the world war. It was our misfortune that the leaders we had didn't understand the importance of technical weapons at the right time.'[24] Had he been in command, he said, Germany would have won the war.

He won a regimental award for exceptional courage in face of the enemy during May 1918, and three months later the Iron Cross, first class. But he never rose above the rank of corporal, and throughout most of the war he was a lance-corporal. According to Oberleutnant Wiedemann,

By military standards Hitler really didn't at that time have potential for promotion. I'm disregarding the fact that he wouldn't have cut a specially good figure as an officer in peacetime; his posture was sloppy and when he was asked a question his answer would be anything but short in a soldier-like fashion. He didn't hold his head straight – it was usually sloping towards his left shoulder. Now all that doesn't matter in wartime, but ultimately a man must have leadership qualities if you're doing the right thing when you promote him to be a non-commissioned officer.[25]

But Hitler never lost his taste for wearing uniform. During the Second World War, as we see from innumerable newsreels, home movies and photographs, he often wore a peaked military cap and a uniform jacket when he could have relaxed in civilian clothes. In a snapshot taken during a Baltic cruise he is wearing a peaked cap and boots while taking a nap in a deckchair.[26]

As a soldier he saw hundreds of wounded and dying men – 'a reminder that life is constantly a cruel struggle'.[27] He said this was the most instructive experience that war had given him. He had learnt that life 'has no other object but the preservation of the species. The individual can disappear provided there are other men to replace him.'[28] This was an argument he often used to justify brutality towards individuals – and sometimes large groups of individuals. Reminded how many newly commissioned officers were being killed in 1943, he said: 'But that's what the young men are there for.'[29]

6

Thundering Demon

Leaving civilian deaths out of account, about 8 million people were killed in the First World War, but it ended less like a tragedy than a farce. The Communist revolution started in the navy when the naval high command, without consulting the government, ordered the fleet into action. This provoked a mutiny at the Kiel naval base, followed by scattered uprisings all over Germany.

The Kaiser took refuge at the army headquarters in Spa, where, on 8 November 1918, a telegram arrived in the evening from the Chancellor, Prinz Max von Baden, who said he could not keep the rebellion in check unless the Kaiser's abdication was announced in the morning papers. But Kaiser Wilhelm had gone to bed, saying he did not want to be disturbed, and nobody dared to wake him. In the morning he refused to abdicate, and he left for Holland the next day in his private train. At the frontier he had to surrender his sword to a Dutch customs official.

In Munich, hearing that all his troops had either deserted or gone over to the rebels, the seventy-three-year-old King of Bavaria, Ludwig III, took a box of cigars and made for the car in the royal garage, only to find that his chauffeur had absconded with the petrol. A private garage supplied him with a car, but it ran off the road outside Munich and got stuck in a potato field.

Within a few days all the other German kings and archdukes had abdicated, deferring meekly to the workers' and soldiers' councils that suggested they no longer had a function. The King of Saxony is said to have told the delegation: 'All right, you can clear up the mess yourselves.'

It was not simply the war that had got Germany into this mess. During 1917 the internal balance of power shifted. By the end of the year, the Kaiser and the Chancellor were no longer in control: decisions were taken by the Reichstag and the military Supreme Command. They could work effectively together so long as Germany seemed to be winning the war, as it did until August 1918. The army penetrated so deeply into Russia during the summer that it looked as if the whole country could be subjugated, and though the United States had declared war on Germany during the spring of 1917, American troops scarcely made their presence felt till the summer of 1918. But by August, the German army was exhausted and demoralised. British troops were being reinforced by Canadians and Australians, while tanks were helping them to break through the German positions.

During 1917, when the Kaiser and Chancellor lost most of their power, it had not been on account of any constitutional change; but the idea of making one was mooted at the end of September 1918, when the Foreign Minister, Paul von Hintze, met General Erich von Ludendorff. Appointed Chief of Staff in 1914, Ludendorff had become Hindenburg's first Quartermaster General in 1916, and in 1918 he had planned the spring offensive against the Russians that nearly won the war for Germany. Hintze suggested that Germany should be democratised by empowering the Reichstag to depose the government with a vote of no confidence. Since Germany would soon have to surrender, the Allies might give better terms to a country that was inclining, however belatedly, towards democracy. Ludendorff, who was in favour of this idea, saw that it would be advantageous for the army because it would be the Reichstag that would have to take the blame for wanting to surrender.[1]

The new government was made up mainly of Social Democrats and Liberals under the leadership of Max von Baden, a liberal aristocrat. Reluctantly he started suing for peace, while the army was still fighting on the Western Front and nothing had been done to prepare the German people for the news that the war was lost. There was soon talk of a 'stab in the back': the army seemed to have been betrayed by the politicians.

* * *

Karl Marx had expected Germany to produce the first prole-
tarian revolution, and to Lenin it seemed tragic that none of
the left-wing parties could lead the workers into insurrection.
But the only party to favour revolutionary violence of the Soviet
variety was the Spartacus Union, which had been founded in
1916 by Karl Liebknecht and the Polish revolutionary Rosa
Luxemburg.

In 1917–18 the Spartacists and the USPD (*Unabhängige
Sozialdemokratische Partei Deutschlands* – German Independent Social Democratic Party) had both been fomenting agitation.
The USPD had been formed by Social Democrats who defected in
1914 when their party supported the war loan, but most people,
tired of the war, had become politically lethargic, and it was not
until October 1918 that rebellion broke out in the navy.

On 17 October Hungary had proclaimed its independence
from Austria, and on 3 November Austria signed an armistice
with the Allies. Since the German army was still fighting, the
leader of the USPD, Kurt Eisner, saw his opportunity and seized
it. A small man with steel-rimmed spectacles and a long wispy
grey beard, Eisner was a Jewish drama critic who had been
working in Berlin till he abandoned his wife and five children
to live with a woman journalist in Munich, where he founded
a branch of the Independent Socialist party. Eisner had been in
prison till mid-October for his anti-war agitation. In Munich,
on the day that Austria signed the armistice, he addressed a big
crowd in the Theresienwiese demanding that a new Bavarian
regime instituted by the people should proclaim peace together
with the German republicans of Austria. He got such a positive
response from the crowd that four days later, rallying support
from soldiers and members of the Bavarian Peasants' League, he
succeeded in capturing all the military headquarters in Munich.
By the end of the day, red posters were being plastered on walls
all over the city proclaiming a Bavarian republic.

The rebellion that had started in the navy reached Berlin on
9 November, when a general strike was called and workers
marched on the Reichstag, demanding peace but unsure of what
else they wanted. The man who stepped out to make a speech
from the balcony was Philipp Scheidemann, joint leader of the
Social Democrats with Friedrich Ebert, a former saddle-maker

and inkeeper. On the balcony Scheidemann promptly declared a republic, though Ebert had promised to help Prinz Max von Baden fight the social revolution.

By the afternoon, when the two men met, Prinz Max had announced the abdication of the Kaiser and unconstitutionally appointed Ebert as Chancellor. Stubbornly monarchistic, Ebert asked Prinz Max to act as regent. But he refused. Like the King of Saxony, he was fed up with the mess. Ebert would have to call a Constituent Assembly to establish constitutional foundations for a democratic Germany.

In Bavaria, a council of People's Delegates assumed power two days before the armistice was signed on 11 November. Some of Eisner's most prominent supporters were Communists, and many were Jewish – Felix Fechenbach, Edgar Jaffé, Eugen Leviné, Ernst Toller, Erich Mühsam and Arnold Wadler. These were the men whom Hitler later derided as 'the November criminals'; what he did not admit was that he had been working for them.

At the end of the war an officer who knew Hitler well, Captain Karl Mayr, sized him up as a time-server. He would 'have been just as glad to work for a Jew or a Frenchman as for an Aryan. The first time I met him he was like a stray dog looking for a master.'[2]

First he volunteered for guard duty at a prisoner-of-war camp in Traunstein, near the Austrian border. There he joined the regiment's propaganda department, and at the end of February 1919 went on a political training course. According to Guido Knopp, he committed himself to socialism, and after Eisner was assassinated on 21 February 1919, Hitler, wearing the uniform of a lance-corporal with the red armband of the Bavarian soviets, marched in the funeral procession following the coffin. (Later these facts were suppressed, and it was not until 1995 that German television audiences saw a sequence of film showing him in the procession.)[3] Anton Joachimstaler contends that Hitler was never in the red army.[4]

In Berlin the Communist rebellion that began on 5 January 1919, led by Karl Liebknecht and Rosa Luxemburg, was crushed within ten days; but in Munich, on the day after Eisner was killed, the Soldiers' and Workmen's Council declared Bavaria a soviet republic. On 15 April, when workers, peasants and soldiers all had to elect spokesmen, Hitler was elected as a *Soldatenrat* – soldiers' representative – in the so-called Demobilisation Company of the 2nd Infantry Regiment.

Friedrich Ebert's instincts were conservative, and if he could not preserve the monarchy, at least he could suppress the revolution. Though he got himself appointed as head of a six-man Council of People's Delegates, he was trying simultaneously to use the army against the rebels. But the returning troops were no longer obeying orders, and many were joining the rebels. The solution proposed by a young major who had been on the general staff, Kurt von Schleicher, was to recruit volunteers from men who had been demobilised, and organise them as Freikorps units under the command of former officers. Then it would not be the army that was firing on the crowds.

Many of the men who volunteered were of the type later described by Goering as 'fighters who couldn't be debrutalised', and some would later become Nazi stormtroopers. By the end of 1918, General Ludwig Maercker, former commander of an infantry division, had recruited 4,000 men. At the beginning of 1919 the rebellion was crushed in Berlin, and in cities all over the country the workers' and soldiers' councils stood no chance against the ruthless private armies.

In Bavaria the soviets survived longer than anywhere else, but in April 22,000 men advancing southwards towards Munich encountered little resistance. It was a mixed army, led by a Prussian major general and consisting partly of troops belonging to the Federal government, which was answering an appeal from Johannes Hoffman, Prime Minister of the *Landtag* (provincial parliament), partly of troops from Württemberg, and partly of private armies such as Franz Ritter von Epp's Bayrisches Schützenkorps and the Freikorps Oberland.[5] They took control of the city on 1 May, and within the next few days the red flags disappeared as Bavaria was integrated into the Weimar Republic; the name derived from a February 1919 meeting of the National Assembly in Goethe's home town.

The democratisation of Germany failed to soften the demands of the victorious Allies. At Versailles on 7 May the German delegates were presented with a peace treaty which they found unacceptable. Intent on punishing and subduing a Germany that no longer existed, the Allies inflicted devastating terms. Germany had to admit guilt for the war, surrendering all guns, warplanes and ships, and to pay not only reparations but also the cost of maintaining the Allied troops occupying the Rhineland.

Fighting an election at home in December 1918, the Liberal British Premier, David Lloyd George, had promised to 'squeeze the German lemon until the pips squeak'. The French and the Conservative majority in his coalition government were more anti-German than he was, and the final terms of the treaty were so harsh that he predicted another war would have to be fought within twenty-five years at three times the cost. It began only twenty years later. 'Something was wrong with the peace,' wrote Klaus Mann. 'Nobody seemed to like it. In fact people now looked more apprehensive even than during the war.'[6]

The Weimar Republic preserved the Federal structure of Bismarck's Reich. While the central government controlled foreign and economic policy, individual states had jurisdiction over matters affecting the citizens' daily life and welfare. Education, public health and policing were the responsibility of the seventeen separate states.

In times of crisis and anarchy it is a relief to hold a single government responsible, but the chaos that prevailed in post-war Bavaria could be blamed either on the Reich President, the Reich Chancellor and the Reichstag in Berlin or on the Bavarian President, Prime Minister and the *Landtag* in Munich. Prussia, which was predominantly Protestant, was the largest of the seventeen states, with 38 million inhabitants – two-thirds of the republic's total population.

For ordinary peace-loving Bavarians, it would have been dangerous to have so many armed men in the streets even if the economy had not been so depressed. Food and fuel were in short supply; the shooting and looting that had been commonplace during the war did not suddenly stop. Crime was uncontrollable. In Munich soldiers were selling their weapons and their uniforms. Not only shops but barracks were being looted. Men in uniform were more likely to be committing crimes than keeping the peace.

Though it imposed a limit of 100,000 on the German army, the Treaty of Versailles failed to establish any jurisdiction over paramilitary groups. The Allies pressed for these private armies to be suppressed, but the terms of the treaty had been so humiliating that the Germans could not be expected to cooperate in enforcing them, and in Bavaria the number of mercenaries rose to a formidable 300,000 thousand – three times the number of soldiers in the army, which maintained underground links with these groups.

While law-abiding army officers wanted to obey the rules laid down by the treaty, loyalties were divided. The treaty was designed to weaken the German army, which could remain strong only through secret activity. Of the officers in the 2nd Infantry Regiment who set out to disobey the rules the most dangerous was Ernst Röhm, later head of the SA but now a captain on the staff of the district command in Munich. He organised a board of inquiry to investigate what had been going on during the revolutionary period and what was currently going on inside the splinter groups that had been proliferating since the war and calling themselves political parties. About fifty of them were extremist; it would be advantageous for the regiment to keep an eye on these, ostensibly to restrain them but actually to form secret links with the ones that might be useful.

When Bavaria's red army was disbanded, Hitler was among the soldiers arrested and interrogated by the 2nd Infantry Regiment. One of the men working for Röhm was Captain Mayr, who had been keeping an eye on the stray dog, and when Mayr was put in charge of an 'enlightenment commando', a kind of counter-intelligence unit to counteract the influence of Marxist ideas on soldiers returning to civilian life, he enlisted Hitler to report on those who had taken orders from the soviets. As an informer on his former comrades, he was useful to his new master, and Mayr selected him for an anti-Communist political education, together with a training in agitation and public speaking.

In June 1919, sent for a week of political instruction at Munich University, Hitler attended a lecture by an anti-Semitic engineer, Gottfried Feder, who had theories about loan capital and the international stock exchange. 'Right after listening to Feder's first lecture, the thought ran through my head that I had now found the way to one of the most essential premises for the foundation of a new party.'[7]

As a trainee speaker, Hitler made rapid progress. One of the teachers on the course was Karl Alexander von Müller, a historian, who was leaving the hall one day after a lecture he had given when he heard someone talking passionately in a strangely guttural voice. A group had collected round him, and he seemed excited by the excitement he was arousing. 'I saw a pale, thin face under a drooping, unsoldierly strand of hair, with close-cropped moustache and strikingly big pale blue eyes gleaming coldly with fanaticism.'[8]

In June 1919, while Hitler was turning his back on Communism, Angela was offered a job in the kitchen of a Vienna hostel for Jewish students. Elfriede was now nine, Geli eleven and Leo twelve. Deciding that they were old enough for her to take a full-time job, she accepted the offer. Though she was afterwards criticised for failing to mention that she was Hitler's half-sister, there was nothing to mention: he was still far from being a well-known anti-Semite.

Situated in Zimmermannsdamm, the hostel was owned by the board in charge of Jewish high schools. The food had to be kosher, and the two cooks, Angela and an orthodox Jewish woman, were supervised by a representative of the board. Angela did her work conscientiously, and when a girl who came to work in the kitchen failed to carry out the orthodox rituals, Angela threatened to sack her.[9] Working a long day, Angela could not spend enough time with her own children, but at last there was more money in the household.

While she was working throughout the summer in a hot kitchen, Hitler was impressing his instructors. In August he was sent to another training course, at Lechfeld, where one of the officers commented in his report on 'a very beautiful, lucid and passionate lecture by Lance-Corporal Hitler on capitalism, touching on the Jewish question'.[10] Captain Mayr was pleased with him. 'I have given a start to some very able young men,' he wrote in September 1919. 'A Herr Hitler, for example, has become a powerful force, a first class popular orator.'[11]

It was the board of inquiry that sent Hitler to inform on one of the splinter groups – the German Workers' Party, which had been founded in January 1919 by Anton Drexler, a machinist in the local workshop of the Federal Railways. More like a beer-drinking discussion group than a political party, the German Workers described themselves as classless, socialist and 'led by only German leaders' – in other words nationalist.

Hitler attended a meeting on 12 September, at which the main speaker was the anti-Semitic engineer Gottfried Feder. Only about forty people were in the audience, and during question time a man said that Bavaria should be separated from Germany and united with Austria. This infuriated Hitler, who made such a vehement speech that Drexler ran after him at the end of the meeting, gave him a pamphlet entitled *My Political Awakening* and asked him to come back soon.

Lying on his bed in the barracks and throwing crusts of bread to the mice, he read the pamphlet, which argued that the world had been corrupted by the Jews. Though he had not applied for it, he received a membership card through the post, and he was invited to a committee meeting in a shabby pub. When the party's funds were counted at a table 'in the dim light of a broken gas lamp', they amounted to seven marks and fifty pfennigs.

The six committee members wanted to co-opt Hitler and put him in charge of recruitment and propaganda. After two days of hesitation, he said yes. He was still in the army, and he was not the only soldier to join. Röhm became a member too.

Making lists and typing letters in the barracks, Hitler did all he could to recruit members and promote the party. He made his mark as a speaker when he addressed a meeting attended by 111 people. 'I spoke for thirty minutes, and what before I had simply felt within me without in any way knowing it was now proved by reality. I could speak. The people in the small room were electrified.'[12] When he had an audience his rhetoric made him more passionate, while his passion made him more rhetorical.

He was lucky that Drexler's original plan had been to fuse socialism with nationalism, but it had not occurred to Drexler that the words 'nationalist' and 'socialist' ought to feature in the party's name. Hitler went on receiving his army salary till the end of March 1920, but over the next twelve months his life increasingly revolved around the party.

In the early summer of 1921, when he paid a second visit to Berlin and stayed there for six months, he was fanatical in his hatred of the fashion-conscious frivolity, the dancing and the decadence. Metropolitan nightlife struck him as proving that the Jews were undermining German values. 'The Jew makes night into day,' he grumbled, and he attacked theatres as 'hotbeds of vice and shamelessness'. Provincial in outlook, Hitler was more at home in Munich.

During his absence, Adolf Drexler had tried to consolidate his hold on the party that had once been his, but he was out-manoeuvred when, after returning to Munich, Hitler strategically resigned on 11 July. Three days later, he offered to rejoin, but only on condition that he became First Chairman with dictatorial powers. He got what he wanted. The appetite inside the party for strong leadership was indicative of the appetite outside. At a meeting on 29 July he was hailed as 'our Führer', and, profiling him in the *Völkischer Beobachter* on 4 August, Dietrich Eckart called him 'selfless, self-sacrificing, devoted and sincere'.

It was thanks to Eckart that the party had acquired the *Völkischer Beobachter* in December 1920. Until 1919 it had been called the *Münchener Beobachter*, and, as the organ of the racist Thule Society, had been the most important of the anti-Semitic papers. Now, as the party's official newspaper, with Eckart as editor, it played a major role in manufacturing and propagating the Hitler myth.

During August he founded the SA; though the letters originally stood for *Sport Abteilung*, he had little interest in creating a division for sport and gymnastics. His twofold ambition was to recruit uprooted, disenchanted soldiers as party members and to form a private army. The SA was put under the command of a former naval officer, Lieutenant Johann Klintsch of the Ehrhardt Brigade, one of the private armies, and the mid-August issue of the *Völkischer Beobachter* proclaimed the objective of bringing 'young party members together into an iron organisation whose strength will be available as a battering ram for the entire movement. It should uphold the military ideals of a free people and protect the work to be done by the leaders'.[13]

Within three months the SA had demonstrated its strength and brutality in a series of beer hall brawls, and in November the *Sport Abteilung* became the *Sturm Abteilung*. Membership grew rapidly. Hitler had always known how exciting war games could be, and he now gave unemployed teenage boys the chance to take part in street battles, parades and cross-country trips in vans as well as to participate in propaganda activities by writing up slogans on walls and putting up posters. Some could improve their riding in the equestrian corps, while others drove cars, played musical instruments, took part in athletic activities or rode in bicycle squads.[14] By September 1922 there were 15,000 men in the SA. Within eighteen months of becoming a civilian, Hitler had a big army of his own, and he declared his intention of recruiting only those prepared to obey their leaders and to face the danger of death.[15]

Without connivance from the police, the SA could not have done what it did. Like the Minister of Justice, Franz Gürtner, the police commissioner, Ernst Pöhner, was a nationalist who consistently turned a blind eye on the violent criminality of the right-wing extremists. The two men effectively gave Hitler *carte blanche* to turn Munich into a playground for adult war games in which people could be killed. Death was doubly helpful to Hitler, who terrorised his fellow-citizens while reminding them of the breakdown in the state machinery for maintaining law and order. Intimidation in the streets reinforced rhetoric at the rallies.

> Cruelty impresses. People need a good scare. They want to be afraid of something. They want someone to make them afraid, someone to whom they can submit with a shudder. Haven't you noticed, after a brawl at a meeting, that the ones who get beaten up are the first to apply for membership of the party? What is this rot you talk about violence and how shocked you are about torture? The masses want that. They need something to dread.[16]

In no other period of German history could this combination of rhetoric and violence have been so effective. After defeat and the humiliating peace settlement, the people were depressed and desperate. Morale could not recover while they had no defence against starvation, crime and inflation.

The Allies had insisted on reparations of 20 billion gold marks by May 1921, but the gold mark was not a coin; it was a concept based on pre-war money markets in which a mark was worth four dollars. By 1921 the dollar was worth sixty marks. To raise money the Weimar government issued newly printed paper currency, which accelerated devaluation. By 1920 the mark had only a tenth of its pre-war value against the dollar, and by January 1922 a hundredth. By October 1923 the cost of printing a banknote was higher than its value. As Alex de Jonge puts it, 'If defeat, abdication and revolution had begun to undermine the traditional values of German culture, then the inflation finished the process so completely that in the end there were no such values left.'[17]

Huge fortunes were made by speculating against the currency, and people who had borrowed money to buy property or finance commercial enterprises could easily pay off their debts, while pensioners and owners of small businesses were reduced to penury. By the end of 1923 beggars were rejecting 100,000 mark notes as worthless, while fifty American dollars were enough to buy a row of houses in the most expensive district of Berlin.[18] Nationalists blamed the crisis on the high reparations payments, but the origins of the problem went back to 1914, when the war had been financed not by raising taxes but by printing paper money.

From any ordinary viewpoint, Hitler had been unlucky in having the boyhood he had. He had accumulated a huge reservoir of bitterness from having a grandfather who may – for all he knew – have been Jewish, from having hunchbacks and half-wits in the family, a bastard father who beat him, a servant-like mother who could not assert herself, a half-brother who ran away and afterwards served two prison sentences for stealing, and a schooling that made him feel even more inadequate. But the bitterness was useful to him as a speaker. He could draw on it to fulminate against the Jewish politicians

of Eisner's soviet republic and against the foreigners who had
made Germany into a nation of beggars.

There was a strongly erotic element in the excitement that
Hitler generated. Konrad Heiden describes his power:

> Suddenly this man, who looked awkward while he was
> standing around, has begun to speak, filling the room with
> his voice, riding over interruptions or contradictions by his
> domineering manner, sending cold shudders down the backs
> of everyone present by the savagery of his manner. . . . Awed,
> the listener feels that something new has come into the room.
> This thundering demon was not there earlier; this is not the
> same shy man with contracted shoulders.[19]

His bitterness came over as anger, but he was saying what the
audience wanted to hear. As Otto Strasser put it,

> Hitler responds to the vibrations of the human heart with the
> delicacy of a seismograph, or perhaps of a wireless receiving
> set, enabling him, with a certainty with which no conscious
> gift could endow him, to act as a loud-speaker proclaiming
> the most secret desires, the least admissible instincts, the
> sufferings and personal revolts of a whole nation. But his
> very principle is negative. He only knows what he wants to
> destroy. He pulls down the walls without any idea of what
> he will build in their place.[20]

The President of the Danzig Senate, Hermann Rauschning, made
the same point:

> It was interesting to watch Hitler talking himself into a fury,
> and to note how necessary to his eloquence were shouting
> and a feverish *tempo*. A quiet conversation with him was
> impossible. Either he was silent or he took complete charge
> of the conversation. Hitler's eloquence is plainly no natural
> gift, but the result of a conquest of certain natural inhibitions
> which, in intimate conversation, still make him awkward. The
> convulsive artificiality of his character is specially noticeable

in such intimate circles; particularly noticeable is his lack of any sense of humour. Hitler's laugh is hardly more than an expression of scorn and contempt. There is no relaxation about it. His pleasures have no repose.[21]

Mothers and Daughters

Settling back into the civilian world, Hitler built his career and his social life around his oratory. Needing a substitute for the solidarity he had enjoyed in the army, he spent most of his time in male company. His tendency was to surround himself with civilian replicas of the fellow-soldiers who had been adult replicas of the younger boys who played war games. As a boy he had imaginary soldiers who took his orders; in the army he had real soldiers who did not. He now had real men who did – men who might once have been non-commissioned officers and would now be effective fighters in a brawl.

He spent much of the day sitting around with them in bars and cafés, eating cakes and drinking – not alcohol but coffee and mineral water. Apart from Putzi Hanfstaengl, the one gentlemanly member of his entourage was Hermann Goering, who had been an air ace during the war and had an attractive Swedish wife. Hitler hated to be alone, but had few close friends, though his platform charisma won him plenty of admirers.

Many of them were women, and if his feelings about women were expressed most clearly in similes and metaphors, none was more revealing than the statement about audiences lusting for domination.

Like a woman whose psychic feeling is controlled less by abstract logic than by undefinable sentimental yearning for complementary strength, who will submit to the strong man in preference to dominating the weak one, the masses love the man who commands, not the man who begs . . . They understand neither the audacity used to terrorise them spiritually nor the outrageous infringement of their human freedom, for they are totally unaware that the doctrine is delusional. They see only the unreasoning force, the brutality and the purpose of its manifestations, and in the end they always give in.[1]

Mastery over audiences gave him erotic satisfaction. In spite of – or maybe because of – his basic contempt for women, he addressed himself chiefly to them. At rallies the visual and musical build-up to his speech was blatantly masculine – the drumbeat and blaring brass in the marches, swirling banners on long flagstaffs, a disciplined parade of jackbooted men – but all this impressed the women.

As Hermann Rauschning summed it up, 'women's gushing adulation, carried to the pitch of pseudo-religious ecstasy, provided the indispensable stimulus that could rouse him from his lethargy. It is curiously reminiscent of the feminine adoration lavished on the arid and unattractive Robespierre.' At rallies the front rows were regularly packed with 'elderly women of a certain type, married and single. Anyone looking down from the platform on those front seat women and watching their expression of rapturous self-surrender, their moist and glistening eyes, could not doubt the character of their enthusiasm.' Stormtroopers on guard duty referred to them as 'the varicose vein squad'.[2]

At the beginning of his political career Hitler had a beautiful voice, which fascinated admiring women. But electronic amplification was unavailable till the end of the twenties, and he progressively made himself hoarse by shouting.[3] At the beginning of a speech he would talk quietly, rocking backwards and forwards on his heels. 'He begins in a low, slow tenor voice, and after about fifteen minutes, something occurs that can be described only by the ancient primitive metaphor – the spirit enters into him.'[4] The writer René Schickele compared his oratory to rape and murder. Using repetition and insistent rhythms, he would pummel the audience's emotions, pushing it relentlessly towards a climax that has often been called orgasmic. This is the word Hanfstaengl uses:

There was a curious tinge to the finale. It was gradually being borne in on me that Hitler was a narcissus type for whom the crowd represented a substitute medium for the woman he did not seem able to find. Speaking for him represented the satisfaction of some depletion urge, and to me this made the phenomenon of his oratory more intelligible. The last eight to ten minutes of a speech resembled an orgasm of words.[5]

Women formed the same impression. One, describing a rally at the Berlin Sport Palace, commented on the 'erotic character not only of the words but also of the accompanying gestures'.[6] He sweated profusely while speaking, and by the final climax his shirt was soaking.

It is inconceivable that he cared as much about bringing a woman to orgasm as about delivering rhetorical thrusts. 'By feeling the reaction of the audience, one must know how exactly when the moment has come to throw the last flaming javelin which sets the crowd on fire.'[7] We could ask whether he needed any other form of sexual satisfaction when he was kept busy as a speaker, but this would reverse the point that needs to be made. If he was often impotent over long periods, he needed an alternative way of releasing tension.

To make himself sound more masculine, he used mainly the lower register of his voice.[8] His performance was carefully prepared. He would pace up and down, pausing only to rearrange the bits of paper on which he had written notes. When dictating to his secretaries he began with quiet intensity, but as he went on he threw himself like an actor into rehearsing the display of emotions, not holding back on the outbursts of rage. He gave no sign of being aware that he did not yet have an audience. When he got to the end, it was as if he had rid himself of a burden.[9]

Dominating a mass audience involved his sadism. He was excited not just by the excitement he could arouse but by the way he could control it, increasing and then reducing the tension like a lover delaying a climax. Hitler alternated between whispered declarations of love for his audience and explosions of rage, which were received gratefully and masochistically. Wielding his rhetorical whip, he was the master.

In cafés and bars, too, surrounded by cronies and admirers, he did most of the talking. Holding court like a monarch, he was not merely delivering monologues, but his companions contributed little more than comments and questions. Incapable of conversational give and take, he needed to dominate, as he had when talking to Kubizek.

Of the subordinates who formed the inner circle in Munich during the middle twenties, Emil Maurice was the one who came closest to being a friend. Eight years younger than Hitler, he had worked as a watchmaker's apprentice, had served in the army and had joined the party shortly after Hitler. He had also been a horse dealer, a nightclub bouncer, a chauffeur and a butcher's apprentice. Joachim Fest sums him up as a 'typical bar-room and meeting-hall brawler'. He became Hitler's driver in 1921, took part in the abortive putsch of 1923 and, when they were imprisoned in the Landsberg, took dictation when Hitler was working on *Mein Kampf*.

The only intellectual among Hitler's companions was Dietrich Eckart. Twenty-one years older than Hitler, he was one of the party's first members, and in the early quarrels between Hitler and Anton Drexler it was usually Eckart who persuaded Drexler to make peace by giving in. Eckart was educated, literate and literary – a poet and playwright. He translated several of Ibsen's plays into German, and his version of *Peer Gynt* earned substantial royalties, some of which he funnelled to the party. He was a *bon viveur*, fond of women, food and especially drink – 'a big bear of a man,' said Hanfstaengl, 'with sparkling eyes and a genuine sense of humour'.[10]

Eckart had influential friends and introduced Hitler to many of them, including the forty-six-year-old Helene Bechstein, whose husband, Edmund, was a son of the famous piano manufacturer and now joint owner of the company. They had a big house in Berlin, where Hitler met them during the summer of 1921, and they often came to Munich. Invited to dinner in their private suite at a hotel, he turned up in a blue suit to find them in full evening clothes. 'The servants were all in livery,' he told Hanfstaengl, 'and we drank nothing but champagne before the meal. And you should have seen the bathroom, you can even regulate the heat of the water.'[11]

He had little idea of how to dress, and his dandyism had taken an odd turn. Franz Felix Pfeffer von Salomon, who had been a captain in a private army and was later to be leader of the SA, had heard a lot about him, but was so appalled on seeing him that he refused to be introduced. Hitler was wearing an old frock coat, yellow shoes and a knapsack on his back.[12]

Hanfstaengl describes an outfit consisting of a blue suit, a purple shirt, a brown waistcoat and a red tie. The bulge at Hitler's hip was caused by a revolver in its holster: he may have been modelling himself on Karl May's cowboys. Invited to coffee at the house of Hanfstaengl's sister, Erna, Hitler stopped in the narrow hallway to discard his whip, his velour hat and his trenchcoat, hanging his cartridge belt, which had a revolver attached to it, on a coat-hook.

Wagner's granddaughter, Friedelind, never forgot her first impression of this man

> in Bavarian leather breeches, short, thick woollen socks, a red-blue checked shirt and a short blue jacket that bagged about his unpadded skeleton. His sharp cheekbones stuck out over hollow, pasty cheeks, and above them was a pair of unnaturally bright-blue eyes. There was a half-starved look about him, but something else too, a sort of fanatical look.[13]

He had always had a strain of fanaticism, but during his teenage period of dandyism it had not counteracted his lethargy. This now vanished into a farrago of activity. In 1922 he often made ten or twelve speeches at different meetings in one evening. He had, as he claimed, 'the gift of simplification'. He liked to say: 'Difficulties exist only in the imagination',[14] and he made it sound as if he could provide straightforward answers to complex problems.

The threat of violence was always present, sometimes in his tone, sometimes in the substance of his speeches. 'They say we're a bunch of anti-Semitic rowdies. So we are! We want to stir up a storm. We don't want people to sleep, but to know a thunderstorm is brewing. We won't let Germany be crucified. Call us brutes if you want to. But if we save Germany, we'll have carried out the greatest deed in the world.' This was what his audiences wanted to hear, and their enthusiasm egged him on. The violence spilled out into action. Hecklers were brutalised, brawling spread into the streets, bloodshed became commonplace. 'We're brawling our way to greatness.'

In January 1922 he was sentenced to three months' imprisonment for causing a disturbance at a meeting of the *Bayernbund*, the Bavarian League, whose leader, Otto Ballerstedt, was beaten up. Confined in the Stadelheim prison on 21 June, Hitler was released after serving just over a month of his sentence. On making his first public appearance after his release from prison, he was given a tremendous ovation and carried to the podium like a popular hero.

Impressed by his intensity and touched by his shyness, Helene Bechstein thought of adopting him as her son. Her husband did not like the idea,[15] but when Hitler went back to Berlin during May 1922 and could not get into the Hotel Excelsior she invited him to stay with them. She wanted to buy him a dinner jacket, a shirt with a starched front and patent leather shoes, but Hanfstaengl warned him that, as leader of a working-class party, he could not afford to be seen in such clothes.

Eckart was so often missing from the office of the *Völkischer Beobachter* that Hitler replaced him with Alfred Rosenberg, a former student of architecture and pupil of Wagner's son-in-law, Houston Stuart Chamberlain. Previously Eckart had edited an anti-Semitic journal called *Auf gut Deutsch (In Plain Language)*, and in 1924 he collaborated with Hitler on an anti-Semitic pamphlet, *Bolshevism from Moses to Lenin*. It was one of the main premisses of their anti-Semitism that Communism was part of the Jewish conspiracy to take control of the world. Normally reluctant to admit that anyone had influenced him, Hitler acknowledged Eckart as the joint creator of National Socialism: *Mein Kampf* was dedicated to him.

If it had not been for Eckart and the Bechsteins, Hitler would never have rented a house in Obersalzberg. During the winter of 1922–3, a warrant was issued for Eckart's arrest after he had slandered Friedrich Ebert. Eckart had been hiding in Munich. A party member, Christian Weber, was staying in Obersalzberg at the Pension Moritz. Its proprietors, the Büchners, were sympathetic to the party, and Weber suggested it as a hiding place for Eckart. There was still a lot of snow on the mountains, and he was not keen on going there, but let himself be persuaded.[16]

A tiny Alpine village on the north-east slope of the Hoher Goll above Berchtesgaden, Obersalzberg was a fashionable tourist resort with spectacular views of the mountain peaks, the Salzburg plain and the Königsee. There were six inns, a sanatorium for children and eleven villas. Named after its first owner, Mauritia Mayer, whose father had called her Moritz, the little hotel was the first to be opened. Previous guests had included Brahms, Freud and Schnitzler. The largest of the villas belonged to the Bechsteins, who came in the summer for hiking and in the winter for skiing, but otherwise spent little time there.[17]

Not a big town, but big in comparison with Obersalzberg, Berchtesgaden had begun to grow when the salt mines were developed in the early sixteenth century. The old priory had been converted sumptuously into a palace, and in 1923 Crown Prince Rupprecht, commander-in-chief of the Bavarian forces during the First World War, moved in.

The first time Hitler went to Obersalzberg, he was appalled at the steepness of the narrow mountain path. What did they think he was? An antelope? But he was so impressed by the scenery that he asked Eckart when it was at its best. 'He told me it was marvellous at seven-thirty. He was right – what a lovely view over the valley. A countryside of indescribable beauty! . . . I didn't stay there long, and went back to Munich. But every time I had a few free days I used to return up there.'[18]

This terrain was especially appealing to a Pan-German Austrian aspiring to political power in Germany and harbouring expansionist ideas. Berchtesgaden is almost due south of Salzburg, but the frontier (which has not changed) curves round to extend the south-eastern tip of Germany into land that had once been Austrian. This extension of Germany is framed on three sides by a lake, the Steinernes Meer, and two mountain chains – the Watzmann, which is almost 9,000 feet high, and the Hagengebirge. The area had belonged to a priory of Augustinian monks governed by the archbishopric of Salzburg until 1803, when the priory was secularised, and in 1809 the land was annexed by the kingdom of Bavaria.

At the Pension Moritz Hitler and Eckart were using assumed names. Eckart called himself Dr Hoffmann, and Hitler was using his favourite alias, Herr Wolf.

On 3 April 1923 an article appeared in the *Münchener Post* about women who, 'infatuated with Hitler', gave money to the party, or donated jewellery and antiques for sale or auction. In 1923 an agreement was made with a Berlin coffee merchant, Richard Frank, who loaned it 60,000 Swiss francs, receiving as security a variety of objects including a platinum pendant set with diamonds and an emerald on a platinum chain, a platinum ring set with a sapphire and diamonds, a solitaire diamond ring, a fourteen-carat gold ring with diamonds set in silver, a piece of seventeenth-century handstitched Venetian *grospoint*, and a Spanish silk piano runner, red with gold embroidery.

Many ladies contributed to this collection. Helene Bechstein donated several items, while another Munich socialite, Frau Gertrud von Seydlitz, not only gave funds but persuaded friends to do the same. The fifty-seven-year-old daughter of a Romanian prince, Frau Elsa Bruckmann was married to a rich publisher, and their salon was one of the most exclusive in Munich. Often invited, Hitler met rich and influential people, but she was jealous of his other admirers and, if we can trust what he later said, stopped inviting him after she had noticed how a beautiful guest was looking at him. We can believe his claim that, though the beautiful lady found him interesting, there was nothing between them. There were also men, such as the industrialists Fritz Thyssen and Emil Kirdorf, who made substantial contributions, but his female admirers were more fanatical.

Hitler prided himself on being able to arouse passionate devotion. Without mentioning her name, he boasted about an admirer who became hoarse with agitation whenever he spoke to another woman in her presence. At one point, apparently, he lay with his head in Helene Bechstein's lap and let her stroke his hair, saying he needed someone to look after him. But there was no question of becoming her lover: abandoning the idea of adopting him as her son, she thought of marrying him to her daughter.

Now in his middle thirties, he never became involved with women of his own age. The patronesses were older, the girls who attracted him younger. Sadists and incompetent lovers are better off with inexperienced women. Unwilling or unable to offer as much pleasure as they take, such men create more resentment with women who want their fair share. Some Freudians explain Hitler's sexual problems in terms of ambivalence towards his mother. Seeing the bond as an infantile attachment based partly on dependence and partly on hostility but involving little love, the psychologist Karl Menninger argues that the sexuality of men with this background is rarely normal. 'If they consort with women at all, it is women who are much older or much younger than themselves and are treated either as protecting mothers or as inconsequential childish amusements.'

Hitler never courted women in their thirties unless he was sure they were unavailable. Left alone with the attractive blonde Helene Hanfstaengl, he knelt down to proclaim himself her slave. He adored her. What a shame they had not met when she was still free! She persuaded him to stand up, and later described the incident to her husband. 'I told her to ignore it and just treat the whole affair as an aberration of loneliness.'[19]

Hitler had made similar overtures to other women. He 'had found no outlet to his personal repressions, although that did not prevent him from indulging in the preliminaries'. This tallied with Helene's first impression of him. 'Putzi,' she had said, 'I tell you he's a neuter.'[20] It also tallies with his behaviour over Stefanie. Nearly twenty years had elapsed, and he was now more self-confident, but he still had a blind spot for the borderline between sexual fantasy and reality.

Women varied in their reactions to him. Kukuli von Arent, wife of a theatrical designer, who had known Magda Goebbels since her first marriage, said: 'As a woman, when you talked to Hitler, you felt no sexual attraction.'[21] But Eva Braun's elder sister, Ilse, found that 'when he looked at me, beads of sweat formed between my breasts',[22] and at the end of the war several of the women in the bunker offered to die with him.

In Munich, though no longer short of money, he was still living in the Thierschstrasse flatlet, to which he invited neither rich friends nor impressionable girls. On the bookshelf were 'editions of a semi-pornographic nature . . . discreetly shrouded in Edgar Wallace thrillers. Three of these well-thumbed volumes consisted of the curious studies of Edward Fuchs – the *History of Erotic Art* and an *Illustrated History of Morals*.'

In Berlin, taking him to the National Gallery, Hanfstaengl noticed his reaction to Correggio's *Leda and the Swan*.

> It was the sensuous portrayal of the two central figures that fascinated him. . . . Over the course of time I discovered that the subject of this picture was almost an obsession with him. In later years this, almost the most obscene of classical subjects, was sure to obtain a gold medal for any German artist who used it as his subject at one of the Nazi exhibitions.

In fact Hitler bought a picture called *Leda and the Swan* from a German painter, Paul Mathias Padua.[23]

Hanfstaengl also took Hitler to a funfair that featured a group of women boxers.

> This seemed to appeal to him, so in we went and watched several matches . . . with the women in abbreviated trunks and vests, mincing around and landing the occasional tap. It was all pure circus, but Hitler was riveted. He managed to keep his face expressionless and made a few superior comments about boxing being a very fine thing, that this was only a put-up job and not the right thing for women and so on. But we had to stay till the show was over.[24]

Female boxing has little in common with the films Leni Riefenstahl made during the thirties and forties, but Hitler's taste, which did not change, shaped the pornographic underside of Nazi iconography. In her two films about the 1936 Olympic Games, which were held in Berlin, close-ups of the athletes' faces make them look like statues, while high divers against the sunlight are contrasted with quivering flags and Olympic torches. The exploitation of well-shaped bodies, male and female, is shamelessly voluptuous, as it is in the work of many third-rate painters and sculptors who enjoyed Hitler's patronage. After Geli's death he commissioned a portrait, based on photographs, from Adolf Ziegler, who painted nude female bodies with a combination of pornographic relish and pedantic precision. Told that Ziegler was known as 'the master of German pubic hair', Hitler retorted: 'Ziegler is the world's best painter of flesh.'[25]

Hitler took a lot of visual pleasure in the female body. According to Ernst Röhm, 'He thinks about the peasant girls. When they stand in the fields and bend over at their work, so that you can see their buttocks, that's what he likes, especially when they've got big round ones. That's Hitler's sex life. What a man!' Emil Maurice told an interviewer that he and Hitler had 'chased girls together' and had sometimes gone to see models posing in the nude at the art academy. 'Hitler circulated quite at his ease among all this nudity.'[26]

Röhm implies that Hitler did not go beyond staring at fleshy girls, but Maurice says they went out together, looking for women in nightclubs and streets. Hitler, he said, would call himself Herr Wolf; sometimes Maurice would pass on one of the girls he had picked up. Hitler, he said, 'always offered flowers, even when he had no money', and did take women to his room in Thierschstrasse, paying them twenty marks each.[27]

His secretiveness encouraged speculation based on the assumption that he had something to hide. According to an anonymous leaflet published during the summer of 1921, 'When asked by members what he lives on and what his former occupation was, he always became agitated and flew into a rage ... so his conscience cannot be clear, especially since his excess in relations with women, to whom he has often referred to himself as "King of Munich", costs a great deal of money.'

Attacks like this were helpful. What mattered was to be talked about, and his claim to be 'King of Munich' was part of his self-promotion. His book, which was popular, provided a base for the legend, and his glamour was enhanced by gossip about escapades with girls. He was rumoured to be having an affair with Jenny Haug, sister of a man who sometimes acted as his chauffeur. She was said to be so devoted that she carried a small pistol in an armpit holster in case he ever needed her protection. Both Konrad Heiden and William Shirer believed these rumours, but Hanfstaengl thought it was no more than a mild flirtation.

More characteristic of Hitler's behaviour with women was an incident at the Pension Moritz. Frau Büchner was tall and blonde. Failing to arouse her interest by pacing up and down, striking at his thigh with the whip he always carried, he started talking loudly about Jewish corruption and malpractice in Berlin. 'I almost imagined myself to be Jesus Christ,' he said, 'when he came to his father's temple and found it taken over by moneylenders. I can well imagine how he felt when he seized a whip and scourged them out.'

But strenuous displays of masculinity and right-mindedness were counter-productive. Hitler's reputation was itself a powerful aphrodisiac, and opportunities were plentiful. According to Emil Maurice,

> very often girls in their teens threw themselves under his car in the hope of getting injured and subsequently being comforted by him. Others presented themselves in Berchtesgaden, often almost naked under their light coats or their BDM [Young Nazi Girls] uniforms, bent on offering their virginity to the Führer. Others tore open their blouses when he passed.

Aware of his charisma, he shrewdly enhanced it by refusing to let anyone photograph him.

> The effect of his camera-shyness was quite sensational. Everybody was hearing and reading about him, but nobody had ever seen a picture of him. They came [to party rallies] out of curiosity; but they left as enrolled members of the movement. For Hitler had the gift of making every single member of the audience feel that he was being personally addressed.[28]

None of Munich's photographers pursued him more persistently than Heinrich Hoffmann, who had started his international career at the Bavarian court before the turn of the century and had sold photographs to most of the fashionable magazines. He had taken studio portraits of the Kaiser, the English King Edward VII, the tenor Enrico Caruso and the composer Richard Strauss. His studio was in Schellingstrasse, opposite Adolf Müller's press, where the *Völkischer Beobachter* was printed, and in 1922, when an American newspaper offered Hoffmann a hundred dollars for a photograph of Hitler, he approached him – only to be rebuffed.

Later, when an American agency was offering 20,000 dollars for exclusive rights to photographs of Hitler, Hoffmann resumed the quest. Hitler's car was an old green Selve with seaweed stuffing spilling out of the upholstery. One day a horse-drawn cart pulled up behind the parked Selve. Mistaking the seaweed for hay, the horse started nibbling, and, by warning the driver, Hoffmann got into conversation with him. Asking him not to drive Hitler away too soon, Hoffmann fetched his camera, a 13 x 18 Nettel, waited in a doorway, and snapped Hitler when he came out, escorted by three men.

> The next moment I found my wrists gripped by pretty rough hands. The escorting three had flung themselves on me. One of them grabbed me by the throat, and a furious struggle ensued for possession of the camera which I was determined not to surrender at any cost. But the men took out the plate and exposed it to the light and ruined it.[29]

There was nothing Hoffmann could do till he heard that Hermann Esser, a journalist who had succeeded Rosenberg as editor of the *Völkischer Beobachter*, was going to get married. Hoffmann knew him, and Hitler, who had given him the job when he was only twenty-one, was certain to be at the wedding. By offering to provide a sumptuous wedding breakfast at his home in Schnorrstrasse, Hoffmann made sure he would meet Hitler, who turned out, he says, to be 'a charming and witty conversationalist', though he refused to make a speech at the party. 'In a small, intimate circle, I never know what to say.'

There was a marzipan effigy of Hitler in the middle of the wedding cake, and, inviting guests to help themselves, Hoffmann noticed how careful they were to keep the knife away from the effigy. Meeting Hitler and discussing the offer of 20,000 dollars, he was told: 'On principle I never accept offers. I make demands. Anyone who accepts an offer without further ado simply loses face, as the Chinese say.' Hitler promised, though, that when he was ready to be photographed Hoffmann would be the first to know. But a moment later his assistant came in with a photographic print and a plate. Hoffmann had secretly snapped Hitler during the reception. By smashing the plate on the edge of a table he impressed Hitler, who asked whether he could call on him, and began to call regularly.[30]

Hoffman boasted that 'it was a friendship that had nothing to do with politics of which I knew little and cared less'. In fact he had been the 427th member of the party, joining in April 1920. The friendship, he said, 'flashed into being at the contact of two impulsive natures, and was based partly on a mutual devotion to art and partly, perhaps, on the attraction of opposites – the austere, teetotal non-smoking Hitler on the one hand and the happy-go-lucky, bohemian *bon viveur* Heinrich Hoffmann on the other'.[31]

Baldur von Schirach, the Nazi youth leader who was to become his son-in-law, describes Hoffmann as 'stocky, with strikingly broad shoulders and bright, rather shifty eyes'. Later dubbed by Eva Braun 'the mad drunkard of the Third Reich', he was exuberant and convivial, as fond of jokes as he was of food and wine. In no danger of being rebuffed or patronised, Hitler could relax with him as he did with his entourage.

8

Putsch

Five years after the end of the war, the wound inflicted at Versailles was festering. Germany had fallen into arrears over reparations, and the French premier, Raymond Poincaré, was taking an aggressive stance, arguing that since the Germans had defaulted on shipments of coal and timber, the French were entitled to occupy the Ruhr – the principal manufacturing and mining region. Depending on France to protect British interests in the Middle East, the Conservative Prime Minister, Stanley Baldwin, was in no position to restrain Poincaré, and on 11 January 1923 100,000 French and Belgian soldiers marched into the Ruhr.

The Germans responded with strikes and massive demonstrations in the streets. 'The anger is fearful,' wrote Thomas Mann, 'deeper and more united than that which caused the downfall of Napoleon.'[1] Crowds gathered around statues of Bismarck and other national heroes to shout insults at the foreign troops and sing '*Deutschland, Deutschland über Alles*'. Passive resistance led to sabotage, and provoked retaliation. Industrialists and union leaders were arrested; saboteurs were shot. This boosted the popularity of the extremist parties. At a Nazi rally in Munich during November 1922, Hitler had an audience of 50,000 people.

The Nazis' first 'Reich Party Rally' was held at the end of January 1923, and in February Hitler became involved with a formidable new conglomeration of right-wing groups, the *Kampfbund* (Combat League). Founded by Röhm, it gained prestige when Ludendorff accepted the presidency. The combination of the SA with the other private armies gave the

Kampfbund a huge fighting force, but there was also a less militant right-wing conglomerate, the *Vereinigte Vaterländische Verbände*, the United Patriotic Organisations, led by the former Prime Minister of Bavaria, Otto von Kahr, and a high school teacher, Hermann Bauer.

It was mainly because of the Nazis – the word came into use at this time – that street life in Bavaria was rowdier than in any of the other German states, where the party had been banned, and on 15 March 1923 the Weimar Republic's Supreme Court upheld the ban. But in Bavaria, where the party was still legal, it grew by about 35,000 between February and November 1923, while membership of the SA increased by about 15,000.[2]

The Bavarian state government looked on approvingly at the party's growth, and high-ranking officials attended its meetings. Hitler was asked privately not to stage a coup, but people were talking openly about the possibility of a march on Berlin.[3] On May Day the extreme right staged a counter-demonstration to the celebrations of the trade unions. Defying the ban on street processions, Hitler plotted with Röhm for the SA to be armed with weapons from the army barracks, and armed SA detachments mustered on the Oberwiesenfeld. But General von Lossow, the district commander, sent troops and police to repossess the weapons and disperse the SA. Hitler had to give in. As a non-German, he could have been expelled from Bavaria if the nationalistic Minister of Justice, Franz Gürtner, had not ordered the state prosecutor to have the case postponed 'until a calmer period'.[4] Hitler hid his discomfiture by withdrawing to Obersalzberg for several weeks.

Certainly this was not a calm period. Passive resistance in the Ruhr had put an end to Germany's self-sufficiency in coal, and on 5 June French troops seized railways in the region. The currency crisis was deepening. During the first three weeks in June the mark lost half its remaining value, and by the 22nd a pound sterling was worth 622,000 marks. On 9 June an egg cost 800 marks, and a pound of tea over 27,000.

The crisis sharpened the rivalry between the federal government and the state government. There were separatists who wanted to restore the kingdom of Bavaria as an independent state under the old dynasty, the Wittelsbachs. There were militarists who wanted to defy the restriction on the size of the German army. And there were nationalists who wanted to make the Weimar Republic strong enough to expel the French from the Ruhr. All three factions rallied support at the end of October when the French, in what was virtually an act of war, occupied the Rhineland areas of Bonn and Wiesbaden. Rioting broke out in Berlin as police clashed with demonstrators protesting about unemployment, and shops were looted when the price of a four-pound loaf rose to 340,000 marks.

Hitler needed support from other nationalist leaders whose objectives were different from his, while they wanted his support but wished neither to confide in him nor to treat him as an equal partner. It was obvious that a right-wing rebellion was imminent, but it was hard to predict which group was going to take the initiative.

Throughout Bavaria, 'German Days' were held at weekends – nationalistic rallies with speeches and militaristic parades. Hitler told audiences that the only choice was between the swastika and the red star. The republic was tottering, and soon it would be time for a march on Berlin to inaugurate a national dictatorship.[5]

On 26 September the Bavarian Prime Minister, Eugen von Knilling, tried to avert a civil war by proclaiming a state of emergency, suspending civil rights and appointing Kahr as State Commissioner with dictatorial powers. Because this constituted a threat to the authority of the federal government, Friedrich Ebert had to follow suit, declaring a state of emergency the same day. He delegated executive powers to the Minister of Defence, Otto Gessler, and to the commander-in-chief of the army, Hans von Seeckt, making them responsible for maintaining law and order throughout Germany. From now on, much would depend on whether the army leaders remained loyal to the republic or sided with the radical right-wingers.

In Bavaria Kahr invited the *Kampfbund* to cooperate, but vetoed fourteen rallies that Hitler had organised. On the other hand, when Seeckt wanted the *Völkischer Beobachter* to be banned, Kahr took no action against it, and when Ebert, with Seeckt's support, dismissed one of his generals, Otto von Lossow, Kahr defiantly appointed him as military commander of Bavaria. Much now depended on how he would use his forces.

Ambivalent about Hitler, Lossow met him and declared himself to be in agreement with him on nine points out of ten. But Hitler was not invited to the meeting that Kahr convened with police and heads of patriotic organisations on 24 October in the Ministry of Defence, where he said he was in favour of a march on Berlin and the creation of a national dictatorship. But he wanted all patriotic organisations to be incorporated into the army or the police.

Hitler was effectively being excluded from a triumvirate consisting of Kahr, Lossow and Colonel Hans von Seisser, head of the state police. On 8 November they held a meeting at Munich's biggest beer hall, the Bürgerbräukeller, where they had an audience of 2,000 people, including the Bavarian Prime Minister, von Knilling, several other ministers and the police commissioner.

Instead of absenting himself, Hitler used his stormtroopers to hijack the meeting. Kahr was halfway through his speech when Hitler arrived with about 600 men, who surrounded the building. After appearing in the doorway with a trenchcoat over evening clothes, a stone beer mug in his hand and a machine gun at his side, he threw the mug to the ground and rushed with a squad of stormtroopers to the centre of the floor. Here he stood on a table, silenced the audience by shooting at the ceiling and announced that the national revolution had begun. Using the pistol, he ordered the triumvirate into another room, where he told the three men to choose between dying with him now and fighting with him tomorrow. Pressing the point of his pistol to his forehead, he said: 'If I'm not victorious by tomorrow afternoon, I'm a dead man.'

Failing to intimidate them, he returned to the audience and worked his charismatic magic there. Alexander von Müller has described how he turned 'the mood of the meeting completely inside out . . . like a glove, with just a few words. I have seldom experienced anything of the kind.'[6] Hitler was not a Bavarian and had no interest in Bavarian sentiment except as a means to an end, but, talking to an audience of Bavarians, he knew how to manipulate its emotions. Ever since Bismarck had created the Second Reich, Prussia had overshadowed Bavaria, but the march from Munich to Berlin would inaugurate a new Reich with a different balance between the two states and the two capitals. Calling Berlin a sinful Babylon, Hitler made out that Kahr, Lossow and Seisser had promised him their support. 'Tomorrow morning will either find Germany with a German nationalist government – or us dead!'

The arrival of Ludendorff helped Hitler to win over both the triumvirate and the audience.

> Now I am going to carry out what I swore to myself five years ago today when I lay blind and crippled in the army hospital: neither to rest nor to sleep until the November criminals have been hurled to the ground, until on the ruins of the present pitiful Germany has been raised a Germany of power and greatness, of freedom and glory. Amen!

He had taken off his trenchcoat, revealing a black tailcoat and waistcoat, cut in Bavarian provincial fashion. In spite of the Iron Cross on his lapel he looked like a waiter or a tax collector at a wedding party, but it was only in repose that he seemed mediocre. When he was talking and gesticulating, his command over the audience was total. Before the meeting broke up, Knilling, the other ministers and the police commissioner were taken prisoner.

Overnight, Lossow changed his mind, and Kahr announced that what he had said had been extracted from him at gunpoint. Hearing nothing from them and getting no reply to the messages he sent, Hitler began to panic. Fest writes:

> As always, when he found himself blocked or disappointed, Hitler's sensitive nervous system gave way. With the collapse of this one project, all his projects collapsed. . . . He then went through a strange alternation of moods, first apathy, then violent despair, histrionics that anticipated the convulsions and rages of later years. Finally he let himself be persuaded to order a demonstration the following day. 'If it comes off, all's well, if not, we'll hang ourselves,' he declared, and this statement, too, anticipated those of later years, when he swung from one extreme to another, from total victory to downfall, from conquest of the world to suicide.[7]

In the morning there were plentiful signs of public support. Swastika flags had appeared on blocks of flats and office buildings. But, less courageous than on the previous evening, Hitler dithered until Ludendorff's resolution got the marchers started. In the Odeonsplatz they were confronted with an armed police cordon. The exchange of shots lasted only a minute. Fourteen marchers and three policemen were killed. Hitler, who had linked arms with Max Erwin von Scheubner-Richter, one of the men shot, had his shoulder dislocated as he was pulled to the ground. But he scrambled to his feet, ran as fast as he could and escaped in an ambulance.

He hid in the attic of the Hanfstaengls' house at Uffing on the Staffelsee, thirty-five miles from Munich. He was expecting to be picked up and taken to safety in the Bechsteins' car, but before it arrived, two lorry-loads of green-uniformed police appeared in front of the house. Helene Hanfstaengl went up to the attic, where Hitler pulled out his revolver and said he would shoot himself rather than let those swine get hold of him. But knowing enough jujitsu to get the revolver out of his hand, she threw it into the big barrel of flour they kept for use during shortages.[8] Hitler pinned his Iron Cross to the lapel of his jacket before letting himself be led away.

Hanfstaengl, Goering and other prominent Nazis escaped to Austria. When they got in touch with Hitler's lawyer, Lorenz Roder, they were told to stay out of Germany: it would only add to Hitler's problems if more of his followers were arrested. In Vienna, before Christmas, Hanfstaengl made efforts to locate Angela. He was curious to find out more about Hitler's background, and, still wanting to make him more presentable in Munich society, was hoping his half-sister could help in weaning him away from some of his more unsavoury companions.

Angela was living with the children 'on the third or fourth floor of a crumbling tenement block'. Though more money had been coming in now that she was working at the Jewish hostel, she still felt degraded by her poverty. Instead of asking her visitor into the flat, she opened the front door only a couple of inches and spoke to him through the slit. 'Even through this crack I could see the place was bare and dirty and that on the floor of the hall there was nothing but a decrepit straw mattress.' When he invited her out to a café, she made him wait on the landing until she came out with Geli, who looked 'probably about sixteen'. In Hanfstaengl's eyes Angela was so dowdy that 'it was rather as if I had taken my charwoman out for a meal. The mother was diffident and confused, but the daughter was quite bold and pretty. They were dressed in cheap, nondescript clothes.'

We do not know whether Angela complained about Hitler's refusal to help while she was bringing up Paula and her own three children on not much more than a widow's pension. Even if she did not, it was obvious that the five of them had been living in poverty for years. Like most people who met Elfriede, Hanfstaengl had nothing to say about her, but he offered to take Geli out. At fifteen and a half she was rather young to spend an evening with a man her mother had only just met, but Angela let them go to an operetta. It was a second-rate production, he says, but, inexperienced in theatregoing, Geli had seen nothing to compare it with. Liking the fat tenor and enjoying the sentimental ballads, she applauded enthusiastically. Hanfstaengl decided that her mind was 'mediocre'.[9]

If the putsch was a fiasco, the trial was a triumph. When Hitler said later that the defeat of 9 November 1923 was the greatest stroke of luck he had ever had, he meant that without it he could not have made himself into a popular hero, as he did by defending himself in the courtroom.

By 24 February 1924, when proceedings began, the political and economic situation was less favourable to the Nazis. Inflation had been halted, and under the new Chancellor, Gustav Stresemann, the federal government was once again in control. But at the trial Hitler was praised for his

> honest endeavour to reawaken the belief in the German cause among an oppressed and disarmed people. . . . His private life has always been clean, which deserves special approbation in view of the temptations which naturally came to him as an acclaimed party leader. . . . Hitler is a highly gifted man who, coming from a simple background, has, through serious and hard work, won for himself a respected place in public life. He dedicated himself to the ideas that inspired him to the

point of self-sacrifice, and as a soldier he fulfilled his duty in the highest measure.[10]

This is not an extract from a speech by the counsel for the defence; it comes from a speech made on 21 March by the State Prosecutor, Stenglein, and it gives some indication of how biased the court was. Assessing its mood accurately, Hitler took the risk of declaring: 'I consider myself not a traitor but a German, who desired what was best for his people.'

He was not a German, and once again, as after the illegal parade of armed stormtroopers on May Day, he was in danger of being expelled from Germany. Since 1922 the Bavarian Minister of the Interior, Franz Schweyer, had been trying to get rid of him, but had been overruled, as he was now, by the Minister of Justice, Franz Gürtner. For Gürtner, as Lothar Gruchmann concludes in his book about judiciary authorities, justice was 'a purely political question'.[11] Gürtner called the Nazis 'flesh of our flesh', and since the beginning of the twenties he had been consistent in his support for Hitler.

Not that Gürtner and the police chief, Ernst Pöhner, were mavericks. As Ian Kershaw has written, 'The Nazis were able to utilise the nationalist sympathies of the Bavarian police, judiciary and army leadership in a state which saw itself as a bastion of the patriotic Right against rampant socialism in Prussia, Saxony, Thuringia and elsewhere.'[12] This helps to explain the bias in the courtroom, and it should not surprise us that Kahr, Lossow and Seisser were not put on trial. They merely had to appear as witnesses, which gave Hitler an opportunity to point out the fundamental injustice in the assumptions behind the trial.

Instead of pleading innocence, he defended himself by attacking the 'November criminals' who had installed a pernicious 'system' that could be overturned only by violence. The National Socialists, he argued, had been acting in the best interests of the nation and of the army. Making the dock into a rostrum, Hitler had no difficulty in winning rounds of applause with his rhetorical affirmation that the future belonged to him.

The army we have trained is growing from day to day, from hour to hour. At this very time I hold to the proud hope that the hour will come when these wild bands will be formed into battalions, the batallions into regiments, the regiments into divisions. . . . Then from our bones and our graves will speak the voice of that court which alone is empowered to sit in judgment on us all. For not you, gentlemen, will deliver judgment on us; that judgment will be pronounced by the eternal court of history, which will arbitrate the charge that has been made against us. . . . That court will judge us, will judge the Quartermaster General of the former army, will judge his officers and soldiers as Germans who wanted the best for their people and their Fatherland, who were willing to fight and die. May you declare us guilty a thousand times; the goddess of the Eternal Court will smile and gently tear in two the brief of the State Prosecutor and the verdict of the court; for she acquits us.[13]

The trial, which lasted until April, became a social event. Photographers waited outside the courtroom, flowers were presented to the prisoners in the dock, while army officers in full dress demonstrated their sympathy with Ludendorff, who was acquitted. The presiding judge was barely able to convince the three lay judges that Hitler should be found guilty, and the sentence finally passed on him was the lowest possible for high treason – five years, with the possibility of parole after six months. This should have been unavailable to a man who had already served a prison sentence, and the law demanded that, as a foreigner who had caused trouble, Hitler should be deported. But the court decided to make an exception of a man 'who thinks and feels in such German terms as Hitler'.[14] When the verdict was pronounced, there were shouts of 'Bravo!' in the courtroom, and Hitler showed himself at the window to the cheering crowd outside.

Imprisoned in the Landsberg fortress, he had a laurel wreath on the wall of his cell, and instead of treating him like an ordinary prisoner, warders greeted him: '*Heil Hitler!*' when they came in.[15] He took his meals in the large common room, sitting at the head of the table, surrounded by his retinue, with a swastika banner on the wall behind him. The forty-odd Nazis who had been imprisoned with him included Emil Maurice, the former sergeant, Max Amann, and Rudolf Hess, who had volunteered for military service during the war and afterwards, as a student at Munich University, had attended one of the party's rallies and fallen under the Führer's spell.

Hitler was exempted from manual work, as he was from participation in prison sports. He delivered a daily speech to his fellow-prisoners at ten in the morning – sometimes it lasted for an hour – and spent much of his time dictating letters and working on his book. Maurice shared his secretarial duties with Amann.

On 17 June, when Angela, Leo and Geli arrived at the prison to visit Hitler, they must have been astonished at the respect he commanded. The visit was probably made at Hanfstaengl's suggestion: he may have been hoping to edge Hitler into offering financial help.

On 20 December, thanks to intervention by Gürtner, Hitler's sentence was remitted. He was free again less than nine months after being sentenced to five years.

9

Reaching My Peak

Though the party, which had been banned, was relaunched on 26 February 1925, and the *Völkischer Beobachter* was revived, Hitler could not simply pick up from where he had left off. If the movement was to regain the impetus it had lost, a lot of campaigning and internal reorganisation would be necessary. Thanks to rallies, parades, recruiting evenings, athletic displays, cookfests and talkfests, membership had risen to 55,000 by the summer of 1923; but it had sunk to less than 28,000 by 1925. Hitler went quickly into action, speaking on 27 February, only to find ten days later that he was forbidden to make any more public appearances in Bavaria. The ban was soon extended to Prussia, Saxony, Baden and Hamburg.

The party's prospects deteriorated still further on 26 April, when the seventy-eight-year-old Field Marshal Paul von Hindenburg became President of the Republic in spite of his anti-republican views. Thomas Mann called him 'a knight at arms from antiquity', but he was a national hero and an almost monumental embodiment of traditional values.

His election prepared the ground for a workable alliance between Catholics, conservatives and right-wing liberals, while the economy appeared to be recovering, thanks to the government's success in stabilising the currency and to money pouring in from American investors. Between 1924 and 1929, Germany received about 25 billion marks from America and paid out only 10 billion in reparations.[1] Serving as Foreign Minister after his stint as Chancellor, Gustav Stresemann had established a good relationship with his French counterpart, Aristide Briand, preparing for the admission of Germany to the

League of Nations. Unemployment was falling, while industrial production was rising. By the middle of 1927, membership of the National Socialist Party's Munich branch had dwindled to 700.

Though the trial had boosted Hitler's popularity in Bavaria, Gregor Strasser was better liked in northern Germany. 'Hitler's nature', wrote Hermann Rauschning, 'was incomprehensible to the North German. The big, broad Strasser, on the other hand, a hearty eater and a hearty drinker too, slightly self-indulgent, practical, clear-headed, quick to act, without bombast and bathos, with a sound peasant judgment: this was a man we could all understand.'[2] In 1925–6 Strasser was principal speaker at nearly 100 meetings, and when Hitler appointed him as Reich organisation leader, Strasser took full advantage of his new powers.

The party was short of funds, and Hitler had decided unilaterally on a new strategy. Though he had no qualms about using violence, from now on he wanted a semblance of legality in everything the party did. Having been put on four years' probation when he was released from prison, he could not take too many risks, and he no longer believed that he could win power by marching on Berlin. He must defeat democracy with its own weapons.

The party had been neither conceived nor developed as a parliamentary party, and it seemed unlikely to win an outright majority in the Reichstag. Nor could Hitler, as a non-German, be elected as a deputy. But his aim was to make the NSDAP more powerful than any of the other parties.

Returning to the Pension Moritz at Obersalzberg early in 1925, he told the Büchners he needed somewhere quiet to work; they installed him in the small annexe. The only mountainside telephone was in the Bechsteins' villa, but they let him use it, and when calls for him came through, their housekeeper, Frau Irlinger, had to run up the path to fetch him. One day, wanting to reward her, he asked whether there was a shop within walking distance. She directed him to the small general store at the foot of the mountain. The double journey took him about an hour, but he came back with a box of chocolates for her and sweets for her two small daughters. She was surprised and embarrassed: 'But that isn't necessary, Herr Wolf. We know you have no money.'[3]

In the summer of 1925 the Bechsteins invited him to the Bayreuth Festival.

> I had all the pleasures of popularity without any of the inconveniences. Everybody put himself out to be nice to me, and nobody asked anything of me. By day I'd go for a walk in leather shorts. In the evening I'd go to the theatre in a dinner jacket or tails. Afterwards, we would prolong the evening in the company of the actors either at the theatre restaurant or on a visit to Berneck. My supercharged Mercedes was a joy to all. We made many excursions, going once to Luisenberg, another time to Bamberg and very often to the Hermitage.[4]

Bavarian leather shorts bulked large in his life at this time. In 1942 he said:

> The healthiest clothing, without any doubt, is leather shorts, shoes and stockings. Having to change into long trousers was always a misery to me. Even with a temperature of ten below zero I used to go about in leather shorts. The feeling of freedom they give you is wonderful. Abandoning my shorts was one of the biggest sacrifices I had to make. I only did it for the sake of North Germany.[5]

Another of his favourite pastimes was picnicking. 'One of my greatest delights', he said in 1942, 'has always been to picnic quietly somewhere on the roadside.' But by then he was often 'pursued by a crowd of motorists eager to see their Führer off duty'.[6] The Königssee is beautiful, a long, narrow lake with dark waters and steep banks, but finding it 'too reminiscent of the Norwegian fjords', he preferred the Chiemsee, 'whose blurred tints are so restful to the eye'.[7] Though sixty miles from Munich and nearly forty from Obersalzberg, it was his favourite spot for picnicking, a pleasure he was to enjoy even more when the party included Geli.

It was Baroness Abegg who introduced him to mountain climbing. Her friend Dietrich Eckart said she was the most intelligent woman he had ever known. 'Without her,' said Hitler, 'I'd probably never have been on the summit of the Jenner. She was indefatigable and could climb like a goat. . . . She was as blonde as flax, with blue eyes and excessively long canine teeth, like an Englishwoman.' She alternated between depressed lethargy and petulant hyperactivity. 'She'd fly into a rage, sweep out like a whirlwind, climb up somewhere and come rushing torrentially down again.'[8]

In 1925 Geli paid her first visit to Munich. She was sixteen, and she was on a school outing with a teacher and classmates. Naturally she wanted to see the uncle who had cut such a fine figure when he was a prisoner in the Landsberg. Too preoccupied with other people to spend much time with her, he briefed one of his two adjutants, Julius Schaub, to take her on a sightseeing trip around Munich.[9]

One of Hitler's links with Obersalzberg was severed in 1926 when the Büchners sold the Pension Moritz to a Saxon called Dressel. Disliking the man, his cooking and the way he ran the little hotel, Hitler moved to the Marineheim, where the Bechsteins were staying. But he did not feel at ease there. Calling it pretentious, he moved down to Berchtesgaden, where he stayed at a hotel called the Deutsches Haus. 'I lived there for nearly two years, with breaks. I lived there like a fighting-cock. Every day I went up to Obersalzberg, which took me two and a half hours' walking there and back.'[10]

Dividing his life between Munich, where he still used his room in Thierschstrasse, and Berchtesgaden, where the hotel was like a home, he was finding a new equilibrium and a new space for private pleasure between the crust of political aggression and the core of private insecurity. At the age of thirty-seven, while staying at the Deutsches Haus, he had what was probably his first affair and was certainly the first to last for more than a few days. Maria Reiter was blonde and only sixteen: he was now old enough for girls of a younger generation to be nubile.

Though he found it easy during his twenties and early thirties to make friends with children and with women in their forties and fifties, he was nervous of being rebuffed or humiliated by women of his own age. But at thirty-seven he was old enough to treat a teenage girl as if she were a child. With Maria, once they were sufficiently relaxed in each other's company, there was nothing to stop them from making love. With Geli the age-gap was almost exactly the same.

Maria Reiter had attended a convent school and now worked in a dress shop opposite the hotel. It had belonged to her mother, who had recently died, and Maria's sister Anni was running it. The youngest of four sisters, Maria was walking their dog, Marko, in the Kurpark when Hitler was walking his Alsatian, Prinz. Like so many dog-owners who are introduced to each other by their pets, Hitler and Maria started chatting. He invited her to a concert, but she could not accept without asking her sister, and when they went into the shop, Anni said Maria was too young to go out with an older man.

A political meeting had been arranged at the hotel, which gave him a chance to impress both girls by inviting them to hear him speak. Maria felt uncomfortable when he kept looking at her during his speech, but she said she had enjoyed it. Immediately more relaxed, he started addressing her with affectionate Austrian diminutives – Mimi, Mitzi, Mitzerl.

The favourable reaction to his speech encouraged him to start flirting, but he did this gauchely, saying that her eyes were like his mother's. He too, he told her, had been orphaned when he was sixteen (in fact he was eighteen). He said it must be significant that the date of Mitzi's birthday was the date on which his mother had been buried. He offered to go with her to her mother's grave, and in the evening, while they were walking their dogs, he tried to impress her with his forceful masculinity – he beat Prinz for disobedience. At the end of the evening, when she would not give him a goodnight kiss, he stuck out his arm in a Nazi salute, gruffly shouting: '*Heil Hitler!*'

The account she later gave of their liaison is more reliable than most of the stories told by women who claimed him as their lover. She gave an interview to a journalist, Günter Peis, who made a tape-recording, which he used as the basis for an article that appeared in both *Stern* and *Time*. The facts and the handwritten letters she received from Hitler were checked by Eugen Kogon, author of *Der S.S. Staat*.

When she went to the cemetery with Hitler, he stared down at her mother's grave and surprised her by saying he had not yet arrived at that state (*'Ich bin noch nicht so weit'*). Gripping his riding whip, he told her to call him 'Wolf'. Once, when they went for a walk in the woods, he made her romp with him like a child. Afterwards he wanted her to stand still in front of a tree. After arranging her as if she were an artist's model, he told her she was his woodland spirit, and when she laughed, she was told never to laugh at him. He then kissed her passionately and said he could squeeze her to bits.

They probably became lovers when she visited him in Munich. He spoke of renting a flat and living with her, but nothing came of these plans, and by July 1927, when she was in Berchtesgaden again, he was no longer living in the hotel. What she had in common with Geli was that she was too young and inoffensive for him to feel threatened. If she laughed it would mean that she was either embarrassed or having a good time.

They kept in touch while he was arranging to rent the house in Obersalzberg. Called the Haus Wachenfeld, it had been built in 1917 by an industrialist with the title Kommerzienrat (Councillor of Commerce). His name was Winter, and Wachenfeld was his wife's maiden name. They lived near his factory in Buxtehude, just outside Hamburg. Reminiscing in 1942, Hitler said it was in 1928 that he heard the house would soon be available for renting. Though his memory was extraordinarily retentive, he was vague about dates, and it must have been in 1926 or early in 1927. By then Winter was dead, and his widow, who still lived in Buxtehude, no longer used the house. Hearing that it was empty and available, Hitler rented it for 100 marks a month (the equivalent of 720 marks or £320 in 1996). He would have liked to buy it, but she was hesitant about selling.

A few weeks before he moved in, he received a present from Mitzi, which meant he must write to her. His letter is affectionate but pompous and patronising. He obviously wants to avoid any sort of commitment.

My Dear Good Child,

    It wasn't until I read your painfully dear letter that I realised how wrong it was of me not to write to you immediately after

my return. . . . Before I turn to the content of your last letter, I
want first to thank you for the sweet present with which you
took me by surprise. I was really happy to receive this sign of
your tender friendship towards me. I have nothing in my flat
the possession of which will give me more pleasure. It will
always make me think of your cheeky little face and your
eyes. . . . So far as your personal anxieties are concerned,
you can be quite sure that I sympathise with you. But you
shouldn't let it weigh down your little head with any sadness,
and you must just realise and believe that if even fathers often
no longer understand their children, because they have grown
up, not just in years but also in sensitivity, they really still
have the best intentions towards them. Happy though your
love makes me, I ask you from the bottom of my heart for
our sake just to go on listening to your father.

And now, my dearest treasure, all the most affectionate greetings from your Wolf who is always thinking
about you.[11]

In early March Franz Gürtner persuaded the Bavarian Prime
Minister, Heinrich Held, to lift the ban that stopped Hitler
from speaking in public. It had been in force for two years.
The news took Hitler by surprise. Had he known he would be
able to resume campaigning so soon, he might not have based
himself in such an isolated spot. Berchtesgaden is 111 miles from
Munich, and the steep mountain road up to Obersalzberg was
full of potholes.[12] By car, the journey from Berchtesgaden to
the Haus Wachenfeld took about twenty minutes.[13] But the
decision had been taken, and Angela moved in two days before
the ban was lifted.

When he had offered her the job, knowing that she would
bring her two daughters, he may already have guessed that Geli's
presence might matter more to him than the work her mother did.
Or he may have been trying to model his domestic life on that of
the charismatic Viennese Burgomaster, Karl Lueger, who used
his two sisters as housekeepers.

For Angela, after eighteen years of hardship, it must have
felt humiliating that she had to work for the man who could
so easily have given her and Paula an easier life. Cooking and

housekeeping for Hitler, she would not even enjoy the same status as men like Maurice, who were treated in roughly the way that Hitler had treated Kubizek. But pride was a luxury that Angela had never been able to afford, and in the Waldviertel during her childhood it had not been unusual for girls from impoverished families to work as servants for less impoverished relations, as Klara had for Alois. Besides, Geli and Elfriede would both get off to a better start in life. Or so it appeared. And it may have been of some consolation that, so far as the land registry was concerned, the house was to be rented jointly by Hitler and her. This is what appears in Hitler's tax declaration for 1929, and possibly there was some financial advantage for him in having her as his co-tenant. What seems odd is that he did not want her to call herself Frau Raubal, but Frau Wolf.[14]

She arrived at the Haus Wachenfeld in March 1927. With his fondness for puddings and cakes, he was unlikely to have forgotten what a good cook she was. If he had, he was soon reminded. Henny Hoffmann describes her as 'a kindly, sympathetic woman, an expert in cooking Austrian specialities. She could make feather-light puff pastry, plumcakes with cinnamon, spongy poppyseed strudel, and fragrant vanilla pancakes – all the irresistible things her brother loved eating.'[15] Christa Schroeder was especially enthusiastic about Angela's apple cakes.[16]

Geli was still in Vienna, completing her last year at school. She was nineteen when she took her *Abitur*. Hitler then went to fetch her, and it was in Obersalzberg, during the summer, that they began to enjoy each other's company. He called her his princess, while she usually called him 'Uncle Alf' and sometimes 'Uncle Wolf'. She had a much better time when he was at home than when he was away. She and Elfriede presumably helped Angela with the housework and the cooking – Geli was to become a good cook herself. She did crossword puzzles in newspapers, but must have found it hard to keep herself occupied in such an isolated spot.

In the summer, when she arrived, she had probably assumed that she was going to settle with her mother and sister in Obersalzberg, but in October Hitler moved her to Munich, where he found her a furnished room and she enrolled at the university as a medical student. Never taken seriously by her or anyone else, her studies were only a pretext for settling her in Munich. She could have enjoyed herself there more than in Obersalzberg, had she been given a degree of freedom. But Hitler liked her too much to liberate her. He probably moved her either because he was expecting to spend more time there himself than in Obersalzberg, or because he wanted to stop Angela from interfering in their relationship.

The house in Obersalzberg had replaced the hotel in Berchtesgaden as Hitler's Alpine base, but he was still dividing his life between the mountains and the city. He did not give up his room in Thierschstrasse until 1929, but according to Fest, he

> rarely left his rural retreat; when he did it would be to attend the Munich opera with his niece or to visit friends in the city . . . He might have been secretly hoping to repeat the game he had played so successfully while in the Landsberg, when he encouraged rivals, promoted antagonisms and actually increased his own authority by slackening the reins.[17]

But he would not have settled Geli in Munich if he had not been planning to spend plenty of time there. He also needed to do a great deal of political work. With its bracing air and its superb views, the Haus Wachenfeld was a good place for writing speeches and thinking out plans; but during the winter of 1927–8 Hitler had to prepare for the elections of May 1928, and between the spring of 1927, when the ban was lifted, and the end of the year he made fifty-six public appearances.[18]

Apart from electioneering and recruitment of new members for the party, he had to do a lot of manipulating and bullying to make the other Nazi leaders accept his new parliamentarianism. This meant spending time not only in Munich but in Berlin, where Gregor Strasser and his journalist brother, Otto, were pressing for National Socialism to be more socialistic. They wanted the biggest industries and properties to be nationalised, but Hitler was anti-capitalist only in so far as he equated capitalism with 'international Judaism'.

The Strassers had at first had the support of a young literature graduate who had failed to find work as a journalist. In his abrasive way, Josef Goebbels used to argue that the 'petty-bourgeois

Adolf Hitler' was not really a socialist, and ought to be expelled from the party. But when Goebbels came to Munich in April 1926, Hitler succeeded in winning him over and channelling his formidable skills as a propagandist into support for the new policies.

The other major problem facing Hitler in 1927 was that the republic looked too stable for his prophecies of disaster to be taken seriously. After holding a successful rally at Nuremberg in August 1927 the Nazis did badly in the elections of May 1928, winning only 2.6 per cent of the vote and only twelve seats in the Reichstag. They had won thirty-two seats in May 1924, though when another election was held at the end of the year they lost eighteen of them. But they had never previously had as few as twelve seats. This made it clear – even to Gregor Strasser – that the party should not base its political hopes on the working class. It must recruit more support from the Protestant middle class and the peasantry: propaganda and organisation would have to be altered accordingly.[19]

Hitler needed to make his presence felt in Munich, both at the Brown House (Nazi headquarters) and in public places. Much as he loved using cafés for meetings and discussions, it must have been inconvenient that his only private space in the city was the small, shabby room in Thierschstrasse, and he must have resented the length of the double journey when he wanted to work in Munich and sleep in Obsersalzberg. Not that he ever gave any indication of regretting his decision to rent the house. Enjoying the altitude and the scenery, he may have found that possession of the house made him feel more proprietorial about the landscape. It was in Obersalzberg, he said later, that all his great projects had been conceived and ripened.[20]

The Bavarian Alps are awe-inspiringly beautiful, and there seems to be a freakish magic in the way they disappear behind clouds to reappear only seconds later. The Watzmann is the second highest peak in Germany. Seen from above, the villages in the valleys look minute, and the buildings – grey, beige and brick – seem intrusive among the natural colours. The geometry of the human domain looks irrelevant to the massive mountains. Some of the peaks are jagged, some bristle with dark and distant trees.

Mist mingles with cloud. Tracks or cracks up the mountainside lead into snow that merges with the mist.

Hitler may have been identifying in a naively romantic way with Nietzsche's superman, or his Zarathustra, who leaves his lakeside home to live in the mountains for ten years, rejoicing in his spirit and his loneliness. The Alps had contributed more than a background to Nietzsche's book. The metaphor of mountain-climbing is recurrent, as he keeps urging his readers – and himself – to become hard. 'To see *much*, one must learn to look away from oneself – every mountain climber needs this hardness. . . . I have not reached my peak until I can look down on myself and my stars.'[21]

The Haus Wachenfeld was small, wooden and pleasing. Speer has described arriving there:

> It had a wide overhanging roof and modest interior: a dining room, a small living room, and three bedrooms. The furniture was bogus old-look. A brass canary cage, a cactus and a rubber plant intensified this impression. There were swastikas on knickknacks and pillows embroidered by admiring women, combined with, say, a rising sun or a vow of 'eternal loyalty'. Hitler commented to me with some embarrassment: 'I know these are not beautiful things, but many of them are presents. I shouldn't like to part with them.'[22]

Hermann Rauschning thought the setting 'combined good middle-class taste with highland scenery and refined peasant style, as was customary in our pre-war middle class. Dimity curtains and what is known as rustic furniture. Everything small and dainty. Not really the right background for the future liberator of Germany.'[23]

But Hitler loved being in the house. In 1933, soon after he became Chancellor, the British ambassador presented his son, Anthony Rumbold, who was 'struck by the paleness of his blue eyes and his podginess'. Hitler was telling his guests about the virtues of salt. 'He was saying that whenever he felt out of sorts he tried to go to the Obersalzberg, his hideout near Berchtesgaden, under which of course there were a lot of salt-deposits, and he invariably recovered his health and spirits.'[24] Only here,

he said in 1936, could he 'breathe and think – and live! . . .
I remember what I was, and what I have yet to do, if only
my strength lasts, and God and Fortune remain with me to
the end!'[25]

10

A Darling Thing

What did Geli look like? Snapshots contradict each other, and so do the people who knew her. Some photographs make her look plain, plump and peasantlike; others show her as sexy and spirited. Apparently humourless in some, she appears in others to be bubbling over with high spirits, and in some she looks much older than twenty-three – the age at which she was to die.

The features are those of an unexceptional country girl: she seems wholesome, appealing, likeable, good-natured and lively. But was she beautiful? In Vienna an American journalist tracked down an old woman who had once lived in the same block of flats as Geli. 'I was walking down the street and I heard her singing. I saw her and I just stopped dead. She was just so tall and beautiful that I said nothing. And she saw me standing there and said, "Are you frightened of me?" And I said, "No, I was just admiring you."'[1]

Obviously we cannot trust all the photographs; can we trust any? According to a young friend of Geli's, Henny Hoffmann, the daughter of Hitler's photographer, none of the pictures captures Geli's charm. Born in February 1913, Henny was only fourteen when Geli arrived in Obersalzberg and only eighteen when Geli died; but Henny was perceptive, intelligent, and, unlike most people in Hitler's circle, honest. Geli, she says,

was a Linz woman, and the women from the Upper Danube – the Upper Austrian women – are famous for their beauty. Hitler said that the Greeks, migrating northwards centuries ago, had settled here, for the Greek profile was to be found

here: only in Upper Austria was the physiognomy to be found
in its purest form. Linz women are gentler, more refined, more
tender than Viennese women.[2]

But Geli was often taken to be Viennese. 'It wasn't that she
was so very pretty,' said Rudolf Hess's wife, Ilse, 'but she had
the famous Viennese charm.'[3]

Other reactions are at odds with the photographic evidence.
Emil Maurice testifies: 'People in the street would turn round
to take another look at her, though people don't do that
in Munich.'[4] During March 1928, after arriving from Berlin,
Goebbels wrote: 'Yesterday I met Hitler, and he immediately
invited me to dinner. A lovely lady was there.' The lovely
lady was Geli.[5] Before Christa Schroeder started working for
Hitler, she 'saw them together at the beginning of 1930 during
the festival at the Prinzregententheater, where Geli, wearing a
white fox fur, struck me as especially beautiful'.[6]

Hitler was reminded by her face of the Sphinx in the Upper
Belvedere, one of the two early eighteenth-century Baroque
palaces in Vienna built for Prince Eugene. But Patrick William
Hitler said: 'Geli looks more like a child than a girl ... You
couldn't call her pretty exactly, but she had great natural charm ...
She usually went without a hat and wore very plain clothes, pleated
skirts and white blouses. No jewellery except a gold swastika given
to her by Uncle Adolf, whom she called Uncle Alf.'[7]

Konrad Heiden describes her as 'a buxom young country girl
from Upper Austria with fair curly hair',[8] but people who knew
her disagree about its colour. Hanfstaengl agrees that she was
blonde, but Baldur von Schirach, the Nazi youth leader who
later married Henny, describes Geli as a brunette,[9] while Eva
Braun's American biographer, Nerin Gun, who interviewed
Emil Maurice, quotes him as saying: 'Her big eyes were a
poem and she had magnificent black hair.' She was proud
of her dark complexion, he said, and despised 'stupid blonde
Bavarian girls'.[10] John Toland, after interviewing several people
who had known her, concluded that her hair was light brown,[11]
and brown is the colour given in the 1952 biography of Hitler
by Görlitz and Quint.[12] None of the witnesses says she was in
the habit of dyeing her hair.

One of the most careful descriptions comes from the adjutant
Julius Schaub, who says she was a brown-eyed brunette, five
foot seven inches tall, well built, with a blooming appearance,
exceptionally full of animal spirits, with a pleasing voice.
'Because she had always been together with boys in her school,
she had no inhibitions, and by nature she was an open character,
always ready for a joke. You could say she was a big child of the
sort you'd like to have. She was extraordinarily self-possessed,
sometimes inclining towards obstinacy.'[13]

While Lord Bullock gives Geli's age as seventeen in 1928, and
Joachim Fest says she was seventeen when she moved into the
Haus Wachenfeld, Gun, who visited her grave in Vienna's Cen-
tral Cemetery, quotes the inscription on the tombstone: 'Here
sleeps our beloved child Geli. She was our ray of sunshine. Born 4
June 1908 – died 18 September 1931. The Raubal Family.'[14]

Today the grave is no longer there. Geli was buried in
Arkadengruft No. 9, opposite the entrance to the Lueger-Kirche,
the church which is the focal point of the cemetery. Her mother
paid for the funeral and for the maintenance of the grave, but
only till the beginning of 1938. It was undisturbed throughout
the war, but the site was a valuable one, and after Geli's remains
had been disinterred in their zinc coffin on 11 March 1946 at the
discretion of Abteilung 43, the department of the city magistracy
dealing with graveyards, a vault was installed under a marble
altar to the Virgin Mary with space for a dozen adult tombs
and the same number of tombs for children. The zinc coffin was
moved to position no. 73 in the second row of the small graves
in area 23E. But there are no graves there today. In the sixties
the burial mounds were levelled; trees and bushes were planted
on the flattened earth.[15] From then on, the only way of tracing
the individual graves was through a grid in a diagram.

A prosperous Viennese furniture restorer, Hans Horváth, who
claims he located the zinc coffin with a metal detector, started
a campaign to have it disinterred. He enlisted support from a
professor at Vienna University's Institute for Forensic Medicine,
Josef Szilvássy, but the civic authorities refused permission,
nervous perhaps that Geli's new grave, for which Horváth
was offering to pay, would become a shrine for neo-Nazis. The
prospects for her remains deteriorated further when plans were

announced to redesign the cemetery, transferring the contents of unmarked graves to a mass burial pit.[16] It may be whimsical, but it is hard not to think of this as typical of what posterity had in store for Geli, who has been forgotten while the unmemorable Eva Braun is remembered.

The dates on the tombstone show that Geli was nineteen when she arrived during the summer of 1927 in Obersalzberg. Gun's book came out in 1969, but several biographies of Hitler, including one by Kurt Petzold and Manfred Weissbecker, published in 1995, follow Fest in giving her age as seventeen when she moved in,[17] while Lord Bullock's 1993 revision of his 1991 book *Hitler and Stalin* says she was seventeen in 1928 when her mother came to Obersalzberg. But Angela arrived in March 1927.

Usually, as Rauschning said, Hitler's laughter was not much more than an expression of contempt, and his pleasures had no repose, but he and Geli soon found they could make each other relax. Though he had enjoyed the proximity of attractive girls, he had never had one living under the same roof, and had shown even less talent for intimacy with women than with men.

Having treated Mitzi like a child, he treated Geli similarly, but less patronisingly. Gauche though he was with the children he petted in front of cameras, he got on well with the children of friends such as the Hoffmanns, the Hanfstaengls and the Wagners.

Henny, whom he called 'My sunshine', was only nine when he met her. One day, answering the bell, she opened the front door to find him on the step. Her father was taking a nap, and she had been practising the piano. When she grumbled that practice was boring, Hitler surprised her by sitting down to play her a Strauss polka. She started to dance, but he stopped her – she must listen. Afterwards he told her stories about Rhinemaidens and the dwarf Alberich. When Hoffmann came downstairs Henny was reluctant to let Hitler go, but he offered to make a bargain with her. He was going to come every afternoon, read the newspaper while she practised, and then play something for her. Their friendship continued, and when she was twelve he took her to the Bayreuth Festival, where they saw *Parsifal* and the *Ring*.[18]

Egon Hanfstaengl had equally happy memories:

Hitler was my fondly loved 'Uncle Dolf'. At that time I liked
playing with toy trains. He got down on his hands and knees
to be my tunnel, and I crawled under him while Uncle Dolf
made train noises. He was wonderful at imitating geese and
ducks, not to mention the mooing of cows, the neighing of
horses, the baaing of sheep and the bleating of goats. My last
meeting with him was at the wedding of a high-ranking S.A.
leader. While everybody approached him with *'Heil Hitler!'*,
my mother and I said only *'Grüss Gott, Herr Hitler'*. We
were making a great mistake. Hitler withdrew his hand and
looked over my head, no longer meeting my eyes. Instead he
started barking out orders to everyone in the room. For me
that was bad. It was the last meeting with my fondly loved
Uncle Dolf.[19]

Hitler had an equal flair for mimicking people, and this was
one of the ways he could make Geli laugh. Her ready laughter
endeared her to many other people besides him, but not to
Egon's father. Hanfstaengl was a frequent visitor, but he never
got to like Geli, even when he came to know her better. He
thought her 'an empty-headed little slut, with the coarse sort
of bloom of a servant girl without either brains or character.
She was perfectly content to preen herself in her fine clothes,
and certainly never gave any impression of reciprocating Hitler's
twisted tendernesses.'[20]

Nearly everyone else liked her. Schirach found her 'sweet,
unaffected, irresistibly charming',[21] and according to Julius
Schaub she was 'intelligent, cultured, good at handicrafts and
made most of her own clothes'.[22] Heinrich Hoffmann calls her
'an enchantress'. At the Café Heck, where Hitler spent a lot of
time surrounded by supporters, he dominated the conversation
only until she arrived: he was glad to let her take over. 'Geli
was a magician. In her natural way, which was devoid of any
coquetry, she managed just by her presence to put everyone at
the table into the best possible mood. We all loved her, and
most of all her uncle, Adolf Hitler.'[23]

Generally, says Hoffman, who is not a trustworthy witness,
Hitler's attitude could not have been more respectful: 'Geli
was deeply revered, indeed worshipped, by her uncle. To him

she personified perfect young womanhood – beautiful, fresh, unspoiled, gay, intelligent, as clean and straight as God had made her. He watched and gloated over her like some servant with a rare and lovely bloom, and to cherish and protect her was his one and only concern.'

Her talent for rapport extended beyond people to animals and birds. She could even win the love of a wounded jackdaw.

> The little Haus Wachenfeld had a big wooden verandah where breakfast was served. If crumbs were left on the table, big black mountain jackdaws swooped down to peck at them. With pine kernels we lured the jackdaws into the room. One came once with a broken wing. It stayed, and Geli trained it. She stuck a little red cloth to the wall between the bookcases and taught the jackdaw to respond to a particular call by pulling the bit of cloth away with its beak. The jackdaw carried it in his beak and flapped above the table with it, hopped to Geli in little jumps and laid it in front of her. Then the trainer pursed her lips and gave the jackdaw a kiss.[24]

She transformed Hitler's life, not only in the house but outside too. He happily took her out shopping and on picnic excursions; she was his regular companion on visits to the opera, the theatre and the cinema. He started to buy books and to search in antique shops for pictures he could snap up at bargain prices.

> He followed her into millinery shops and watched patiently while she tried on all the hats and then decided on a beret. He sniffed at the sophisticated French perfumes she enquired about in a shop on the Theatinerstrasse, and if she didn't find what she wanted in a shop, he trotted after her . . . like a patient lamb. She exercised the sweet tyranny of youth, and he liked it, he was more cheerful, happier.[25]

Henny's view of what happened in shops does not quite coincide with that of Hitler's driver. Emil Maurice says: 'He was obviously embarrassed at having to follow Geli out of a store, laden with parcels.'[26] Many variants were told of stories about Geli in hat shops. According to Hitler, she was liable to try on every hat in the shop without feeling under any obligation. If he told her: 'You can't carry on like that and then go away without buying anything,' she would answer: 'That's what the salesgirls are there for.'[27]

Maurice noticed how glad Hitler was to have her as his companion: 'He liked to show her off everywhere; he was proud of being seen in the company of such an attractive girl. He was convinced that in this way he impressed his comrades in the party, whose wives or girlfriends nearly all looked like washerwomen.'[28]

On her side Geli was proud to have captivated him and to be seen with her hand on his arm. Now that photographs of him were at last appearing in the papers, no one could fail to recognise him. His moustache and the lank hair over his forehead were like badges of identity, and everyone seemed glad to serve him, wait on him, chat with him. He had been right to hold out against the pressure of well-wishers such as Hanfstaengl, who thought the moustache was 'a ridiculous little smudge which made it look as if he had not cleaned his nose'. Trying to groom him for Munich society, Hanfstaengl said he would look more dignified if he either let the moustache grow full out, or clipped the full width of it. Hitler said he was setting a fashion: in time people would be pleased to copy it.[29]

Narcissistic though he was, Hitler was not vain about his looks. He knew his appeal lay in his power as a speaker, but the charisma he had acquired under the floodlights extended into his everyday life, and Geli knew that other women would have been delighted to swap places and have him as their escort.

In Vienna, two years previously, she could not have pictured herself in this role, going into expensive shops and restaurants with a famous man doing his best to give her a good time and buy her anything she wanted. Or almost anything. He rarely bought jewellery. Around her neck she usually wore a simple chain with either a gold cross or swastika, and the white fox seems to have been her only stole. Hitler did not like fur coats. He said Jewish furriers were so greedy that the most beautiful breeds of animal were being exterminated, and besides, as a non-smoker, he had such a fine sense of smell that he could not bear the stink of furs. In any case, as leader of the party he should not be seen with a woman in an expensive fur coat.[30]

In October 1927, when Geli moved out of the Haus Wachenfeld to live in Munich, Hitler found her a furnished room in Königinstrasse, which runs up the west side of the Englischer Garten.[31] The Haus Wachenfeld was so small that Angela knew about everything Geli did, even if she could not control it. From how on, Angela would find out only what they told her.

Geli registered in November as a medical student at the university, but her studies were broken off early in the new year. She had no doubt been expecting a big city to provide more entertainment and a wider range of choices than Obersalzberg. Now she was no longer living under the same roof as her uncle, he could not be quite so proprietorial. Though he cross-questioned her about what she had been doing, he could not keep her under constant surveillance. On 5 July 1928 she returned briefly to Linz because her passport had to be renewed, but when she settled back in Munich on 5 August, Hitler rented a furnished room for her in the house of his Thierschstrasse neighbours, the Vogls, at no. 43.[32] Adolf Vogl, a singing teacher, was a long-standing member of the party.

During the years she shared with Hitler, Geli changed a great deal. When she arrived, she was still a teenager, spirited and full of curiosity about life, but inexperienced and unsophisticated. Only two when her father died, she had been brought up by a mother too impoverished and overworked for her natural kindliness to flower. Geli had met few people, and though she had a talent for enjoying herself, it had developed on a narrow base.

In Obersalzberg and Munich between 1927 and 1931, the girl grew into a woman. One thing that did not change was her lack of interest in politics. The impression Henny formed was that Geli never read *Mein Kampf*, or at most only the early chapters dealing with Hitler's childhood and youth.[33] She rarely attended rallies or political meetings, and once, when the two girls went together to a rally at the Circus Krone, Geli

watched the fantastic theatricality of the entrance parade, the flags with golden eagles on them, heard the singing and the

stormy ovations as her uncle went up to the speaker's lectern
in his dark blue suit. But this was a foreign world that she
was confronting – foreign and strange. She wasn't wearing
a badge. She wanted to live and enjoy herself. Perhaps her
uncle struck her as weird.

Of course, she did her best to seem relaxed when she appeared
with him at social gatherings. In 1928 they turned up together
at a Christmas party held by National Socialist students in the
banqueting room of a Munich hotel. Schirach had invited Hitler
without seriously expecting him to come,

but now he was suddenly standing amongst us, and I have
rarely seen him looking so happy. And in his tone of voice
there was a mixture of pride and tenderness as he introduced
'My niece, Fräulein Raubal.'
   The girl at Hitler's side was of medium size, well developed,
had dark, rather wavy hair, and lively brown eyes. A flush
of embarrassment reddened the round face as she entered
the room with him, and sensed the surprise caused by his
appearance. I too stared at her for a long time, not because
she was pretty to look at but because it was simply astonishing
to see a young girl at Hitler's side when he appeared at a large
gathering of people.

Schirach had been told she addressed Hitler as 'Uncle Alf', but
had not believed it until they

sat at the long table with candles and white tablecloths with
Adolf Hitler on her left and me on her right, and she said in a
bright, cheerful voice 'Uncle Alf'. It shocked me, and I didn't
understand why. He chatted animatedly to her, patted her
hand and scarcely paused long enough for her to say anything.
Punctually at eleven o'clock he stood up to leave the party
with Geli, who had gradually become more animated. I had
the impression Geli would have liked to stay longer.[34]

Naturally other men were attracted to her, and one of
these was Josef Goebbels, who lived in Berlin. When he

met her in Munich at the end of March 1928, he was carrying on two affairs. One was with a married woman in Weimar; the other was with a teenager, Tamara von Heede, who worked at the party's Berlin headquarters. But he immediately thought of Geli as someone who might settle down with him.

Unaware of Hitler's interest in her, he propositioned her and apparently found her responsive. 'Arrive Munich 5 A.M. . . . Then I meet Geli Raubal. She wants to come to Berlin. A darling thing! We've laid plans.'[35] In July, accepting an invitation from Hitler, he made a trip to Heligoland with him, Angela and Geli. Glad to join them, Goebbels did not compete with Hitler.

Other men did. Though always sporadic in exerting himself, Hitler had to work at keeping the party under control, and when he used underlings like Emil Maurice to chaperone Geli, he would not monitor what happened in his absence. He had been encouraging Maurice to find himself a wife. 'I'll come and have supper with you every evening when you're married,' he promised. Though Maurice must have known what was going on between Hitler and Geli, he was undeterred. The story, as he tells it, is: 'Following his advice, I decided to become engaged to Geli, with whom I was madly in love, like everybody else. She gladly accepted my proposal.'[36]

Maurice even confided in some of the others, including Goebbels.[37] But she was unfaithful to him, according to Hanfstaengl. 'Maurice was furious to find her one day *flagrante delicto* with a student, whom he threw out of the room neck and crop.'[38]

Not that this proves her interest in Maurice was merely casual. Henny, who thought she was seriously in love with him, rated him much more highly than Hanfstaengl did. 'He was a sensitive man,' says Henny, 'not just someone who took pride in fighting, and there was a genuine tenderness behind his affability.'[39] This tallies with the impression formed by Nerin Gun that Maurice was still in love with Geli thirty-seven years after her death.[40]

What drove Geli into Maurice's arms, according to Konrad Heiden, was Hitler's flirtation with Winifred Wagner, the

English wife of Wagner's only son, Siegfried. He was a homosexual, and forty-six when he married Winifred, who was eighteen. Since 1923 she had been declaring herself to be pro-Hitler, and he often paid incognito visits to Bayreuth, though Siegfried was said to disapprove of him. The Wagner children called him 'Uncle' and spoke to him in the familiar second person singular. Hitler was shorter than Winifred, who was a very large woman, but there were rumours that she was going to leave her husband and marry him. When Geli protested, Heiden says, he locked her up. After Siegfried Wagner died in 1930, the rumours gathered force. Angela Raubal said that Winifred wanted to consolidate the Berlin–Bayreuth axis dynastically, and Hitler joked ungallantly about her size: 'The only person I can fittingly marry as Führer is the lady Wagner. Then it would be a national undertaking.'[41]

At first it was hard for other people to know whether he was aware of Geli's affair with Maurice. Hanfstaengl wondered:

> Was he really as unsuspecting as he made himself out to be, or was it a case of the same 'mousetrap' tactics he often used – it seemed he was generously overlooking moral shortcomings in his immediate surroundings so that he'd get an opportunity of using the people involved as unresisting instruments in his secret plans? Was he waiting till he could take a suitable revenge?'[42]

That he did know what was going on is clear from a letter Geli wrote on Christmas Eve 1927.

> My dear Emil,
>   The postman has already brought me three letters from you, but never have I been so happy as I was over the last. Perhaps that's the reason we've had such bad experiences over the last few days. . . . Uncle Adolf is insisting that we should wait two years. Think of it, Emil, two whole years of only being able to kiss each other now and then and always having U.A. in charge. . . . I can only give you my love and be unconditionally faithful to you. . . . I love you so infinitely

much. . . . Uncle Adolf insists that I should go on with my studies. . . . Uncle A. is being fearfully nice. I'd like to give him great happiness, but I don't know how. . . . But Uncle A. says our love must be kept completely secret. . . . Uncle A. has promised me we'll often see each other and also often be alone together. He's wonderful. . . . And that's mainly thanks to Frau Hess . . . She was the only person who believed you really love me. . . .

All the best from *your* Geli. I'm already happy![43]

Arlyn Imberman, the graphologist to whom I showed Geli's handwriting, found it sensual but said that if I had not told her it was a woman's, she might have thought it was a man's. She found an obsessive quality in it, a rigidity, and a lack of spontaneity. She got the impression that Geli had been given a strict upbringing, with a lot of punishment, and had developed a strong sense of duty together, possibly, with a desire to be dominated.

Having so much power over both of them, Hitler could easily have stopped them from seeing each other. But without allowing them to carry on an affair, he was not trying to separate them, and he let things go on like that for at least ten months. In October, Goebbels was chatting with a *Gauleiter* who had befriended him at the beginning of his party career, Karl Kaufmann. 'He tells insane stories about the Boss. Him and his niece, Geli, and Maurice. The woman tragedy. Why must we all suffer so much over women?'[44]

How is Hitler's behaviour to be explained? He had engineered an awkward triangle in which all three of them felt cramped. But, as Geli says in her letter, Hitler was 'in charge', and if he could not monopolise her, that was the best consolation available. His intermittent impotence was probably more of an obstacle than her being his half-niece. If he wished her to go on thinking he was wonderful and go on wanting to give him great happiness, he could neither sack Maurice nor forbid them to be alone together. But he could keep her goodwill while imposing strict limits on her freedom.

She was an affectionate, tactile, sexy girl, and there may have been more fondling and flirtation between her and Hitler than

she admitted to Maurice. Hitler may have wanted to make love
whenever he could, and in promising Maurice that she would be
'unconditionally faithful' she was making the highest possible
bid; but we do not know how much she had told him about her
relationship with her Uncle Alf, while, in any case, the promise
was only a promise, and if she could not make love to Maurice,
fidelity did not amount to much.

In spite of his intermittent impotence, Hitler was not prepared
to let Geli have another man. He behaved differently towards Eva
Braun. Fifteen years later she was told to find herself another
lover since he could no longer satisfy her. For her, says Albert
Speer, in whom she confided, 'it was out of the question. . . .
Her love for him, her loyalty, were absolute.'[45] Hitler probably
knew this, and possibly would not have made the offer if he had
thought she was going to take advantage of it. To Geli, who
would have used all the freedom he gave her, he offered only
a little.

He may at the same time have been getting vicarious and
masochistic satisfaction from her relationship with Maurice.
He may have felt like a shareholder in it, as he did in the
marriages he organised between people dependent on him.
According to the youngest of his secretaries, Traudl Humps,
a former ballet dancer who was twenty-two when she joined
his staff in November 1942, 'He always tried to marry off
his assistants.'[46] After six months of working for him she
let him manipulate her into marrying one of his two valets,
Obersturmführer Hans Junge, who had also let Hitler talk him
into the liaison. Both he and Traudl would have preferred to
take more time before committing themselves, 'but the Führer
wouldn't have it. He was going to have us marry, or else. I
don't really know why.'[47]

Encouraging another secretary, Gerda Daranowsky, to marry
a colonel, Eckhardt Christian, Hitler promoted him to the rank
of general, and he married off Eva Braun's younger sister, Gretl,
to an SS general, Hermann Fegelein. The pleasure that Hitler
took in matchmaking may have involved a complex strategy
of self-deception: he may have been trying to convince himself
he did not envy men who were not impotent. If there was an
element of masochism in setting up the marriage between Gretl

and Fegelein, it was sadistically complemented two days before he married Eva: when Fegelein was caught trying to escape from Berlin, Hitler gave orders for him to be shot.

Watching Geli with Maurice, knowing how frustrated they both were under the veto he had imposed, Hitler was indulging both his sadism and his masochism.

11

The Forest Glade

It was partly because of Geli and partly because of Hitler's growing popularity that he started to enjoy picnicking more than ever. His open Mercedes was well known. Recognising it outside restaurants, people came inside to stare at him and, if possible, start a conversation. Geli loved to go picnicking whenever it was warm enough, and Henny never forgot the endearing smile that appeared on her face when she put her arm around Hitler's neck to say: 'Uncle Alf, do let's go for a picnic on the Chiemsee.' He seldom refused.

Maurice drove, with Hitler in front next to him. Usually they both wore leather shorts, white linen shirts and pale blue linen jackets with horn buttons. Geli sat on the back seat with the other girls. When the long-legged Hanfstaengl came he joined them there, while the other men – Schaub, Brückner, Hoffmann, perhaps – sat in the folding middle seat. Henny often came, and sometimes Anni Rehborn, a champion swimmer. To protect the girls' hair from the wind, Hitler kept a collection of tight-fitting caps in the glove-box – white linen in the summer, brown leather in the winter. Also stored in the glove-box was a supply of peppermints, acid drops and Bahlsen biscuits in their red, white and blue wrapping paper. Woollen rugs and white linen tablecloths were taken to spread on the ground. The food and drink would be packed in picnic hampers – roast chicken cut into portions and packed in greaseproof paper, cheese and salami sandwiches, a big apple tart, Apollinaris mineral water for Hitler, and vacuum flasks of tea and coffee.

His favourite spot for picnicking was between the woods and the lake, but he never swam. As a boy, he said, he used to bathe in the Danube, but he had been too thin to stay in the water for long. The main deterrent was his fear of looking undignified. As President of the Republic, Friedrich Ebert had not improved his image by letting himself be photographed in a bathing costume. (Later, Hitler would take Mussolini as his example of a statesman who had rashly posed in bathing gear for photographers.)

More circumspect, the Führer discarded only his shoes and socks, exposing his white feet and paddling in shallow water. He also enjoyed the schoolboy game of sending flat pebbles skimming across the surface of the lake. Sometimes he managed to make a pebble bounce ten or twelve times before it sank. 'It must certainly be a game that was played in olden days,' he declared.

He liked talking about town and country planning projects that would be realised when he came to power. A motorway would run from Munich to Salzburg, and here on the shores of the lake would be a big restaurant, designed by his Bavarian architect, Degano. None of his audience had known him in the days when he intended to rebuild Linz, giving it 'a bridge unequalled anywhere in the world', but little had changed either in the predilection or the compulsion to talk about it. The difference was that he now stood a chance of realising his fantasies. Using a stick to draw in the fine white lakeside sand, he sketched out his plan for a modern university with sporting facilities, a heated swimming pool and a yachting school. Within a few years, he said, men would travel to the moon on a rocket that had already been designed by Hermann Oberth and Max Valier.

Sometimes Emil Maurice brought out his guitar from the boot of the car and, accompanying himself, sang Irish folk songs he had learnt, while the others – all except Hitler – hummed the refrain. When a friendly fisherman offered them fish from his catch, Maurice built a barbecue and grilled them. When Hanfstaengl came, he would bring a thick bundle of foreign newspapers and tell Hitler what people were saying about him all over the world. When Heinrich Hoffmann came, he brought the German papers, and, after they had eaten, the men would find a spot where they could read. Hitler often took a book: one of the books that impressed him was a biography of Trotsky. It was brilliantly written, he said.

Only the girls went swimming. Concealed behind bushes at a suitable distance, they took off their clothes, hanging them on sloe trees, and walked through the soft sand to the lake. After swimming naked, they let the sun dry their bodies, wanting to get as brown as they could. Henny remembered how

one day a cluster of butterflies settled on the naked Geli. We made ourselves garlands of strawberry leaves and put them on. For us the world was a garden, a forest glade, with fairies dancing in the moonlight and fauns with goat feet making music. We thought life was a party that was just beginning. We didn't know the forest glade was a battlefield you couldn't leave till you were defeated. We didn't know the world was rough and mean and stupid. Hitler knew.[1]

In the car during the day, he was boyishly competitive: hating to be overtaken by another driver or a motorcyclist, he nagged Maurice to go faster.[2] But during the long summer nights they drove slowly and silently, halting to watch an eagle in the sky or a buzzard on a tree stump. Sometimes they saw shooting stars, sometimes deer and hares. Often Hitler would turn round in his seat to say: 'You'd better talk or sing to keep the driver awake.' They sang whatever came into their heads – the latest popular hits or old folk songs or, if Geli was taking the lead, songs from Viennese operettas. Hitler never joined in.

He and Geli often went to spend the weekend in a country house belonging to Adolf Müller, the *Völkischer Beobachter*'s printer. He had two daughters, Lotte and Else, who were friendly with Geli and Henny. The house was in St Quirin, on the shore of the Tegernsee, thirty miles south of Munich. Built in the style of a Bavarian farmhouse, it was luxuriously furnished. 'The house smelt of cedarwood, and the big, leather-upholstered chairs, the corner seat, the big round table, the speckled handwoven carpet in fine colours, the winding staircase all created the atmosphere of a Bavarian play by Ludwig Thoma.'[3]

Hitler and Geli were often seen together at the opera and at Philharmonic concerts. He even took her to Bayreuth. When he went to Obersalzberg for the weekend, visitors usually found her there too, and people were saying he had more than avuncular feelings for her. 'But these rumours were only whispered by party members behind their hands. For Hitler it would have been no joking matter.'[4]

Most of the men around Hitler had no desire to sneer or grumble.

> We liked her. When she was there, Hitler almost never started on the dreadful and often really painful scenes with endless monologues and uninhibited recriminations he bestowed not only on political enemies but also on friends and fellow-fighters. Geli's presence relaxed and released him. In front of favoured guests he let her perform her speciality act with the mountain jackdaw – when she called, the bird flew in through the open window – and he enjoyed seeing her romp about with his Alsatians Blondi and Muck. Geli was allowed to laugh at her Uncle Alf and adjust his tie when it had slipped. She was never put under pressure to be specially clever or specially witty. She could be simply what she was – lively and uncomplicated.[5]

On 21 June, the day of the summer solstice, Hitler, Geli, Henny and some of the men were in the car with Maurice at the wheel when they saw what looked like a house in flames. Driving closer, they found it was a St John's fire. The custom was to pile dry branches together on the mountainside or in a field, and light the fire at sunset. Sitting in a circle around the blaze, boys and girls would go on singing till enough of the wood had burnt to make it feasible for the bravest couples to hold hands, take a run and leap over the flames with a yell of defiance, hoping the girl's dress would not be singed. It was both a test of courage and a ritual with an erotic charge.

Maurice parked the car, and they all wandered towards the fire. With his arms crossed, Hitler prowled around the outside of the circle. Sparks were flying, and there was a strong smell of burning wood. Suddenly one of the boys took Geli's hand, challenging her to leap over the flames. Without hesitating, she held on to his hand as they took a couple of paces backwards, ran towards the fire and jumped with a triumphant yell. The motor horn was then sounded twice, which meant that Hitler wanted to leave. Reluctantly, the others climbed into the car.[6]

Hitler knew that under the restrictions he had imposed, Geli's passion for Maurice would gradually die down, and that it would eventually be easy to end the arrangement by which they were waiting for each other. 'All he did,' says Hanfstaengl, 'was make Geli move out of the quarters in which she had so much freedom and into the monitorship of Frau Elsa Bruckmann, who'd been born as the Princess Cantacuzene, while Maurice to all appearances went on performing his duties as if nothing had occurred.'[7]

  There are three versions of what afterwards happened to Maurice. Hanfstaengl's is that, instead of sacking him, Hitler 'gradually started to freeze him out, fell behind in paying his wages, and in the end Maurice himself made the break'.[8] Otto Strasser's is that, by pressing her ear to the door, Geli overheard a conversation in which Hitler told Maurice he was never to set foot in the house again, and Maurice replied: 'Sack me, and I'll take the whole story to the *Frankfurter Zeitung*!' Hitler gave in to the threat.[9] The third version is that Hitler threatened to sack Maurice unless he broke off the engagement, and implemented his threat when Maurice tried to defy him. It is possible that all three stories are untrue. Hitler may have succeeded in keeping the relationship Platonic long enough for one or both of them to become more interested in someone else.

  Whether it centred on Geli or not, the financial quarrel with Maurice ended a friendship that had begun in 1919, when they both joined the party. Maurice sued Hitler for arrears of salary amounting to 3000 marks. When the case was heard at the *Arbeitsgericht* in Munich, the court dealing with disputes over employment, Hitler was ordered to pay Maurice 500 marks. He used the money to set himself up as a watchmaker, but he did not leave the SA, transferring later to the more elite SS, and in 1935, when the Gestapo investigated his ancestry and alleged that he came from Jewish stock, Hitler intervened secretly to save his life and allow his career in the SS to continue.[10] The allegation may have been unfounded.

The man who replaced him as chauffeur was Julius Schreck, who had previously had twelve men under him in Hitler's personal *Stabswache* (bodyguard) which had been formed in March 1923. Speer liked Schreck's 'peasant sanity' and noticed that Hitler let him make 'caustic remarks about the fawning courtiers who surrounded him. He was the only person who was allowed such liberties.'[11]

Now that Hitler had installed Geli in Munich, he could take her out as often as he liked. Even when things were going well for the party, he did not devote the whole day to work: he was never cured of 'his congenital inability to keep to an orderly daily time-scale . . . His whole life was lived in this impromptu Bohemian style. He would turn up at the Brown House at eleven or twelve as it suited him. He would come announced and unannounced and would keep people waiting for hours.'[12] Some of the most crucial discussions took place around his regular table at the Café Heck.

Hitler saw himself not as an ordinary statesman but as a world-historical man as defined by Hegel, or an artist-politician as defined by Nietzsche. In Hegel's view, Alexander, Caesar and Napoleon were heroic by virtue of having accepted their vocation from the inner spirit that bursts the outer world into pieces. Their words and their actions were the best of their period.

For Nietzsche, the future belonged to the leader who was making practical politics into an art. In *The Genealogy of Morals*, discussing 'the master race that conquers' and 'the blond beast of prey', he rejected the idea of a social contract that had been evolved in the seventeenth century by Hobbes and Locke. Nietzsche asked:

The man who is by nature commanding and masterful, who is violent in deed and manner – how much does he have to do with contracts? Men like this are unpredictable; they come like fate without reason or calculation. They appear like lightning, abrupt, forceful, so dissimilar to anything else that they attract no hatred. They work by creating instinctively and imposing form. Their artistry has nothing to do with willpower or consciousness.[13]

This is how Hitler liked to think of himself, but Nietzsche, who hated both anti-Semitism and totalitarianism, would have disliked everything about Hitler, including his taste for Wagner and operetta. Geli went with him regularly to both. They rarely missed the first night of a new production at the opera house, and spent a lot of time together in theatres, cinemas, restaurants and cafés.

Hitler's favourite restaurant was the Osteria Bavaria, which had opened at the turn of the century, when Schwabing – Munich's most bohemian district – was enjoying its heyday. Italian culture, Italian food, Italian wines were all the rage. Designed to look Italian, the Osteria had a bunch of illuminated blue glass grapes above the entrance. On display inside were a Parma ham and a big Gorgonzola cheese, surrounded by Chianti bottles. There were grissini on every table, a fading photograph of Paganini on one of the dark, panelled walls and a romantic picture of the Gulf of Naples on another. Hitler approved of the way spaghetti was cooked – 'not too soft and not too hard'.

Hoffmann, who lived nearby, had recommended the restaurant, and Hitler now had a long corner table reserved for his use in one of the two back rooms. Friends were welcome to join him and Geli when they ate in the late evening. During the summer they dined out of doors in the little courtyard, which had a red tiled floor, two Doric columns painted red and a fountain with water coming through the mouth of a red marble lion.

After going to a show, Hitler and Geli usually ate either here or at the table reserved indoors. At the opera house and the Kammerspiele, his favourite seat was in the sixth row of the stalls.[14] He was equally addicted to cinema-going, and his taste was as unsophisticated as hers. In later life two of his favourite films were *King Kong* and Walt Disney's *Snow White and the Seven Dwarfs*, while one of the tunes he often whistled came from another Disney movie – 'Who's Afraid of the Big Bad Wolf?' His favourite actress was Shirley Temple.[15]

One night Hitler took Geli, Henny and the older of his two adjutants, Wilhelm Brückner, to a Western. (Brückner was four years older than Hitler and fourteen years older than Schaub.) Afterwards they ate in the courtyard of the Osteria. Geli did not like the star of the film, and, rarely subtle when he wanted to play masochistic games, Hitler asked her what sort of looks would please her most in a man. He never carried money or a pen on him, but Schaub and Brückner were always equipped with petty cash and writing materials. When Brückner produced a pen and a white card, Hitler sketched a male profile. Would a man like this appeal to her? She shook her head. He drew another profile, which failed to please her, and then another with a beard. After all three sketches had been rejected, he repeated his question. How would she like a man to look? She said: 'That's what's wonderful – you never know what he'll look like, the man you're going to love.' Hitler tried to hide his disappointment,[16] but even if he had not been trying to provoke a rebuff he had launched himself on a line of questioning that could hardly have produced any other kind of response.

If he was possessive, it was only to be expected, and at first it was tolerable, but it was hard for both of them to acclimatise themselves to the situation. Self-involved and inexperienced in personal relationships, he was insensitive to other people's needs. More concerned with his public image than with anyone's private pleasures – even his own – he liked being seen with a young and attractive woman. He later encouraged photographers to snap him in opera houses, theatres and other public places arm in arm with a variety of personable women, including starlets. Now, for the first time, he was dating one woman steadily, and it was luxurious to have her permanently available. In August 1929 he took her to the annual party conference at Nuremberg, and on the evening before it opened Goebbels was invited to dine with them in their suite at the hotel. His diary comment on Geli was 'A pretty child.'[17]

She was usually, but not invariably, good-tempered, and while her only ambition was to fall in love, he was the most driven of political careerists, however bohemian he was in his habits. Like a man who keeps tapping the barometer to see whether the needle has moved, he kept checking the newspapers for changes in the political situation. She would have been happy to do nothing, so long as someone was doing it with her. She was not interested in reading and, though she enjoyed cooking, dressmaking and crossword puzzles, she did not like being left on her own for long. In Obersalzberg the presence of her mother and sister had made it easier for her to get through the day. She could chat while cooking or helping with domestic jobs. In Munich she was on her own and, though she was quite good at making friends, Hitler was not prepared to let her.

He realised he must find something to occupy her. She had a pleasant singing voice: with his passion for Wagner and his capacity for fantasy, it was natural for him to think she could develop into an opera singer. Why should she not have lessons from her landlord, Adolf Vogl? Vogl's star pupil had become a successful opera singer. (Her stage name was Bertha Morena, and Hitler admired her too much to believe Hanfstaengl, who said her real surname was Meyer and both her parents were Jewish.) But according to Christa Schroeder, it took a long time for Hitler to persuade Geli.[18] Singing lessons would be less boring than the lectures on anatomy and comparative zoology that she had to sit through as a medical student, but she was not passionately committed to the idea. One day Henny asked: 'Do you really want to be a singer and have to stand on the stage and be able to sing every note by heart and make out you're dying or something and then, when the curtain falls, get up again and bow when the people clap?' Geli answered: 'Oh yes, it's wonderful if you can have so many lives – if you can be Salome and ask for the head of John the Baptist on a silver platter because you want to kiss John the Baptist's lips, or you can be a Valkyrie on the flaming rocks, or Isolde, dying of love.'[19]

Though Vogl was in his fifties, his wife was pregnant, and Geli was her first visitor in the hospital where she had the baby. She never forgot what Geli said: 'I can't tell you how much I'd like to have a little baby too – you know whose baby I'd like it to be.'[20]

According to Henny, Geli was never in love with Hitler, though he was in love with her.[21] But since we are analysing the shifting emotions of two human beings between the summer of 1927 and the autumn of 1931, such a statement would be simplistic, even if were not questionable whether Hitler was capable of loving. Geli was, and, if she was thinking about Hitler as the father of her unborn child, she was clearly in love with him at the time. But could a healthy, normal, sexy girl have gone on loving a man like Hitler for over four years?

What eventually disillusioned him with Adolf Vogl was the teacher's scepticism about Geli's future as a Wagnerian soprano. Her next teacher, Hans Streck, said her voice was better suited to Lieder. He had a studio in Gedonstrasse, near the Englischer Garten, and it was arranged that he would give her twelve lessons a month for 100 marks. Another of his pupils was Helene Hanfstaengl, and Putzi, who sometimes collected her from the studio, chatted with Streck, who said Geli was the laziest pupil he had ever had. 'Half the time she rings up to say she can't come, and she learns very little when she does.' She never practised at home, but Hitler, taking a proprietorial interest in her progress, sometimes arrived early when he was picking her up, and listened to the lesson from the entrance hall.[22]

Before her twenty-first birthday, she had received an offer of marriage from a man whose name we do not know. After her death, in the room which Hitler kept exactly as she had left it, Christa Schroeder found a shoebox full of letters from various men. After breaking off her unofficial engagement to Emil Maurice, Geli accepted another proposal. But as a minor, she could not marry without permission from Angela, who could not defy Hitler, and he used the same tactic as before – not forbidding the marriage, but delaying it. This time, since her twenty-first birthday was approaching, he asked only for twelve months.

Having appropriated one of these letters at the end of the war before Julius Schaub could carry out the order to destroy them, Schroeder quotes from it at length:

Now your uncle, who knows how much influence he has over your mother, is trying to exploit her weakness with boundless cynicism. Unfortunately we won't be in a position to fight back against this blackmail until after you're twenty-one. He's putting obstacles in the way of our mutual happiness although he knows that we're made for each other. The year of separation your mother is imposing on us will only bind us together more closely. Because I'm always very strict with myself about thinking and behaving in a direct way, I find it hard to accept when other people don't do that. But your uncle's behaviour towards you can only be interpreted as egoistic. He quite simply wants you to belong to him one day and never to anyone else. . . . Your uncle still sees you as the 'inexperienced child' and refuses to acknowledge that in the meantime you've grown up and want to take responsibility for your own happiness. Your uncle is a force of nature. In his party they all bow down to him like slaves. I don't understand how his keen intelligence can mislead him into thinking his obstinacy and his theories about marriage can destroy our love and our willpower. He's hoping to succeed this year in changing your mind, but how little he knows your soul.[23]

Since she was going to be twenty-one in June 1929, this letter was probably written before Goebbels made the entry in his diary about the Hitler–Geli–Maurice triangle. It would be understandable if, condemned to a Platonic relationship with Maurice, Geli had started to see someone else. The young man was obviously less aware than Maurice had been about what was going on between her and her uncle, and underestimated Hitler's chances of frustrating their intentions.

On one level it was true that 'He quite simply wants you to belong to him one day and never to anyone else.' But nothing would have been simple even if she had not been his half-niece, and even if he had not suffered from intermittent impotence. One of the other problems was that he did not like women. Though he did like Geli, she could produce only temporary and sometimes half-hearted deviations from habitual patterns. According to Erich Fromm, Hitler tended to divide women into two categories – respectable women, distinguished by wealth, social status or artistic fame, and women who were socially beneath him. Stefanie, like the rich women who contributed money or jewellery to the party, belonged to the first category; Geli and Eva to the second.

Fromm concluded that Hitler's 'sexual desires were largely voyeuristic, anal-sadistic with the inferior type of woman, and masochistic with admired women'.[24] Freud had used the term 'anal-sadistic' to characterise the second phase of emotional development, which occurs between the ages of two and four, when the primacy of the genital zones has not yet been established. The connection between sadism and anal eroticism is based on the assumption that, just as the anal sphincter is involved in both evacuation and retention, the sadist wants both to destroy the object and to preserve it by mastering it.

It may be true that anal-sadistic and masochistic elements were prominent, if not dominant, among Hitler's erotic objectives, and if he secretly thought of himself as an inferior type of man, it should have followed that Geli, coming from the same family, was an inferior type of woman. But his behaviour towards her was sometimes masochistic. Perhaps she was the only 'inferior' woman he ever admired.

Even if there was more sexual intercourse and less perverted loveplay at the beginning of their relationship than later on, it is hard to believe that Hitler was a good lover. Even if he could sometimes be gentle, it is unlikely he was ever generous or interested in foreplay. Everything he said about women indicates a misogynistic refusal to recognise them as capable of partnership with men on an equal footing. The one line of Nietzsche he quoted frequently was: 'You are going to see a woman? Do not forget your whip.'[25]

Of the whips that Hitler carried around with him, the three he liked most had been presents from motherly middle-aged ladies. He sometimes cracked his whip, sometimes used it to emphasise a point with a threatening gesture, and sometimes whipped his own hand as if he were a little boy being punished. When he whipped Prinz in front of Mitzi Reiter, he seemed to think she would be impressed by his mastery over the dog and that he could lay its howls of pain like a sacrificial offering at her feet.

Many men, including Speer, were embarrassed by what he said about women when women were present. Eva Braun had to put up with much more boorishness of this kind than Geli. Sometimes he wanted to humiliate Eva; at other times, only half aware of her presence, he was pontificating about the superiority of men. He told the wife of an SA officer: 'A woman must be a nice little cuddly thing, soft, sweet and stupid.'[26] He also said: 'A man must be able to put his mark on every girl. Women wouldn't want it any other way.' 'The world of women consists of men: they think about nothing else.' 'Nothing is more enjoyable than educating a young thing – a girl of eighteen or twenty, as pliable as wax.' He maintained that 'unless a girl has a child, she'll get hysterical or sick', but he had no intention of giving a child to either Geli or Eva.

Though he frequently asked women for a kiss when they had signalled no desire to kiss him, he was outraged if a woman took the initiative. Giving a party on New Year's Eve, Hoffmann had followed the English tradition of hanging up a bunch of mistletoe, but the thirty-four-year-old Hitler stood underneath it without knowing what to expect. Few of Hoffmann's guests were as elegant as the young girls he used as models. Else Brummer was

> one of the most beautiful girls, with a gold-fringed dress and the first silk stockings. She deliberately went up to the young Hitler, who looked at her unsuspectingly. She embraced him and kissed him tenderly on the mouth. The others watched. They found it funny that Hitler was being kissed so openly: he was already known at this time, but there was no talk about his being involved in any love affair. It would have been the most natural thing for him to kiss the girl back, but he didn't do that. As she moved away from him, he gazed at her solemnly, turned round and fetched his mackintosh. (Hitler possessed no overcoat. He said that a pullover and walking fast took the place of a thick coat.) He took his black hat and without wishing anyone a happy new year, went out into the night.[27]

Even the most intelligent women, in his opinion, were too emotional to be capable of thinking objectively or reasoning logically. Though it was pleasant to have beautiful women around him, it was irritating if they tried to join in political discussions, and at the first general meeting of the party, in January 1921, he made it a rule that no woman could ever sit on the executive committee. He had no doubt that men were superior.

In the pleasure a woman takes in dressing up, there is always an admixture of some trouble-making element, something treacherous – to arouse another woman's jealousy by displaying something the latter doesn't possess. Women have the talent, which is unknown to us males, for giving a kiss to a woman-friend and at the same time piercing her heart with a well-sharpened stiletto. . . . Other women are extremely careful of their appearance, but not beyond the moment when they've found a husband. . . . When you marry them, they put on weight by the kilo![28]

His mysogyny must have conditioned his relationship with Geli day and night.

He had in any case little talent for friendship. He was too narcissistic to empathise or look at the life of another human being in the same perspective as his own. Speer, one of the best candidates for friendship, knew Hitler to be incapable of it; Goebbels, another candidate, sometimes wrote excitedly in his diary about his uncertainty whether Hitler was fond of him. Of the four men who spoke to Hitler in the second person singular, one, Ernst Röhm, was killed in the purge of 1934, while August Kubizek, a close friend from 1900, when Hitler was eleven, was discarded without a word of explanation when they were sharing digs in 1908. 'When I returned to Vienna in the autumn, my friend had left our room in the Stumpergasse; he had simply disappeared.' Hitler did not want Kubizek to know he had been rejected again by the academy. They did not see each other for thirty years.[29]

Not unaware of other people's reactions to him, Hitler enjoyed his ability to charm them. Maria von Below, widow of Nicolaus von Below, an air ace who later became his Luftwaffe adjutant, said: 'I don't know why so many people want to deny that extraordinary spark in him. I often noticed later on how aware he was if one was not awed. I mean, if one seemed at ease with him. I think he liked that. He was immediately very nice to me.'[30] One reason he had become fond of Geli was that she never seemed over-awed.

Many of his closest associates described his power as hypnotic. 'All those who worked closely with him,' said Speer, 'were to an extraordinary degree dependent on and servile to him. However powerful they appeared in their domain, in his proximity they became small and timid.' After being with him for any length of time, Speer felt 'weary, exhausted and empty, as if it paralysed any effort to think and act independently'. Assertive enough with everyone else, Hermann Goering admitted: 'I try so hard, but every time I stand before the Führer, my heart drops into the seat of my pants.'[31]

Hitler was capable of magnanimous gestures. When his favourite Englishwoman, Unity Mitford, shot herself after war was declared in 1939, he arranged for her to be nursed in a private clinic, and later had an ambulance specially built for her. It was not only on their shopping expeditions that Geli benefited – more than most other women – from his sporadic generosity. With Eva Braun he was comparatively mean: for her twenty-first birthday, which was celebrated in his absence a week after he became Chancellor, he did not give her the dog she wanted but a set of matching earrings, bracelet and ring made of tourmalines – semi-precious stones.[32] On most of her birthdays he would send out an adjutant to buy cheap jewellery and flowers.[33]

If his behaviour towards Geli was exceptional, his generosity was not extended to other members of the Raubal family. On the Christmas after Geli's death he sent a present to Leo with an affectionately worded note, but in 1942 refused to have him exonerated from fighting at Stalingrad, and when Angela eventually got married again in February 1936 – she was fifty-two and the bridegroom about sixty – it was announced in the press that the Führer was too busy to attend the wedding.

12

Luxury and Terrorism

On 10 September 1929 Hitler took possession of his luxurious new nine-room flat eight weeks before Geli was due to move in. It was in one of Munich's most fashionable squares, the Prinzregentenplatz, a short distance from the Prinzregententheater, where they often went together. There was a statue of Wagner not far from the house, which was big, grey and surrounded by tall trees.

Massive and dark, Hitler's furniture was designed for him by a man he admired, the architect Paul Ludwig Troost, and constructed by the Vereinigte Werkstätte – a company that still has a shop in the centre of Munich. Proud of his new furniture, Hitler never tired of saying he had paid for it out of his savings.[1]

It was only in the room he was preparing for Geli – a corner room next to his – that brighter colours prevailed, and the furniture was daintier, with painted motifs. The walls were pastel green, and the sheets were embroidered. One of the pictures was a watercolour of a Belgian landscape, painted by Hitler during the First World War.[2]

No longer 'identifying himself with the workers and have-nots of the world', Hitler employed a young married couple as servants. Georg Winter had been an orderly in the household of General von Epp, leader of a private army; his twenty-four-year-old wife, Anni, had been a lady-in-waiting to Countess Törring. To make up a staff of four Hitler also took on his former landlady, Maria Reichert, and her deaf mother, Frau Dachs. Anni was both a good cook and a good housekeeper, while her husband was good at waiting at table.

pulled me aside and asked me: 'Haven't you guessed who that gentleman is? Don't you ever look at our photos?'[3]

The elderly gentleman was forty. Next time he appeared in the shop, it was with a bunch of flowers, and he invited her to a matinee at the opera. Trying not to seem too interested, Hoffmann warned her that Geli had a full figure. Eva, he suggested, should stuff handkerchiefs into her bra before going out with her new admirer. At first Hitler took her out only during the day – the evenings belonged to Geli, who moved into the flat on 5 November.

Angela appears to have raised no objection to their living together, possibly because she believed they would end up by marrying. At least, she talked to other people as if she did. Her father had been given Papal dispensation to marry a close relation; why should Hitler not do the same? Besides, the new domestic arrangements suited Angela well. Elfriede was still living with her, and they now had the Haus Wachenfeld to themselves most of the time. Hitler wanted to go on coming there to relax and invite guests, especially over the weekend, but he and Geli would spend less time there than before. After so many years of hard work and poverty, Angela was finally in a comfortable position. It was almost like having a house of her own.

Geli was equally glad to have turned her back on poverty, but she must have felt ambivalent about moving in with Hitler. Probably she had no alternative: he could have refused to go on renting a room for her, now that he had such a big flat. But she knew him well enough to distrust any promises he may have made about allowing her independence and freedom of movement. When writing her Christmas Eve letter to Emil Maurice, she was only nineteen and she still trusted Hitler's promises; two years later she knew him better.

While she was still a minor he had stopped her from becoming engaged by putting pressure on Angela. Though Geli had now come of age, neither Maurice nor any of her other admirers would be able to defend her when her only home was Hitler's flat. Previously he could monitor only some of her movements; now she would have no privacy and no freedom.

Though there is no proof that they were lovers, it is unlikely he would have taken the risk of living with her if they were not. Of the biographers who think they were not, one, John Toland, argues that he was 'too cautious to ruin his political career by taking a mistress into his own apartment – particularly the daughter of a half sister'.[4] But if they were living in the same flat, the risk of scandal did not depend on whether they made love. Other people were not going to know what they did; the only way to avoid gossip would have been to let Geli live somewhere else. But then she would not have been under his control.

If they did become lovers, it may have been before or after she started the affair with Emil Maurice, before or after Hitler rented the room in Königinstrasse for her, before or after he moved her to the next-door house in Thierschstrasse, before or after his gauche attempt to draw a profile of her ideal man, before or after she jumped over the bonfire with a boy. Hitler's possessive jealousy had been aroused again and again. Perhaps, as Henny suggested, he fell in love when he watched Maurice sharing a moment of laughter with Geli. Henny's impression was that Geli grew more and more indifferent to him while he grew more and more passionate about her.[5]

At first he may not have realised how much he wanted her. He may have thought her girlish presence, her *joie de vivre*, her companionship and her full-throated laughter were all he needed. But she was progressively becoming less girlish and more self-assured. Even if he had once believed he wanted nothing more than to stop her from falling into the wrong hands, he was growing uncomfortably aware that nobody else's hands would ever seem right.

Once he came to terms with his desire, there was nothing to hold him back. Whatever she felt, she was in a weak position. In spite of the affair with Mitzi Reiter, Hitler's sexuality had not changed much since the non-affair with Stefanie. Though he had braved gunfire in the trenches and charmed rich ladies in drawing rooms and roused big crowds to frenzied cheering, he was sexually and emotionally inexperienced. Apart from Geli, his only lover had been a girl of sixteen.

He had never been scrupulous about the way he used his

power, and he now had a great deal. He had been in no position to pressurise Stefanie. Though he had had two violent ideas – kidnapping and suicide – both had been fantasies. But there was no limit to the pressure he could exert on Geli. She was unlikely to run away. Where could she go? How could she earn a living? How could she send Angela and Elfriede back into poverty and exile?

If Geli threw her arms round Hitler's neck when she wanted to drive out for a picnic, it is inconceivable that he never asked for a kiss, inconceivable that she never gave him one, and almost inconceivable that they went no further. It is possible that, without being in love with him, she would have accepted a proposal of marriage, had he made one. According to Anni Winter, 'Geli was a flighty girl who tried to seduce everybody, including Hitler, and he merely wanted to protect her.'[6] Anni is also quoted as saying: 'Geli loved Hitler. She was always running after him. Naturally, she wanted to become "Gnädige Frau Hitler". He was highly eligible ... but she flirted with everybody; she was not a serious girl.'[7]

This is contradicted by Helene Hanfstaengl, who regarded her as 'a nice, rather serious girl', and certainly not a flirt.[8] Working in the flat, Anni must have known what was going on, but we cannot trust either her or Hoffmann when they insist that Hitler's only interest was in protecting Geli. He would not have kept Anni in the job unless he could count on her discretion, for which he was no doubt willing to pay a high price. Like Hoffmann, she went on protecting his reputation after he was dead, but so did many of the others who had got into the habit while he was alive.

We have to go on picking our way through the forest of contradictions. According to some reports, Geli's virginity was still intact when she was found dead in 1931; there is also plentiful evidence that she had lovers. In 1973, working on a book about Hitler and Eva Braun, Glenn Infield interviewed one of Adolf Vogl's ex-pupils, Ada Dort, who said Geli was not serious about singing and chatted to her about men.

After we became better friends, Geli told me about her uncle and how he gave her expensive gifts whenever she was 'nice' to him. When I learned that her uncle was Adolf Hitler, the radical politician, I warned her she was asking for trouble. Geli just laughed at me. She said she could wind him around her little finger when she was alone with him.[9]

Infield also interviewed a former SA officer, Wilhelm Stocker, who claimed he had been on guard duty at the Munich flat and had been one of Geli's lovers.

> Many times when Hitler was away for several days at a political rally or tending to party matters in Berlin or elsewhere, Geli would associate with other men. I liked the girl myself so I never told anyone what she did or where she went on these free nights. Hitler would have been furious if he had known that she was out with such men as a violin player from Augsburg or a ski instructor from Innsbruck. After she was satisfied that I wouldn't tell her uncle – and I had a personal reason for not telling him – she often confided in me. She admitted to me that at times Hitler made her do things in the privacy of her room that sickened her but when I asked her why she didn't refuse to do them she just shrugged and said that she didn't want to lose him to some woman that would do what he wanted. . . . She was a girl that needed attention and needed it often. And she definitely wanted to remain Hitler's favourite girlfriend. She was willing to do anything to retain that status. At the beginning of 1931 I think she was worried that there might be another woman in Hitler's life because she mentioned to me several times that her uncle didn't seem to be as interested in her as he once was.[10]

Hitler sometimes used women as chaperones, but often took the risk of using men. If Stocker was telling the truth, he had probably been risking his life: he would not have been treated with the same clemency as Emil Maurice. Even if the story is untrue, it reminds us that a discipline of terrorist intimidation could not always be effective.

Geli does seem to have been involved with another man, though we do not know who he was or how they met. When

Henny asked: 'Which would you prefer – to be loved or to be in love?' the answer came without hesitation: 'What I want is to be in love – of course. Being loved is boring, but to love a man, you know, to *love* him – that's what life is about. And when you can love and be loved at the same time, it's paradise.'[11] At that time, it would seem, she was not in paradise.

During the late twenties, violence was increasing in the Munich streets. Jews were being beaten up brutally, and there was a lot of bloodshed in street battles with Communists. The SA had been reconstructed in February 1925 with the purpose of 'steeling the bodies of our youth, educating them in discipline and devotion to the common great ideal, training them in the organisational and instructional service of our movement'. Instead of being a mere defence corps, the SA became the main engine of mass terrorism. When it took over police duties at meetings and rallies, hecklers were beaten up viciously. All through the last years of the Weimar Republic, battles were fought against Communists in beer halls, meeting halls and streets.

It was obvious that the Nazis were responsible for the violence, which had been going on for ten years, showing that neither the republic nor the state would ever be able to restore stability. It looked as if the only solution was to elect the Nazis: once they were in power, they would have to discipline their uniformed thugs. The catchphrase was *'Besser ein Ende mit Schrecken als ein Schrecken ohne Ende'*. Better to end the terrorism than have terrorism endlessly.[12]

Geli could not have failed to understand the connection between what she saw in the streets and conversations she heard between Hitler and his followers in the Café Heck and the Osteria Bavaria. One member of the *Stosstrupp Adolf Hitler 1923* wrote of the stormtroopers:

> All false sense of fair play and treading softly was alien to them. They remained faithful to the old law of the club – might makes right – and when hard pressed they were inhibited by no commandment. When Joseph Berchtold or his deputy Julius Schreck blew the whistle and when we were called into action by the command 'Shock troop to

the attack! Left, right, step out, forward, march!' the fur
started to fly and in minutes the streets and squares were
swept clean of opponents. We always played rough when
we were let loose, when Berchthold, Schreck and Maurice
let go so that the sparks flew.[13]

It is possible that Maurice had never got rough when he was
alone with Geli, and possible that Julius Schreck was calm and
obedient in his role as chauffeur; but she must have known what
both men were doing in the streets, and if Uncle Alf never took
part in brawls himself, it meant neither that he was devoid of
brutality nor that he would be inhibited about enforcing his
will in a bedroom. She was putting herself at the mercy of a
man she knew to be merciless.

But if he had expected their relationship to improve when they
were living together, he was disappointed. It is possible that his
periods of potency were becoming briefer or rarer; it is possible
that political activity was engaging more of his energy, pushing
him into the same straits he was in when he told Eva Braun
to look for another man. It is also possible that his incipient
interest in Eva was based on the assumption that she would be
less demanding than Geli.

13

Things He Makes Me Do

Hitler often had to choose between spending time with Geli and making an appearance at one of the many events staged to publicise the party and recruit new members. In the manufacture of the Nazi myth, nothing was more useful than martyrdom. When Horst Wessel, a twenty-two-year-old SA man who had moved in with a former prostitute, was killed by Communists called in by her landlady – she was trying to get rid of him – he was no more of a martyr than any of the Communists killed in brawls by SA men, but Goebbels exploited his death so brilliantly that his name was immortalised by the song that was given its first performance by massed choirs at the end of a rally on 7 February 1930.

For the funeral, which Goebbels delayed till 1 March, he arranged a parade which Hitler promised to attend. But when the time, came he opted for a weekend with Geli in Obersalzberg. Goebbels was furious. 'He works too little, and then the woman, the *women*.' Afterwards Horst Wessel's mother complained that Hitler had not even written a letter of condolence.[1]

Goebbels was not the only Nazi leader to think that Hitler was devoting too much of his time and too much of the party's money to his private pleasures. It was the party that paid for a new, open, supercharged Mercedes, and two days after it was delivered, he used it to bring Geli with him to Berlin, where he spoke at the Sport Palace. But the car also had quasi-military uses. One night, after three Communists had been killed by SA men, he was recognised by a group of his opponents when driving in the car with six brownshirts. Constantly nervous of being assaulted, he knew he was in danger, but his driver scattered the enemy by driving the car like a tank.[2]

If the summer solstice caused one crisis of jealousy, the *Fasching* caused another. During the run-up to Lent in such Catholic cities as Munich, Cologne and Vienna, carnival celebrations featured masquerades, formal balls and street parades. On Shrove Tuesday in Munich, the squares were festooned with decorations and lit for dancing in the street, while rich and distinguished people attended parties in the artists' studios of Schwabing. Visitors converged on the city – young Americans, Russians, students from other cities.

In Vienna Geli had seen the street events, but had never been to a carnival party or a ball. In 1930, though Hitler refused to accompany her, she persisted till he agreed she could go to the fancy-dress ball at the Deutsches Theater, on condition that Hoffmann and Max Amann escorted her, and that the three of them left the theatre no later than eleven o'clock.

Once he had capitulated, discussions started about what she should wear. Knowing the theatrical designer Ingo Schröder, who had costumed Henny as an Indian princess, Hoffmann suggested he should design a dress for Geli. He made several attempts, but Hitler rejected all his designs as too provocative.[3] Irritated, Geli tried to design a costume herself, but when he saw her sketch, Hitler said: 'If you want to wear something like that, you might as well go naked.'

According to Ilse Hess, Geli 'got angrier, much angrier than he had ever seen her. She picked up her drawing and ran through the door, slamming it shut. And Hitler was so contrite that within half an hour he was looking for her.'[4] But he did not give in, and she had to settle for a white evening gown from a shop in Theatinerstrasse. The only decoration she was allowed was a silver headband with a white feather.

In the theatre she sat in a box with her two middle-aged escorts – the wide-shouldered photographer and the short ex-sergeant. They were her principal dancing partners. She was not forbidden to dance with younger men who came to the box asking to dance with her, but she was watched while with them. No kissing, no hugging, no chance of letting herself be carried away, like everyone else, by the spirit of a carnival in which strangers exchanged kisses as casually as glances. Most of the time she had to sit in the box with her unattractive chaperones, grimly drinking champagne. When the three of them left punctually at eleven, she was seething with rage.[5]

In the morning Hoffmann was outspoken – or claims he was – in protesting to Hitler. 'The pressure under which Geli lives is burdensome to her, and what makes matters worse is that she's prevented from saying how unhappy she feels. . . . The ball gave her no pleasure. It merely reminded her of how little freedom she has.' According to Hoffmann, Hitler replied:

You know, Hoffmann, I'm so concerned about Geli's future that I feel I have to watch over her. I love Geli and could marry her. Good! But you know what my viewpoint is. I want to remain single. So I retain the right to exert an influence on her circle of friends until such a time as she finds the right man. What Geli sees as compulsion is simply prudence. I want to stop her from falling into the hands of someone unsuitable.

She once started talking to Hoffmann's wife, who had formerly been a cabaret artiste, about a man she had met in Vienna. But she checked herself. 'Well, that's that! And there's nothing you or I can do about it. So let's talk about something else.'[6] As Hoffmann summed it up,

Certainly, it flattered her that her serious and unapproachable uncle, who was so good at hiding his feelings from everybody else, was fond of her. She wouldn't have been a woman if she hadn't been flattered by Hitler's gallantry and generosity. But it seemed simply intolerable to this child of nature that he should want to mother her every step and that she shouldn't be allowed to speak to anyone without his knowledge.[7]

When he came back after an absence from Munich, she had to account for every hour of her time and tell him about everyone she had met. Though Hoffmann may have felt a genuine sympathy for her, he would not have taken the risk of offending Hitler, who had made him rich by appointing him as his official photographer with a monopoly on all the photographs he took. Nor did he ever feel obliged to tell the truth. Even when writing after Hitler's death, he may have been twisting facts to avoid contradicting what he had said earlier. Besides, even if Hitler talked like this about stopping Geli falling into the hands of someone unsuitable, it is unlikely that Hoffmann believed it, or that he had not heard rumours about the perverted love-play that had been integral to Hitler's relationship with Geli since the beginning of 1929 – over a year before the carnival.

The former SA officer Wilhelm Stocker was not the only man to claim she had told him she had been forced into doing things that sickened her. Whether she and Hitler ever made love in the normal way, there is little doubt that he forced her into perverted sex. In the Munich flat, where they had more privacy than before, he was free to involve her in any sexual games he chose. Sadists have more fun when their victims resist. Usually the masochistic partner wants the sadistic partner to enjoy inflicting pain – the suffering and humiliation are part of the loving sacrifice – but we have no reason to think Geli was a masochist.

Early in 1929, before they had moved into the flat, Hitler wrote to her about masochistic and coprophiliac fantasies he had been having about her. We do not know whether she ever received the letter, which fell into the hands of his landlady's opportunistic son, Dr Rudolph. Nothing is known about the blackmail negotiations that went on except that the party treasurer, Franz Xavier Schwarz, was involved in them. He tried to get hold of the incriminating letter through two collectors of political memorabilia.

An anti-Semitic priest who knew Hitler, Father Bernhard Stempfele belonged to the order of St Jerome. Konrad Heiden describes him as 'an armed bohemian in priest's robes', and his partner, the photographer J. F. M. Rehse, as 'a dwarf-like eccentric'. Schwarz asked them to buy the letter from Rudolph, saying they wanted it for their collection. The deal was concluded in April 1929, and Stempfele handed the letter to Hitler in return for a guarantee that from now on the party would take financial responsibility for the collection, employing him and

Rehse as curators. Hitler made out that the party had saved a valuable cultural institution,[8] and, like so many other people who knew too much about his private affairs, the priest was later killed off.

Hitler's perversion may have had nothing to do with any deficiency in his potency, but his sado-masochistic games required no preliminary erection, while another advantage was that they involved no risk of pregnancy. Hanfstaengl had often felt curious about what went on between Hitler and Geli.

> What particular combination of arguments her uncle used to bend her to his will, presumably with the tacit acquiescence of his half-sister, we shall never know. Whether he assumed that a young woman who was already no saint might be brought fairly easily to submit to his peculiar tastes, or whether in fact she was the one woman in his life who went some way towards curing his impotence and half making a man out of him, again we shall never know with certainty. On the evidence available, I incline to the former view. What is certain is that the services she was prepared to render had the effect of making him behave like a man in love. She went round very well dressed at his expense, or, more probably, at the Party's, as a lot of resentment was expressed, and he hovered at her elbow with a moon-calf look in his eyes in a very plausible imitation of adolescent infatuation.[9]

There was no need to postulate an either/or about the two possibilities: she may have been exceptionally successful in arousing him sexually, and may also have been a reluctant partner in perverted sex games.

His sado-masochism was deep-rooted. Probably his father had known what reaction to expect when he took the boy to see weapons at the courthouse in Ried. Alois Hitler may even have been trying to impose on his son something of his own predisposition.

During the early years of the movement, long before Hitler was in a position to make women 'submit to his peculiar tastes', he revealed his misogynist vindictiveness when he designed ten-mark promissory notes for use as receipts when the *Völkischer*

Beobachter floated a loan. The money was to be repaid as soon
as the party came to power. On the left of the note was a picture
of a young man wearing an open-necked shirt. Though he was
clean-shaven and better-looking than Hitler, the resemblance
was unmistakeable. The face was stern and determined. In his
right hand was a sword dripping with blood, while in his left
he held a severed female head by the hair. The caption was:
'Warriors of truth, behead the lie.'[10]

This sado-masochistic strain persisted throughout Hitler's life.
When the time came to execute the unsuccessful conspirators
who tried to kill him in July 1944, he gave specific instructions
for the way they were to be hanged. Instead of having their necks
broken by the ropes, they were to be strangled slowly, and their
trousers were to be lowered so that spectators could watch the
movements in their genitals. A film was made of the execution
and shown several times in the Chancellery.[11]

One night at the theatre, Putzi and Helene Hanfstaengl saw
Hitler and Geli together, watching a Bavarian play by Ludwig
Thoma. According to Putzi, 'They were standing on one of the
side galleries during an interval, with Hitler mooning at her,
thinking he was unobserved, but as soon as he saw me he
switched his face to the Napoleonic look.' Afterwards the four of
them had supper together at the Schwarzwälder Café. Discussing
politics as they walked through the streets after the meal, Hitler

> emphasised some threat against his opponents by cracking
> the heavy dog whip he still affected. I happened to catch a
> glimpse of Geli's face as he did it, and there was on it such
> a look of fear and contempt that I almost caught my breath.
> Whips as well, I thought, and really felt sorry for the girl. She
> had displayed no sign of affection for him in the restaurant and
> seemed bored, looking over her shoulder at the other tables,
> and I could not help feeling that her share in the relationship
> was under compulsion.[12]

Helene formed the same impression – that Geli was not allowed
to organise her life as she wanted to.[13]

In the spring of 1931 Gregor Strasser's brother, Otto, who
had heard that she was free with her favours, invited her to

a carnival ball. She accepted – she usually accepted invitations unless there was a good reason not to – but on the day of the ball a furious Hitler telephoned Otto Strasser: 'I don't allow her to go out with a married man. I'm not going to have any of your filthy Berlin tricks.'

Though they gave up the idea of going to a ball, Strasser turned up at the Prinzregentenplatz flat.

> Geli seemed to have won the argument, but her eyes were red with weeping. His face stony, Hitler stood in the doorway as we left the house to climb into the waiting taxi. We spent a very pleasant, high-spirited evening. Geli seemed to enjoy having escaped from his supervision for once. On the way back from Schwabing to Prinzregentenplatz, we went for a walk in the Englischer Garten. At the top of the Chinese Tower, Geli sat down on a bench and started to weep bitterly. In the end she told me that she really loved Hitler, but she couldn't bear it any longer. His jealousy wasn't the worst thing. He demanded things from her that were simply disgusting. She had never dreamed that such things could happen. When I asked her to tell me, she described things I had previously encountered in my reading of Krafft-Ebing's *Psychopathia Sexualis* when I was a student.[14]

This is what Otto Strasser told the writer Willi Schwarzwalder. Pressed to be more specific, Strasser merely said that Hitler was a sado-masochist. But in May 1943, interviewed by officials of the US Office of Strategic Studies, Strasser went into detail:

> Hitler made her undress. . . . He would lie down on the floor. Then she would have to squat over his face, where he could examine her at close range and this made him very excited. When the excitement reached its peak, he demanded that she urinate on him and this gave him sexual pleasure. Geli said the whole performance was extremely disgusting to her and . . . it gave her no gratification.[15]

Any doubts we might have about the validity of his statement are eroded when we compare it with another piece of testimony collected by the Office of Strategic Studies. The film actress Renate Müller, who starred opposite Emil Jannings in *Liebling der Götter*, confided in the director Adolf Zeissler in 1936 before she committed suicide.

She met Hitler in the autumn of 1932 when she was filming on location near the Danish coast. He watched the shooting all day, and, in the evening, visited the house where she was staying, but his behaviour, when they were together, was distinctly odd. At forty-three, he still seemed ill at ease when alone with a glamorous woman. 'He sat there, not moving at all, looking at me all the time, and then he'd take my hand in his and look some more. He talked all the time – just nonsense.'[16] Later, when she was invited to a party at the Chancellery, he ignored her until everyone was leaving but then took her arm, offering to show her round the building. He pointed out the changes he had made and took her to his wardrobe, where he brought out his tail-coated dinner shit, saying he had never worn evening dress till he came to power.

After this he arranged frequent meetings with her, and the jewellery he gave her included a diamond bracelet more valuable than any of his presents to Geli and Eva Braun. But the demands he made were as unpalatable to her as to Geli. One night, for instance, at the Chancellery, he began by going into detail about Gestapo methods of torture, comparing them with medieval techniques. After they had both taken their clothes off he lay on the floor, begging her to hit him and kick him. She refused, but he went on heaping accusations on his own head, saying he was her slave, unworthy to be in the same room.

Eventually giving in, she started to kick him, abuse him with obscene words and hit him with his whip. Becoming increasingly excited, Hitler started to masturbate. After his orgasm, he suggested quietly that they should both put their clothes on. They drank a glass of wine together and chatted about trivialities. Finally he stood up, kissed her hand, thanked her for a pleasant evening and rang for a servant to show her out.[17]

When she wanted to take a holiday in London, she asked his permission, which was granted, but the Gestapo kept her under surveillance while she was there, and after spending a lot of time with a former lover, Frank Deutsch, who was

Jewish, she found, on returning to Germany, that she had been blacklisted, and it was rumoured that she was to be put on trial for 'race defamation'. While under this pressure, she became addicted to morphine. Eventually she went into a sanatorium and, after being discharged, asked for an interview with Hitler, who refused to see her. Back in the sanatorium, she was looking out of the window one day when a car pulled up in the street below, and four SS officers got out. She killed herself by jumping out of the window. She was thirty.

Had she survived, she could possibly have been dangerous to Hitler in the same way as Geli could: either of them could have damaged him by revealing the truth about his sexual habits. In 1937, when her death was reported in the German papers, they revealed neither that Hitler had known her nor that she had killed herself. According to the *Völkischer Beobachter*, it had been known for some time that she was 'no longer in the best of health'.[18] Hitler did not attend the cremation, but Goebbels sent a wreath.

On the evening when Hitler took Geli to the theatre, Hanfstaengl might not have interpreted her 'look of fear and contempt' in the way he did if his suspicions had not already been aroused. It was early in 1930 that Schwarz first confided in him about an attempt to blackmail Hitler over a portfolio of pornographic drawings he had done of Geli's genitalia. (The other blackmail incident had already occurred, but Hanfstaengl did not hear about it till later.) It was not clear how the second blackmailer had come into possession of the drawings – possibly Geli had confided in someone so desperate for cash that he had stolen them and offered to sell them back. Instead of letting Schwarz destroy them after he bought them back, Hitler insisted on having them kept in a safe at the Brown House.[19]

Evidence of his perversion has mostly been destroyed, but apparently Geli told a girlfriend that he was a monster. 'You'd never believe the things he makes me do.'[20] Inferences can be made from what is known about later relationships with other women. There is evidence that his demands had traumatic effects on some of his short-term partners.

The report prepared for the US Office of Strategic Studies in 1943 by Walter Langer and other doctors concluded that Hitler was subject to 'an extreme form of masochism in which the individual derives sexual gratification from the act of having a woman urinate or defecate on him'.[21] Reviewing Langer's book when it appeared nearly thirty years later, Hugh Trevor-Roper objected that 'There is not a shred of evidence on any of these matters.'[22] But the books by Waite (1977) and Schwarzwalder (1995) contain substantial evidence. If Hitler made demands like these on Geli, it is understandable that she would not go into detail when talking to other people, but it is also understandable that she could not keep silent about it.

14

Like Characters in a Western

We do not know whether Hitler ever talked to Geli about getting married, but Angela went on waiting for their engagement to be announced until the news reached her that her daughter was dead, and Hitler often said – afterwards – that Geli was the only woman he had ever wanted to marry. It is possible that he never considered it seriously till it was out of the question, though he had never come closer to behaving like a normal man than during their relationship, which lasted just over four years. She was twenty-three when she died in September 1931, and he was forty-two.

He never mastered the art of listening to other people as if he wanted to hear what they were saying, but with Geli he approximated more closely than with anyone else to listening, and he enjoyed the commonplace pleasures – eating, drinking, laughing, shopping, going to restaurants, driving into the country, holding hands, cuddling. She had exerted a healthy influence, extending what little talent he had for human interaction. Though the relationship with Eva Braun lasted four times as long, she had less of a hold on his emotions than Geli and less influence on his behaviour.

By the middle of 1931, his relationship with Geli was deteriorating. He was often away from Munich, which made her increasingly restless and truculent. Henny noticed that since she had moved into his flat she was less happy-go-lucky, more withdrawn, more solemn. 'There was nothing she wanted less than to be watched over. She was ready for new adventures, hungry for new experiences.'[1] After four years of treating her as if she were one of his most treasured possessions, Hitler was suddenly – or perhaps not so suddenly – prepared to consider the possibility of giving her more freedom.

In mid-September she rang her singing teacher, Streck, to cancel her lessons for the rest of the month. She was going to Vienna, she said. She would let him know when she came back. Asked to recommend a teacher there, he suggested the man who had taught him, Professor Otto Ro. She also asked a music critic, Willi Schmidt, for letters of introduction to teachers there. Apparently she told him that one of her reasons for leaving Munich was that her uncle was molesting her. Several other people were informed that she was going to consult another teacher in Vienna. Though we do not know what arrangement she had made with Hitler, it looks as if he had agreed either to give her a longer leave of absence than ever before or to let her take control of her own life.

Why, after four proprietorial years, would he suddenly do that? Though she had been in his flat since November 1929 few people knew they were living together, and it was becoming increasingly important to him and the party that the newspapers did not find out. A rumour was circulating that she was pregnant, either by him or by a Jewish lover in Vienna, possibly a singing teacher, possibly a painter or art teacher. In the past, Hitler had usually ignored gossip inside and outside the party. In 1928 a Württemberg *Gauleiter*, Munder, had lost his job because he had been talking indiscreetly. At a meeting of officials, Hitler insisted angrily that, as founder and leader of the party, he was not going to let anyone tell him whether he should let his niece ride in his car.[2] So far as we know, that was the only retaliatory action he ever took over gossip about Geli.

But in October 1929, just before she moved in, the political and economic situation started changing dramatically. During 1926, when he had the affair with Mitzi, and during the second half of 1927, when he was often seen with Geli, he had been glad to have a whiff of scandal surrounding his life. It encouraged people to talk about him, and he had nothing to lose, being such a long way from the gates of power. He was saying that twenty or even a hundred years might have to elapse 'before our idea is victorious'.

He had always expected his life to be a short one. He told

Baldur von Schirach that he was suffering constant pain in the diaphragm and stomach – he thought he had cancer. Frau Bruckmann urged him to see her doctor, but 'like all hypochondriacs, he preferred to remain in the dark about his real or imaginary ailments'.[3]

As leader of a party that wanted to overturn the government without breaking the law, he was on a see-saw: his side went up when the government's went down, and vice versa. While Gustav Stresemann was managing to stabilise the economy and improve Germany's relationships with former enemies, Hitler had appeared to be operating on the lunatic fringe of German politics.

In August 1928 Stresemann agreed to a plan proposed by the American banker Owen Young for paying off war debts. The terms were aimed at giving the German economy a chance to expand by spreading payments over thirty years, and Stresemann persuaded the French, who were still occupying the Rhineland, to consider an early withdrawal. The date eventually settled for the evacuation was 30 June 1930. Though better than any terms previously proposed, these were bitterly opposed by the right-wing nationalists led by the bigoted Alfred Hugenberg, a sixty-three-year-old industrial and newspaper magnate who in 1928 had become leader of the German National party.

Mistaking Hitler for a man he could manipulate, Hugenberg provided what the Nazis needed – massive publicity resources. Hitler's run of good luck started in October 1929. At the beginning of the month Stresemann died, and on the 29th, a week before Geli moved in, the New York Stock Exchange had the disastrous day that was dubbed Black Thursday. Nearly 13 million shares changed hands. By mid-November 30 billion dollars had been wiped off the value of stocks that in September had been worth 80 billion, and dozens of speculators committed suicide.

No one could have told Geli that Stresemann's death and the Wall Street Crash were going to change her life, but the nation suffered abysmally from the worldwide depression that ensued on the crash. The American payments stopped, while short-term loans had to be repaid. During the winter, unemployment reached the point at which the state's insurance scheme could no longer pay benefits. With extremist demagogues and uniformed thugs active in the streets, rattling collecting boxes and wielding truncheons, party membership rose to 120,000 by the end of 1929. In the Reichstag elections of 1928 the Nazis had won only 810,000 votes, but another election was called for 14 September 1930, and they were going to make the most of their opportunity.

At first, naturally, Hitler was happy to collaborate with Hugenberg and leaders of the other nationalist parties, the *Stahlhelm* and the German National Unity party. Together they collected over 4 million signatures in support of a draft law repudiating the war-guilt clause in the Treaty of Versailles, and demanding the immediate withdrawal of French troops. When this so-called Freedom Law was put to a referendum in December 1929, nearly 6 million people voted for it – enough to show that hopes of toppling the government were no longer unrealistic.

Instability in the federal government panicked the state government into revealing its weakness by putting on a show of strength that could be effective only in the short term. Early in June it vetoed private uniforms, and two weeks later, when the Prussian state proclaimed a copycat veto on brown shirts, stormtroopers had to parade in white ones.

Now eighty-two, Hindenburg had come increasingly under the influence of Kurt von Schleicher, who ten years earlier, as a major, had pioneered the idea of the Freikorps, and had since risen rapidly to the rank of general. He was only forty-seven. It was on his recommendation that Hindenburg took a crucial step away from democracy, intervening for the first time in the formation of a government. He appointed Heinrich Brüning, leader of the predominantly Catholic Centre Party, as Chancellor.

Brüning was obsessional about reparations. He was so keen not to go on paying them that he exploited the world crisis, deliberately letting Germany's economy deteriorate. Having no parliamentary majority, he failed to muster enough support for his economic policy, and, rather than abandon it, he dissolved the Reichstag in order to govern by a series of emergency decrees. The moment he chose to do this was unfortunate for Germany, but fortunate for Hitler.

Unemployment was rising, the sense of crisis deepening, and it looked as if the gap between republican constitutionalism and Nazi violence was narrowing. In August 1930 Hitler summoned his closest colleagues to tell them he was on the verge of a breakthrough. Everything he wanted was within reach; the next twelve months would be crucial.

He may have decided that the moment had come to jettison Geli. Throughout most of his adult life he had been saying he could not settle down with one woman; this certainly was not the moment to risk a scandal. If he was reluctant to sacrifice Geli, Goebbels, Gregor Strasser, Himmler, Goering and Schwarz would have gone all out to convince him he had no alternative. If they were on the verge of a breakthrough, he was about to step into the limelight. Newspaper reporters were going to become more curious about his private life, more persistent in asking questions. Someone would find out that he was living with his niece, and the scandal would put paid to his chances of victory.

The elections of September 1930 increased the number of Nazi deputies in the Reichstag from twelve to 107. The entry in Goebbels's diary was '107 mandates at once. None of us expected that.'[4] In non-Nazi newspapers, Hitler and the party had previously been given minimal space, but from now on he was rarely out of the headlines,[5] and it was more important than ever that he should appear to have heroic stature. Attacking the over-privileged capitalists who became cabinet ministers, he made himself out to be a selfless idealist, interested in nothing but the welfare of the German people.

In Catholic, socialist and traditionally conservative papers and pamphlets he was still being denounced. An SPD leaflet called him 'the Pied Piper of Braunau',[6] but it was important not to provide his attackers with ammunition. His image needed to be cultivated in a new way. Hindenburg was regarded as an incarnation of traditional Germanic virtues, while Catholicism was such a powerful force in Bavaria that Hitler must do everything possible to prove that Nazism was not a form of 'neo-paganism'. In 1930 he distanced himself from Alfred

Rosenberg, whose book *The Myth of the Twentieth Century* exposed the party to that charge. Hitler, who was often attacked as an unprincipled rabble-rouser, had to persuade the public that it could count on him not only to fight the anti-religious Marxists but also to uphold high moral standards.

If he had decided to let Geli go, political reasons may have been reinforced by personal ones. Hanfstaengl talked to Karl Anton Reichel, whom he describes as one of the closest intimates at Hitler's regular table in the Café Heck. Hitler had shown him a letter he had recently written to Geli while she was staying in Obersalzberg.

> It was couched in romantic, even anatomical terms and could only be read in the context of a farewell letter of some sort. Its most extraordinary aspect was a pornographic drawing which Reichel could only describe as a symbol of impotence. Why on earth he should have been shown this letter I cannot imagine, but he was not the man to make up such a story.[7]

Some of Hitler's pornographic drawings may still be extant in private collections, but even if none has survived, there is plenty of evidence that they existed. Imminent victory, like imminent defeat, puts a man under emotional pressure, and the crisis of 1930–1 may have had the same effect on Hitler's potency as the war crisis of 1943, when Eva Braun was told to look elsewhere.

The strain in his relationship with Geli is also evident in his need for flirtations with girls likely to be undemanding. It is pointless to speculate about whether the strain caused the need or the need caused the strain; each exacerbated the other. He took Eva to restaurants, cinemas, matinees at the opera and even on picnics. He probably talked more to her about Geli than to Geli about her, and apparently they saw each other only once, in October 1930, when, after a sustained campaign of persuasion, Hitler let Geli go to the Oktoberfest – a gigantic public fair which is still one of Munich's most popular events. In canvas marquees, beer from local breweries is served in tankards, and whole oxen are roasted on a spit. The Oktoberfest lasts for sixteen days and dates from 1810, when Prinz Ludwig of Bavaria announced his engagement to Princess Therese.

Hitler refused to go, but Geli was escorted by Schwarz, Schaub, Schwarz's wife and Schaub's fiancée. They had a good time on the roundabouts, on the swing-boats and in the various show-booths. They were eating roast chicken, drinking beer and enjoying the music in a marquee when Hoffmann appeared with Eva Braun. Unprepared for a confrontation, Geli was furious when Hoffman introduced Eva as his niece. It was at best an unsubtle joke, and Geli took it to imply that she belonged on the same level as a shopgirl.

Schwarz and Schaub did their best to calm her down, but the two women thought she was right to be offended. When Hoffmann and Eva sat down at a nearby table, Geli made fun of her rival, who was wearing a black overcoat with long strands of fur hanging from the collar and sleeves. It looked like monkey fur, and she referred to Eva as 'the monkey girl over there'.[8]

It is hard to assess how Hitler's friendship with Eva affected Geli, who seems to have become more embattled about restrictions on her freedom. Though spending less time with her, Hitler was no less fanatical about stopping her from seeing other people. He also flirted with Henny, who was maturing into a good-looking woman, and the man she later married, Baldur von Schirach, described her as

> a worldly type of girl – bobbed chestnut-brown hair, a make-up that was unconventional for the time, fashionable pullover and short, narrow skirts, silk stockings and high-heeled shoes. I took her for a French girl. Usually she was walking a boxer dog. For me she was the most beautiful girl in Munich.[9]

Her father sometimes used her as a model, and she got a few small parts in films. Hitler frequently came to dinner in their house, both before and after she bobbed her hair.

> He gave himself great airs, with his dark leather coat, his whip and his Mercedes, whose driver waited for him in front of the door. After dinner Hitler – at that time he was still Herr Hitler to us – sat down at the piano and played

some Wagner followed by some Verdi. 'Do you recognise the leitmotiv of *La Forza del Destino*?' He addressed me as *Du*, for I was only seventeen and he was over forty. Then he took his leave and my father went with him.[10]

She was left on her own in the house till the doorbell rang: Hitler had forgotten his whip.

The whip was Hitler's fetish. He took it and planted himself on the red carpet of the ante-room, his broadbrimmed felt hat in one hand and his whip in the other. Finally to my great surprise, he asked me with a very serious air: Will you kiss me? I was mainly struck by the fact that this time he'd called me *Sie* – the first time since I'd known him.[11]

Her answer was: 'No, please, really not, Herr Hitler, it's impossible for me!' He left without trying to persuade her. When Hoffmann came back, she told him what had happened, only to find that he laughed in her face. 'Kiss you? A brat with pigtails? You're having delusions.' He was surprisingly angry. 'You're not to mention this to anyone! Understand? You're to forget the whole thing! Understand? Now go straight to bed.'[12]

Though Henny apparently said nothing to Geli, she must have noticed (as Wilhelm Stocker claims she told him) that her uncle was no longer so obsessed with her.

Eva Braun's schoolteacher father held Hitler in contempt. 'He thinks he sucked in wisdom with his mother's milk. When I see him in the street, I cross to the other side.' Scared that she might be sent back to the Simbach convent where she had been educated, Eva did not tell her parents she was seeing Hitler; but she was quite enterprising in the initiatives she took. One day, as she confided afterwards to Henny, she slipped a note into the pocket of his raincoat: 'I'm sorry you're so sad – Eva.'[13]

Making it clear from the outset that he did not intend to spend much time with her, he said what he had so often said before and would so often say again – he could afford neither to get married nor to risk the scandal that would blow up if he was discovered to be having an affair. As party leader, he had to look like a model of ethical behaviour. Anyway, women had a disastrous influence in politics. 'Look at Napoleon. And the dancer, Lola Montez, who destroyed Ludwig of Bavaria. And Chiang Kai Shek's wife was a madwoman, so full of hatred that she provoked Japan and brought ruin to her country.'

Later on, Eva complained of being 'a prisoner in a golden cage', but, caring less about her, Hitler gave her more freedom than Geli had. When he was away from Munich, Geli was allowed to spend time with Angela in the Haus Wachenfeld, but she was summoned back when he arrived in Munich, even if he was going to be there only briefly. A fortnight before she died she had two enjoyable days with her brother Leo, who was working as a teacher in Linz. He came to Obersalzberg, and they went for long hikes together over the mountains, but she generally had to spend too much time doing nothing.

Both before and after the elections of September 1930, Hitler was busy. He addressed a lot of pre-election meetings, and he went to Leipzig the same month to appear as a witness at the Supreme Court. Three army officers were on trial for distributing Nazi leaflets, which gave him another opportunity to do what he had done after the 1923 putsch – make a political speech in a courtroom. Intending to reassure the army leaders and the general public, he promised that his party would not use illegal methods to gain power. No one could have stopped him from taking Geli with him on at least some of these journeys, but this was not a good time to be photographed with her on his arm or to ignore the feelings of colleagues who complained that she was distracting him from political duties.

Geli got on well with Schaub's fiancée, and before the couple married in May 1931 (when Schaub was thirty-three) Geli not only helped the bride to choose her wedding dress but gave her a chiffon veil as a present. To wear at the wedding herself, Geli chose a dark blue jacket and skirt from a shop in Maximilianstrasse. She also got involved in planning and preparing the couple's home. One day, when the decorators had left a lot of dust and rubbish in the freshly painted kitchen, the two girls worked together at cleaning it up.[14]

They had a lot more free time than Hitler or Schaub, and in the summer of 1931 they spent a couple of days in Obersalzberg with Angela and Elfriede. The three girls crossed the frontier to shop in Salzburg, which is only about twelve miles away. Geli bought a pair of red silk shoes that would match an evening dress she had made for herself, and – at the risk of annoying Hitler – a small ermine fur for another evening dress. She had been invited to Bayreuth with the Bechsteins, and needed the right clothes.

Hitler, too, stayed in Obersalzberg during the summer, and Hoffmann was often invited. One Sunday afternoon they went for a walk in the mountains, taking the two Alsatians, Blondi and Muck. Geli was holding Hitler's arm and carrying her camera, the Rolleiflex he had given her. When she said how much she would like to own a Leica Hoffmann promised to give her one from his shop, but Hitler objected to this. The Leica, he said, was a photographic revolver. All you needed to do was aim it at a subject. No artistry was involved. This might be necessary for newspaper photographers, but not for Geli. She had already taken so many good photographs with her Rolleiflex, and this was the right camera for her. She argued, pouted and pleaded in vain. When she threatened to buy one for herself, he reminded her that she had no money, and he was not going to give her any for a Leica. On the way home she sulked and walked by herself, behind the others. But he did not give in.[15]

The presence of pistols in the Munich flat was taken for granted. Hitler was nervous that he might be assassinated: several threats had been made against him, and one of his dogs had been poisoned. Wherever he went, he was escorted by armed bodyguards; vulnerable inside the flat, he kept a Walther 6.35 in the drawer of his writing table, and had told Geli that, since she was living in a politician's flat, she must learn how to use it.

She was glad about this, because she sometimes felt scared. Nerin Gun says that when she was alone in the flat she kept one of her pistols at her side 'for fear of Frau Reichert'. This 'old woman', he says, 'lived in a maid's room on the same landing' and 'was in the habit of going up and down the stairs of the building with a kitchen knife and a piece of bread in her hand'.[16] In fact Frau Reichert was only forty-five. Her deaf mother, Frau Dachs, could have been called an old woman, but they both lived in the nine-room flat and it is hard to see why either of them would want to go outside with bread and a kitchen knife.

The seventeen-year-old Henny was in no danger from assassins, but together with Geli she was given weapons training, and they were both allowed to carry loaded pistols around with them. They practised shooting on a rifle range just outside Munich; they were taught how to use a safety catch and how to clean a Walther, taking it to pieces and putting it together again. They enjoyed this: it made them feel like characters in a Western.[17]

What seems to have happened shortly before Geli died is that Hitler, who often changed his mind at the last minute, reversed his decision about letting her go to Vienna. It is quite likely that the other Nazi leaders were putting pressure on him. Though they would all have been glad to get rid of her, they may have told him it was unsafe to set her free: she knew too much. They may have found out that she had confided in other men about Hitler's sexual habits, and Schwarz knew she had modelled for his pornographic drawings. If she talked indiscreetly in Vienna, stories might get picked up by the liberal press at the worst possible moment.

Four years earlier, thousands of German girls would have given anything to swap places with her. But now that her uncle was on the verge of a breakthrough, the Nazis could neither let her go nor let her stay. The trap was closing.

Island of Liars

On the morning of Saturday, 19 September 1931, Geli's body was found on the floor of her room in the flat. She had been bleeding from a wound near her heart; her clothes were soaked with blood. She was lying face downwards, with her nose against the floor. One arm was stretched out towards the pistol, a Walther 6.35, which was on the couch. The bullet, which had missed her heart, had pierced her lung. Still in her body, it had lodged on the left side of her back above the level of her hip.[1]

On the table was an unfinished letter, which was not a suicide note. It was addressed to someone in Vienna – either a music teacher[2] or a girlfriend.[3] The tone was cheerful, and the letter broke off in the middle of the word *und*: 'When I come to Vienna – I hope very soon – we'll drive together to Semmering an . . .'[4] Semmering is an attractive health resort outside Vienna.

There are several conflicting accounts of what happened before and after the death. None of them is entirely factual, and the one we can eliminate first as mainly fictional appears in the memoirs of Bridget Hitler, who provides an elaborate fourth-hand account of Geli's last meal with Hitler in the Munich flat. Bridget claims that she heard the story from her son, Patrick; that he heard it from the woman his father, Alois Hitler, had bigamously married; and that she heard it from Hitler's housekeeper. Two obvious mistakes are that the housekeeper's name is given as Josephine Bauer, and that Angela (who was in Obersalzberg) plays a part in the scene.

As they were eating, Geli said calmly, 'I should like to go to Vienna, Uncle Alf.'

Adolf looked at her quickly. 'Why should you go to Vienna? What do they have there you don't have here?' He was beginning their many-times repeated discussion, which always ended in tears for Geli.

But Geli, though her voice was trembling, quietly insisted. 'Dear Uncle Alf, I must go to Vienna for a little while.'

Realising Geli wasn't going to be talked down, Adolf's attitude changed to one of hurt resentment. 'But why? Why do you want to go?'

'I want to see Aunt Paula.'

Adolf pushed aside his plate and sat staring at the tablecloth. Minutes crawled by, but the silence continued. Finally Adolf stood up and began shouting. 'We're getting to the bottom of this right now. You say you have to go to Vienna? Is it to see that filthy Jew, the one who claims to be a singing teacher? Is that it? Have you been seeing him secretly again? Have you forgotten I forbade you to have anything to do with him? Tell me the truth now. Why do you want to go to Vienna?'

Geli looked up into the tortured face of the man who was in love with her. 'I have to go to Vienna, Uncle Alf, because I'm going to have a baby.'

Trying to vary the tone of the dialogue while maintaining the suspense, the writer makes Adolf put his arm around Geli's shoulder to say 'in a low tortured voice: "Please don't worry. We'll find some way out. I'm terribly nervous, but I'll be all right soon. Then we can decide what to do."' Angela, 'relieved that the storm was over', suggests that they should postpone the whole question till Adolf comes back from his electioneering tour in North Germany.

Washing dishes in the kitchen, Josephine Bauer overhears fragments of a quarrel. The phrase 'I can shoot myself' is repeated several times, and she hears the swish of a whip. When Geli starts screaming, Josephine screams too. Hitler locks Geli into her room; Josephine unlocks the door. 'Geli, lying on the bed, smiled briefly and murmured "Thanks", but refused any further assistance except to ask for a small box in which to bury Honz, one of the four canaries given her by Adolf, which had died that day.'[5]

Neither of the two real housekeepers – Maria Reichert and Anna Winter – would have confided in anyone connected with Alois. Hitler had no contact with his half-brother, and never talked about him. But six years after Geli's death, when Bridget visited Hanfstaengl, who was then living in London, she told him 'the immediate family knew very well that the cause of Geli's suicide was the fact that she was pregnant by a young Jewish art teacher in Linz, whom she had met in 1928 and wanted to marry at the time of her death'.[6]

The main concern of the Nazis was to avoid a scandal and keep gossip to a minimum. Statements would have to be made to both the police and the press. The statements did not have to be true, but they had to be convincing and consistent. If Hitler, as he afterwards claimed, was in Nuremberg when he learned about the shooting, a decision had to be taken in his absence about whether to wait for his return or to make immediate contact with the police and the press.

We know that a top-level conference of Munich Nazis was held in his flat during the morning of Saturday, 19 September, though we do not know what time it began or who convened it. Gregor Strasser, Rudolf Hess, Max Amann, Franz Schwarz and Baldur von Schirach discussed what should be done. Eventually Schirach telephoned Adolf Dresler of the press department at the Brown House, instructing him to tell the press that Hitler had gone into deep mourning after his niece's suicide. But they went on arguing about whether this was the best line to take, and they decided it was not. Schirach made another call to Dresler, telling him to say it had been an accident.[7]

Only twenty-five minutes had passed between the two telephone calls, but the second was too late. Dresler had issued a statement to the press. Since it could not be changed, the Nazis now discussed what should be said about motivation. Nothing could be revealed about Geli's relationship with Hitler or restrictions on her freedom of movement. It would be best to say she had been worrying about her future as a singer.

The police need not find out that a discussion had taken place before they were called in. Schwarz, who was a city councillor, stayed in the flat, but the others left before the arrival of two inspectors from the criminal police – Kriminal Kommissars Sauer and Forster, who took statements from the Winters, Maria Reichert and a daily maid, Anna Kirmair.

Georg Winter testified that at 9.30 in the morning his wife had told him that Raubal's door was locked, and that the pistol which Hitler kept on a shelf in the next room was missing. Winter knocked several times on the locked door but got no answer.

> As the thing seemed to me rather suspicious, at ten o'clock I forced the double-door open with a screwdriver. As I broke the door open, my wife, Frau Reichert and Anna Kirmair were present. As I'd opened the door I stepped into the room and found Raubal lying on the floor as a corpse. She'd shot herself. I can't give any reason why she should have shot herself.

Maria Reichert said that, at three in the afternoon of the previous day, she had heard the door of Raubal's room being locked. 'I was in another room, so I can't say whether it was Raubal herself who shut herself into the room. A short time after that I heard a faint noise from Raubal's room as if something had been knocked over. I attributed no particular significance to it.' At about ten she had wanted to turn the bed down, but, finding the door locked and getting no answer when she knocked, she had assumed Geli had gone out. But at nine in the morning, again getting no answer when she knocked, she called Frau Winter, who called her husband. Both women were present when he broke the door open. 'I can't explain why Raubal had killed herself. She was very agitated recently.'

As reported by the police, Anna Winter's statement was even briefer. 'On 18 September 1931 about 15.00 I saw Raubal, very flustered, go into Hitler's room and then hurry back into her own room. This seems to me rather extraordinary. I now presume that she was fetching the pistol from Hitler's room. I was present when my husband forced the door open, I don't know why Raubal shot herself.' Anna Kirmair made the point that the key was still in the door, which had been locked from inside.

After the police doctor, Dr Müller, arrived at the flat, he certified that the time of Geli's death was '18 September 1931 evening', that the cause of death was suicide, and

> that rigor mortis had set in several hours previously. It was a fatal shot that penetrated through the dress to pass directly through the skin above the heart, which it in any case missed. It did not come out of the body but lodged in the left side of the back, rather above the level of the hip, where it could be felt beneath the skin.

Presented by the directorate of the Munich police on 28 September to the Bavarian Ministry of the Interior, the report says that a police decision had been taken that this was clearly a case of suicide.[8] The body was taken from the flat to the East Cemetery some time between two o'clock in the afternoon of Saturday the 19th and eleven in the morning of Sunday the 20th. Though the state legal authorities released it on Monday, they were prompted by newspaper reports to ask for 'further investigation'.

What appeared in the *Münchener Neueste Nachrichten* was:

> According to a police communiqué, a twenty-three-year-old student fired a pistol aimed at the heart in a room of her flat in the Bogenhausen district. The unfortunate young woman, Angela Raubal, was the daughter of Adolf Hitler's half-sister, and she and her uncle lived on the same floor of a block of flats on Prinzregentenplatz. On Friday afternoon the owners of the flat heard a cry but it did not occur to them that it came from their tenant's room. When there was no sign of life from this room in the course of the evening, the door was forced. Angela Raubal was found lying face down on the floor, dead. Near her on the sofa was a small-calibre Walther pistol.
>
> The motives for this action are not yet clear. Some say that Fräulein Raubal had met a singer in Vienna, but that her uncle

would not allow her to leave Munich. Others affirm that the poor girl killed herself because she was supposed to make her début as a singer but did not believe herself capable of facing the public.

The report in the socialist paper the *Münchener Post* appeared under the headline: 'A Mysterious Affair: Suicide of Hitler's Niece'.

In a flat on Prinzregentenplatz a 23-year-old music student, a niece of Hitler's, has *shot herself*. For two years the girl had been living in a furnished room in a flat on the same floor on which Hitler's flat was situated. What drove the student to kill herself is still unknown. She was Angela *Raubal*, the daughter of Hitler's half-sister. On Friday 18 September there was once again a violent quarrel between Herr Hitler and his niece. What was the reason? The vivacious 23-year-old music student, Geli, wanted to go to Vienna, she wanted to become engaged. Hitler was strongly opposed to this. The two of them had recurrent disagreements about it. After a violent scene, Hitler left his flat on the second floor of 16 Prinzregentenplatz. On Saturday 19 September it was reported that Fräulein Geli had been *found shot* in the flat with Hitler's gun in her hand. The dead woman's nose was broken, and there were other serious injuries on the body. From a letter to a female friend living in Vienna, it is clear that Fräulein Geli had the firm intention of going to Vienna. The letter was never posted. The mother of the girl, a half-sister of Herr Hitler, lives in Berchtesgaden; she was summoned to Munich. Gentlemen from the Brown House then conferred on what should be published about the *motive* for the suicide. It was agreed that Geli's death should be explained in terms of *frustrated artistic ambitions*.

Though this reporter had somehow found out that the Nazis met to discuss what they should say about her motivation, he did not find out where she had been living. This was obvious to the two policemen, but, not having access to police files, newspaper reporters were told she had been living in another flat on the same floor. The Nazis' insistence on this point is an indication of how dangerous it would have been for Hitler to go on living with Geli.

The 'further investigation' ordered by the police produced a report by Dr Müller, who had signed the death certificate. He now confirmed:

> On the face and especially on the nose were to be found no wounds connected with bleeding of any kind. Nothing was to be found on the face except dark greyish deathmarks which had proceeded from the fact that Raubal expired with her face to the floor and remained in this position for about 17–18 hours. That the tip of the nose was pressed slightly flat is due entirely to her lying with her face on the floor for several hours. The extreme discoloration of the deathmarks in the face is probably to be explained by the fact that death was primarily consequent on suffocation following the shot in the lung.[9]

The 'further investigation' also produced statements from the two women employed to lay out corpses. Maria Fischbauer had come to the flat, washed Geli's body without taking her clothes off, and, with help from another woman, put the body into a wooden coffin. 'Apart from the entry wound on the breast, I noticed no injuries and in particular I did not notice that the bone in the nose was broken or that the nose was injured in any other way.' Rosina Zweckl, who, with help from a mortuary attendant, transferred Geli to a zinc coffin, 'looked carefully at the body because I had heard that the dead woman was a niece of Hitler. She was very blue in the face. Apart from the entry wound in the breast, I noticed no injuries and in particular I saw nothing suspicious about the nose.'

According to the police report, Maria Reichert testified that Hitler had left the flat about fifteen minutes before Raubal went to her room. The report says that Schwarz gave him the news over the telephone, and that later the police heard he would be available in the flat from about three o'clock if they wished to interview him. Sauer, who went back about half past three, was told that:

his niece had been a medical student but hadn't taken to it and had therefore turned to singing lessons. She was soon to have made her debut, but didn't feel ready for it and therefore wanted further lessons from a teacher in Vienna. He had agreed to this on condition that her mother, now in Berchtesgaden, went with her, and since she did not wish to, he declared himself to be against the plan. She may well have been annoyed about that, but did not seem particularly upset and had taken leave of him quite calmly when he left on Friday afternoon. Once, previously, after taking part in a séance, she had told him that she certainly wouldn't die a natural death. She could easily have taken the pistols because she knew where his things were kept. Her death affected him very deeply, because she had been the only relation who was close to him, and now this had to happen to him.

It was characteristic of him to talk about her death as something unfortunate that had happened to him, but it seems odd that he should have wanted to tell the policeman about the séance.

Hitler would have preferred the public not to know that 'gentlemen from the Brown House' had come to the flat for a conference, but he did not deny it when he wrote to the *Münchener Post* on the day its report appeared, contradicting many of the other points. He also denied what he had admitted to Sauer on Saturday about vetoing Geli's trip to Vienna. The newspaper, he said, had misrepresented the facts:

I therefore demand that in compliance with Clause 11 of the Press Law, you publish the following correction in your next complete edition in the same position in type of the same size:

1. It is untrue that I had either 'recurrent disagreements' or 'a violent quarrel' with my niece Angelika [*sic*] Raubal on Friday 18 September or previously.
2. It is untrue that I was 'strongly opposed' to my niece's travelling to Vienna. The truth is that I was never against the trip my niece had planned to Vienna.
3. It is untrue that my niece wanted to become engaged in Vienna or [*sic*] that I had some objection to my niece's

engagement. The truth is that my niece, tortured by
anxiety about whether she really had the talent necessary
for a public appearance, wanted to go to Vienna in order
to have a new assessment of her voice by a qualified voice
specialist.

4. It is untrue that I left my flat on 18 September 1931
'after a violent scene'. The truth is that there was no kind
of scene and no agitation of any kind when I left my flat
on that day.

Munich, 21 September 1931 (sig) Adolf Hitler

This statement was afterwards reprinted in other newspapers,[6]
and he made a similar statement in the *Völkischer Beobachter*.

The story that Geli was about to make her debut as a singer
had already found its way into the newspapers, but it was pure
fiction, designed to make the suicide seem more plausible. What
about the oddly brief statements of the four witnesses? Had
Maria Reichert, the Winters and Anna Kirmair been briefed
about what they should tell the police? And what about the deaf
old Frau Dachs, Maria Reichert's mother? Unlike the Winters,
Maria Reichert and Frau Dachs lived in the flat. When the shot
was fired, according to Henny, Geli was alone in the flat with
Frau Dachs.[11] If this is true – and the seventeen-year-old Henny
is more trustworthy than the Winters or Maria Reichert – why
was Frau Dachs not in the flat when the police came? Was she
sent out? And why was Frau Reichert not in the flat when the shot
was fired? Had some pretext been found for Geli to be left alone
with the deaf Frau Dachs? Was something about to happen that
Frau Reichert must not see and Frau Dachs would not hear?

In later interviews, Maria Reichert insisted that she was in
the flat when the shot was fired. Early in the night, she says, she
heard a dull sound and a cry, but did not get out of bed. In the
morning, when Geli failed to appear for breakfast, she started to
worry. Finding that Geli's door was still locked, she telephoned
Max Amann and Franz Schwarz, who sent a locksmith to open
the door.[12] This contradicts both her own testimony to the police
and her husband's. They both said he forced the door open, but
later, when they gave interviews, they did not know that the

public would ever have access to the police report in which they both contradict what Ilse Hess told John Toland – that Anni Winter contacted Rudolf Hess, and *he* broke the door down.[13]

There is also some disparity between the accounts given by the two housekeepers of what happened earlier. Talking to Nerin Gun, Anni Winter said that Geli told her

> she did not want to spent the weekend with her mother on the Obersalzberg, as had been arranged, because she had no suitable dress to wear . . . She told me that her uncle Adolf had refused to buy her a new dress, which also meant paying her fare to Vienna, for she bought her clothes only in Vienna and Salzburg. But she did not seem unduly disappointed. Her moods changed so quickly.[14]

It is odd that Anni Winter should say this when some of Geli's clothes were bought in Maximilianstrasse, Munich.

Maria Reichert's version of the story is that before Hitler left the flat Geli went to Obersalzberg, but had only just arrived at the house when Hitler telephoned, summoning her back, though he was about to leave again for a meeting of *Gauleiters* and SA leaders in Hamburg. When she arrived, she was angry about having to come back, and became even angrier when he would not let her go to Vienna. They went on arguing over the spaghetti they ate for lunch.

After storming out of the room (according to Anni Winter), Geli stayed in her own room till Hitler was about to leave. Then, going out on the landing, she said goodbye to him and greeted Hoffmann, who was to be his companion on the trip to Hamburg.[15]

Hitler was afterwards inconsistent in what he said about Geli's death. He rarely talked about it, and in the inner circle it was an unwritten law that no one could mention it unless he did. But he sometimes told Eva Braun that Geli had killed herself out of love for him, and that 'We are all responsible for the death of my dear Geli.'[16] He got confused, though, about where she had shot herself. At one stage he said Geli had wrapped the Walther in a facecloth to muffle the explosion and then fired into her mouth.[17]

He also told Friedelind Wagner that Geli had been scared of guns ever since a fortune teller predicted that a revolver bullet would put an end to her life.[18] This sounds like a variation on the story about the séance, and it contradicts Henny, who says she and Geli enjoyed feeling like characters in a Western.

16

Gentlemen from the Brown House

If the Nazis had reached agreement on the accident story before Baldur von Schirach made his first telephone call to the Brown House, or if Adolf Dresler had waited for twenty-five minutes before issuing a statement to the press, the newspapers would have announced that Hitler's niece had died after shooting herself accidentally, and, almost certainly, the official verdict would have been accidental death. The police would have accepted this story just as willingly as the one they were given.

As it turned out, the public was told that Geli had killed herself, and this is the story that has been inherited by biographers and historians. In their 1952 biography of Hitler, Walter Görlitz and Herbert Quint say he spent the night in a Nuremberg hotel, which he left before the news of Geli's death reached him: 'She had taken her life in his flat during the night.'[1] The story was repeated in 1973 by Joachim Fest, who writes that while Hitler 'was setting out on an election campaign visit to Hamburg, word reached him that his niece Geli Raubal had committed suicide'.[2] According to John Toland, whose biography came out in 1976, Hitler could not have killed Geli 'since he was in Nuremberg'.[3] The cause of death, according to Marlis Steiner's 1991 biography, was more likely to have been suicide than accident or murder,[4] and Alan Bullock's dual biography of Hitler and Stalin, which was published the same year and reissued in 1993, tells us that Geli committed suicide in protest against Hitler's possessiveness.[5]

None of these writers seems to have analysed the discrepancies in the evidence presented by Hitler and his staff to secure the verdict of suicide. Their account of what happened has been recycled many times since the war in a series of unreliable memoirs such as Heinrich Hoffmann's. The witnesses contradict each other so much that studying the evidence is reminiscent of the adage that Bertrand Russell used about the Cretan who says: 'All Cretans are liars.' If this is untrue, he is telling a lie, and if it is true, he is a liar. With the testimony about Geli's death we cannot say that all the witnesses were liars, but they could not all have been telling the truth.

One basic question is where Hitler was when the shot was fired. Anni Winter says she saw him leave the flat, but the only witness who could have given him an alibi was Hoffmann, who claimed that, except for two days after they came back to the flat, he was with Hitler all the time between Friday evening, 18 September, and Saturday, 26 September.

Invited to accompany him on the trip to North Germany, Hoffmann says, he picked him up from the flat during the evening of Friday the 18th. Before leaving the building, Hitler hesitated and went back upstairs in an attempt to pacify Geli before driving off. He stroked her cheek tenderly and whispered something conciliatory in her ear, but she turned away angrily.

According to Anni Winter, Geli went back into the flat after the two men left. She apparently telephoned a friend, Elfi Samthaber, who often visited the Haus Wachenfeld. According to Nerin Gun, Elfi 'maintains that they spoke only about inconsequential things, a dress that was for sale in a boutique, an evening at the theatre'.[6]

In Hoffmann's account of what Anni Winter told him, Geli said: 'I'm really getting nothing at all from Uncle.' While they were tidying Hitler's room together, she searched in the pockets of a jacket he had been wearing and found a handwritten letter on blue paper. She read it and tore it angrily into four pieces which she left on the table, where he could not fail to see them.

After saying she would not want supper because she was going out with friends, she locked herself into her room, leaving the key in the door.[7] Later on, Maria Reichert, who was in the kitchen, heard something smash, and told her deaf mother that

Geli must have picked up a scent bottle from her dressing table and broken it.

Left alone, Anni Winter put the torn pieces of blue paper together to read the letter: 'Dear Herr Hitler, Thank you again for the wonderful invitation to the theatre. It was a memorable evening. I am most grateful to you for your kindness. I am counting the hours until I may have the joy of another meeting. Yours, Eva.'

Hoffmann says the quarrel with Geli had upset Hitler. Sitting next to Schreck in the car, he was silent for a while, but as they were passing the Siegestor he turned round abruptly to say: 'I don't know. I have a nasty feeling today.' To reassure him Hoffmann blamed the nasty feeling on the *Föhn*, the dry Alpine wind that has a reputation for unsettling people. They spent the night in Nuremberg, says Hoffmann, in the Hotel Deutscher Hof.

In the morning, he goes on, they had left the hotel before any message reached them. Maria Reichert testified to the police that it was Schwarz who telephoned Hitler, but according to Hoffmann it was Hess who tried to reach him in the hotel at about 11.45. (The four witnesses had presumably been warned not to tell the police that Hess and the other Nazis had been in the flat.) The car was on its way northwards, says Hoffmann, when Hitler noticed in the driving mirror that another car was following them. (If Hitler was sitting next to Schreck, as he had the previous day and as he usually did, he could not have seen a car behind them without re-angling the mirror.) It was a taxi, and inside it a page-boy from the hotel was gesticulating for them to stop.

When they did, Hitler was told that Hess was in his flat, urgently wanting a telephone conversation. They drove back to the hotel where, throwing hat and whip on a chair, Hitler rushed into a telephone booth.

'Hitler here – has something happened?' His voice was hoarse with agitation. 'Oh God! How awful!' he cried, after a long pause, and there was a note of despair in his voice. Then in a firmer tone, which rose almost to a scream: 'Hess! Answer me – yes or no – is she alive or dead? Hess? Hess?' His voice rose to a scream. He seemed to be getting no answer. Either he was cut off, or Hess had hung up to avoid having to answer. Hitler rushed out of the telephone booth, his hair awry over his forehead and a wild and glazed look in his face. He turned to Schreck. 'Something has happened to Geli,' he said. 'We must go back to Munich – get every ounce you can out of the car. I must see Geli alive again.'[8]

Hoffmann's account of the car journey is written in the same excited style. 'Hitler's frenzy was contagious. With its accelerator jammed to the floorboards the great car screamed its way back to Munich. In the driving mirror I could see the reflection of Hitler's face. He sat with compressed lips, staring with unseeing eyes through the windscreen.'[9]

Soon after half past one, while they were driving through Ebenhausen, which is near Ingolstadt, about halfway between Nuremberg and Munich, they were stopped for speeding. In his report, Hauptwachtmeister Probst said they were driving at almost twice the legal speed. Schreck explained that he had been ordered to drive as fast as he could.[10]

Hoffmann writes: 'At last we arrived at his house and heard the dread news. Geli had already been dead for twenty-four hours.'[11] Since the police were told that Hitler would be available from three o'clock onwards if they wanted to interview him, we can assume that he and Hoffmann arrived there no later than about 2.45. But Hoffmann, who was inexpert in the art of faking evidence, must have been forgetting he had said they left Munich on the evening of the previous day, and saw her alive just before they left. To have been dead for twenty-four hours, she would have had to be shot before 2.45 on the afternoon of Friday, 18 September.

Part of Hoffmann's story is obviously untrue, but which part? It may be true that by 2.45 p.m. on Saturday the 19th she had already been dead for twenty-four hours, though Dr Müller certified that she died during the evening of Friday the 18th and thought that the body had been on the floor for seventeen to eighteen hours. He said that *rigor mortis* had set in some hours before he examined the body (at about 11.30 a.m. on Saturday the 19th), but it is not clear how long she was alive after the shot was fired. According to Hoffmann's summary of what Dr Müller said (though this is not clear from his written report), it might have been possible to save Geli's life had a doctor been called sooner.

In his partly fictional narrative, Hoffmann gives us the most detailed account we have of events in Hitler's life before and after Geli's death. But since he made no statement to the police, Hoffmann cannot be held responsible for a miscarriage of justice – if there was one. What about the witnesses who testified to the police?

Georg Winter claimed to have broken the door down at ten on Saturday morning. According to Hoffmann, the Winters rang Angela before they rang Hess.[12] The conference then had to be convened. Gun says the Winters' first call was to Hess, who arrived with Gregor Strasser.[13] They presumably then telephoned Schwarz and Schirach, who had to come from their homes or the Brown House or wherever they were. The Brown House was in Briennerstrasse, about three miles from Prinzregentenplatz. Schirach made his first telephone call after the first round of discussion, and the second twenty-five minutes later. Then, before telephoning the police, they debated what to say about motivation. Sauer and Forster were then sent to the flat from wherever they were. Dr Müller, who arrived later than they did, examined the body at about 11.30. Could all this have happened in an hour and a half? If not, the evidence was rigged.

For the Nazis, truth was as pliable as plasticine, and history is full of dark holes where propaganda still survives in the absence of evidence that was destroyed and people who were killed for knowing too much. Inside the Third Reich, between 1933 and 1945, the Nazis could confiscate private papers and edit public records. All files kept by the Munich police were at the disposal of Himmler, Heydrich and the later Gestapo chief Heinrich Müller.

But even before Hitler came to power in 1933, the Nazis profited, especially in Bavaria, from preferential treatment. The trial after the putsch was typical. Today we somehow feel reluctant to acknowledge that there could have been so much miscarriage of justice before Hitler came to power. We feel disinclined to believe that the functioning of the police force and the judicial system could have been corrupted so deeply by sympathy for the Nazis. But after Geli's death there was no inquest, and only one doctor examined her body before it was released, taken out of the country and buried in Vienna.

It would have been easy to check whether there were powder burns on her skin or her dress, confirming that the pistol had been fired at close quarters. Questions should have been asked, too, about the trajectory of the bullet, which entered above the heart and ended up slightly above the level of the hip. This means that if she was standing or sitting when the shot was fired, the barrel of the pistol was pointing downwards, and the hand holding it was higher than her heart. Even if she was lying on the couch or the floor, it would not have been easy for her to shoot herself in this way. And why should she want to? Having been taught how to use a Walther, she could, if she wanted to kill herself, easily have avoided such a slow and painful death.

Several other questions were not answered, or even, apparently, asked. Someone must have noticed that Hitler's statement to Sauer did not tally with his statement to the *Münchener Post*, and if the police paid attention to what the paper said about bruises on Geli's face, how could they ignore what it said about the meeting of 'gentlemen from the Brown House'? This should have made it impossible to go on accepting the statements that crowded so many events into the ninety minutes between ten and 11.30.

If the police had made only one or two mistakes or omissions, we could put them down to inefficiency or dilatoriness. But there were so many that it looks as if they were under orders not to press their enquiries far enough to make things awkward for Hitler and the party. It is puzzling that Frau Dachs is not mentioned in the police report. How could the two policemen fail to interrogate the woman who might have been the key witness? It is easy to understand why the Nazis would have wanted to keep her out of the way: old and deaf, she was more likely than her daughter to misunderstand or disobey any instructions she had been given about what to say and what not to say. But it should have been a matter of routine for the police to check how many people were living in the flat. If they failed

Hitler gave Geli her camera, a Rolleiflex.

Less experienced than he was in posing for photographs, Geli did not always appear to be enjoying Hitler's company.

Emil Maurice said 'Her big eyes were a poem,' and Hoffmann called her 'an

enchantress,' but Hanfstaengl said she had the coarse bloom of a servant girl.

Patrick Hitler said she looked 'more like a child than a girl. You couldn't call her pretty exactly, but she had great natural charm'.

The house in Prinzregentenplatz where Geli lived with Hitler for over two years in his nine-room flat on the second floor.

Hitler in civilian clothes playing with one of his Alsatians in front of the house in Obersalzberg.

The new Chancellor. Throughout most of the night on 30 January 1933, crowds surged to the Chancellery where a tired Hitler supported his elbow to give the Nazi salute.

In the crowded visitors' room of the Munich Brown House.

Rudolf Hess sitting erectly between the Nazi Youth Leader Baldur von Schirach and his wife Henriette, Heinrich Hoffmann's daughter.

Magda Goebbels with five of the six children who were all killed by their parents, who wanted to die with Hitler in the bunker.

Two victims of Hitler's sado-masochism: Eva Braun (top) and the film star Renate Müller. The relationship with Eva Braun lasted for sixteen years; Renate Müller met him in 1932 and killed herself in 1937.

to find out that Frau Dachs existed, they were extraordinarily negligent; if they knew of her existence and left her out of their report, they were breaking the law in order to help the Nazis.

The 'further investigation' was remarkably perfunctory, and remarkably quick. It did not start until Monday, 21 September, and the coffin was taken by train to Vienna in time for a funeral in the Central Cemetery on the afternoon of Wednesday the 23rd. The police report was not sent to the Ministry of the Interior until five days later.

According to Hoffmann and Henny, it was Angela who decided that her daughter should be buried in Vienna,[14] but Hitler would have had the final say. One advantage of having the body taken across the frontier was that this would rule out any possibility of exhuming her for an inquest.

The question of the broken nose and the bruises will never be settled. The evidence of the two mortuary nurses would be conclusive if we could be sure they were not given ready-made statements to sign, but the wording suggests that they might have been. The style looks like that of someone more accustomed than nurses would be to writing official reports and using such terms as 'entry wound', while it is noticeable that Maria Fischbauer says: 'in particular I did not notice that the bone in the nose was broken', and Rosina Zweckl says: 'in particular I saw nothing suspicious about the nose'. It is possible that Zweckl heard what Fischbauer said and echoed it; it is also possible that a police official wrote both statements.

Hanfstaengl believed that the nose had been broken, and to Joachim Fest, who queried this in an interview, he said it had been generally known at the time.[15] Henny also believed that the nose had been broken.[16] But the police could hardly have made it easier for the Nazis. As Minister of Justice, Franz Gürtner had the power to call off the investigation and release the corpse. This is what must have happened. In helping Hitler, Gürtner was doing what he had often done before, and in 1932 he was rewarded when, thanks to Nazi lobbying, he was promoted. He became Reich Minister of Justice in von Papen's cabinet, a position he kept when Hitler came to power.

Unable to expect so much goodwill from the press, the Nazis acted quickly and ruthlessly. According to Emil Maurice, they intimidated newspaper editors. Goering, who was in charge of this operation, used stormtroopers. The opposition press later complained that the *Völkischer Beobachter*, which expatiated on the death of any Nazi street-fighter, had kept strangely silent over the death of Hitler's niece.[17] But so had the other papers.

Members of a Gang

At the beginning of September, after his two days in Obersalzberg and his hikes over the mountains with his sister, Leo Raubal had gone back to Linz. He was incredulous when his mother telephoned to say that Geli was dead. Angela was bringing the coffin from Munich to Vienna by train, and he joined her at Linz for the last part of the miserable journey. Once he had got over the first phase of shock, it struck him as odd that his mother and Hitler should not want Geli to be buried in either Munich or Berchtesgaden, and when Angela talked about suicide it seemed that she was holding something back.

At the Central Cemetery, Geli was given a Catholic funeral. The officiating priest, Father Johann Pant, knew both Hitler and the Raubals. Twenty years earlier he had been doing part-time work as a chaplain at the men's hostel when Hitler was there, and he had tried to find someone who would pay for Geli's education when Angela could not afford to. After the funeral, when Leo questioned him, the priest said he could not have done what he just had if Geli had died by her own hand. But he refused to explain.[1] Certainly it was abnormal for a suicide to be given a Catholic funeral. An exception had been made in 1889 for Crown Prince Rudolf, but only after the Emperor, Franz Josef, had intervened.

Hanfstaengl assumed that Geli had been pregnant and Hitler had found out. 'His anti-Semitism would have caused him to accuse her of dishonouring them both and to tell her that the best thing she could do was to shoot herself. Perhaps he threatened to cut off all support from her mother. . . . If so, it would be the first example of many similar instances to follow.'[2]

The biographer Konrad Heiden made the same assumption
about pregnancy and arrived at the same conclusion – that she
might have been bullied into killing herself. But the bully he
suspected was Heinrich Himmler, who might have visited her
late at night and explained how she had 'betrayed the man who
was her guardian, her lover and her Führer in one – according to
National Socialist conceptions there was only one way of making
good such a betrayal'. But this seems no less far-fetched than
Rudolf Hess's theory that she was killed by a jealous woman
who got into the flat during the night.

One of the better arguments in favour of the suicide theory
was advanced by Henny, who saw the shooting as an attempt
to hurt Hitler.

> He fenced her life so tightly, confined her in such a narrow
> space that she saw no other way out. Finally she hated her
> uncle, she really wanted to kill him. She couldn't do that. So
> she killed herself, to hurt him deeply enough, to disturb him.
> She knew that nothing else would wound him so badly. And
> because he knew too, he was so desperate, he had to blame
> himself.[3]

This at least confronts two of the main weaknesses in the
theory. One is that suicide would have been out of character
for Geli, and the other is that, apart from this possibility that
she wanted to revenge herself on Hitler, she had no motive.
She seems to have been neither depressive nor prone to sudden
acts of passionate violence. When Leo was with her, a fortnight
before she died, he saw no sign of despondency.[4]

Many of her other friends, including the Vogls, did not believe
she had killed herself.[5] If she had ever thought of killing herself,
it would have been when she had reason to believe she might
have to spend the rest of her life as a prisoner in Hitler's flat.
For nearly two years after moving in, she really was fenced into
a narrow space, as well as being forced into sexual games she
did not like. But the situation appeared to be changing. He had
agreed to let her visit Vienna, and she had only just found out
that he had changed his mind. It looks as if she felt quite happy
while writing the letter about a visit to Semmering. She was

used to his indecision, and, if he had just changed his mind about letting her go, there was no reason to think he would not change it again. Or so it would have seemed to her: neither he nor anyone else would have told her she knew too much.

At one point, later on, he made his own attempt to explain what might have driven her to suicide. While talking to Henny, he wrote down three possible motives. One was that he was paying for the singing lessons, and she might have thought she was not good enough. The second was that there might have been a conflict over love. Though Henny had forgotten what the third hypothesis was, she remembered that Hitler ended up by crossing out all three.[6]

There is only one piece of evidence which suggests that Geli was depressed just before she died. This comes in an unpublished memoir by Julius Schaub, who gives an account of the last evening in her life, writing about himself in the third person. Contradicting all the other witnesses, he says she went to the theatre with his wife.

> Geli had been expecting Uncle Alf to go, but Hitler was prevented because he had to prepare his speech for a meeting that was going to take place two days later in Hamburg. He told Schaub to drive the two ladies to the theatre in his car. Schaub returned to Hitler and had told the ladies that if he didn't pick them up in the car at the end of the performance, they should take a taxi. That is what happened. The car wasn't there and they took a taxi. During the show . . . Geli was inattentive, sad, indeed almost tearful. In the interval Geli bought refreshments and chocolate at the stall in the theatre. Frau Schaub asked her what was the matter with her, Geli answered that she was upset. Nor did they talk much on the way home. At Prinzregentenplatz, her flat, she got out, spent a long time saying goodbye to Frau Schaub, asked her what she was going to do in the next few days because she was alone, too. Frau Schaub said that she had nothing planned, and would be in her flat. Then came the handshake and Geli vanished behind the front door while Frau Schaub went on alone in the taxi to her flat which was two minutes away. Frau Schaub had only just got home

when her husband arrived and she told him how strangely upset Geli seemed, but they didn't think it was anything serious, they were used to mood-changes in Geli. On the next morning, Schaub said goodbye to his wife because he had to go to Hamburg with Hitler. At about ten o'clock on the following morning, Frau Winter telephoned Frau Schaub to ask whether Geli had spent the night with her and was still there. Frau Winter had been trying to take the newspaper into Geli's room as she did every morning, but couldn't get in, the door was locked and no-one answered when she knocked. She started to suspect that Geli had been out overnight. She then rang her mother up in Obersalzberg, but she wasn't there either. After making several more attempts to get into the room, Frau Winter realised it was locked from inside with the key stuck in the other side of the door. After that she let the locksmith Hatzk break the door open, Geli was found lying in her own blood on the carpet, the revolver next to her, a 6.8 Walter pistol, she had shot herself in the region of the heart.

Schaub's typescript also contains another, briefer account of his wife's outing with Geli. Here, an ambiguous sentence could mean either that Geli died on Thursday, 17 September or that Hitler left Munich on 17 September: 'On the day before the suicide (17.9.31) he left Munich in his car to hold a meeting in Hamburg.' If she died on the 17th, the four witnesses were lying to the police, but Hoffmann was telling the truth when he said she had been dead for over twenty-four hours and the doctor was approximately right about the length of time the body had been lying on the floor.

Hitler habitually wrote nothing down, and one of the ways that Schaub and Brückner made themselves useful was by taking notes and keeping records. If Schaub still had his notes when writing his memoirs, he is less likely to have made a mistake about the date of Geli's death than to have confused the real date with the official date.

The brief narrative also contradicts itself by saying that on the day of the suicide, 'Geli had lunch with Hitler, it was veal Schnitzel, but Geli's wasn't touched, she ate hardly anything.'

Maria Reichert had said it was spaghetti, but what they ate is less important than whether Hitler had or had not left the previous day.

Schaub wrote his memoirs after the war, thinking that they could be sold. They could, but only to a private collector. He has provided evidence that Geli was depressed, but can we trust it?

Neither Hoffmann nor any of the staff say anything about a visit to the theatre on the last evening of Geli's life. If Anni Winter thought Geli might have stayed overnight either with Frau Schaub or with Angela in Obersalzberg, and if she telephoned both women before calling in the locksmith, why did she mention this neither to the police nor to subsequent interviewers? If Geli did spend the last evening of her life in the theatre, why would none of the other witnesses have mentioned this? If she did not, why would Schaub have invented it?

Hitler could not have survived as long as he did without being able to judge whose loyalty he commanded. Closer to him than any of his other aides, Schaub was the man he trusted to burn secret documents. If it had not been for Christa Schroeder, Schaub would have destroyed all the letters in Geli's shoebox. It was not merely that, as an Obersturmführer in the SS, he had taken an oath of lifelong loyalty to his Führer; so had hundreds of others. But Schaub's devotion was like religious zealotry. If Hitler had shot Geli, no one was less likely – even after 1945 – to expose him as a killer.

Christa Schroeder has described Schaub:

He had rather staring eyes, and because some of his toes had been frozen in the First World War, he sometimes walked with a hobbling gait. It may have been this disability that made him so cantankerous. Always suspicious, and full of curiosity into the bargain, and inclined to give a wide berth to everything that wasn't congenial to him, his popularity in Hitler's circle was limited.

From 1925 onwards he was 'Hitler's constant personal companion. He was so devoted to Hitler that he gave up smoking.'[7] Perhaps he was sufficiently devoted to manufacture proof that

Geli was depressed, and, in saying that Hitler had left Munich on the day before the shooting, he may just have been trying to provide a better alibi than Hoffmann did by saying they had left earlier the same evening.

Certainly we cannot believe Schaub's narrative. He is no better than the others at allowing sufficient time for the events that are supposed to have happened before Dr Müller examined the body at 11.30. In this version of the story, it was already ten when Anni Winter telephoned Frau Schaub.

Schaub says it was Herr Klein, the manager of the Nuremberg hotel, who pursued Hitler in a taxi, and he says that Hitler wanted to attend the funeral, implying that he would have done so if he could legally have crossed the Austrian border. (He had forfeited his Austrian citizenship by volunteering for the Bavarian army in 1914, and after the putsch of 1923 the Austrian government had issued orders that he should not be allowed to cross back over the frontier.)[8] Himmler and Röhm represented him at the funeral, and though Schaub did go with him to Hamburg, this was not until 24 September. Schaub contradicts himself about when Hitler left, at one point saying it was on the day before the suicide, at another the following day.

And why are there so many conflicting statements about who broke the door down? Georg and Anni Winter testified that he did it with a screwdriver, Ilse Hess said her husband did it, Maria Reichert said Max Amann and Franz Schwarz sent a locksmith, and Schaub, who implies that Anni Winter sent for the man, provides a name for him – Hatzk. Perhaps the truth behind the confusion is that the door was not locked at the time of the shooting. It may have been locked by the Nazis just in time for them to break it down before the police arrived.

The only extant documentary evidence about Geli's death is the police report of 28 September and the report on the speeding offence. If there were any other documents they have been suppressed, while the people who could have testified are dead. But not all of them died a natural death.

One who did not was a strong opponent of the suicide theory – Fritz Gerlich. A friend of Hanfstaengl's father, he edited the *Münchener Neueste Nachrichten* until February 1928, when it was taken over by the reactionary nationalist Alfred Hugenberg. In 1931 Gerlich was converted to Catholicism and, with money from a prince, Fürst Erich von Waldburg-Zeil, founded an anti-Nazi paper, *Der Gerade Weg*. It was printed, oddly enough, by Hitler's friend Adolf Müller, who also printed the *Völkischer Beobachter*.

Condemning Nazism as a spiritual plague, Gerlich predicted that it would lead to 'enmity with neighbouring countries, internal totalitarianism, civil war, international war, lies, hatred, fratricide and infinite trouble'. In March 1932, he published an 'open letter' telling Hitler: 'On your conscience must lie the burden of a possible civil war.' This issue reached about 1,250,000 readers.

Seeing an opportunity to discredit Hitler, Gerlich used all his journalistic skills to investigate Geli's death. As his suspicions hardened, he collected evidence for publication in pamphlet form. If we can trust the summary of the pamphlet in *The Memoirs of Bridget Hitler*, he got affidavits from Willi Schmidt, the critic Geli had consulted about teachers in Vienna, and from one of the police inspectors who had visited the flat. This man – we do not know whether it was Sauer or Forster – believed that Hitler had been in the flat when the shot was fired. The report mentions a 'police decision' that 'it was clearly a case of suicide', but the decision, which seems to have been taken not by the police but by Gürtner, may have conflicted with the opinions formed by Sauer and Forster.

Gerlich came to the conclusion that, instead of leaving for Nuremburg, Hitler had postponed his trip. Herr Zehnter, the owner of a Munich restaurant called the Bratwurstglöckl, testified that Hitler arrived with Geli on the evening of Friday the 18th, that they were in a private room on the first floor till nearly one in the morning, and that Hitler, who rarely touched alcohol, was drinking beer. According to this summary of the pamphlet, he and Geli went back to the flat, where he threatened her with his revolver and shot her. After reading what Gerlich had written, Leo Raubal went to see him.

At the beginning of 1933 Gerlich was involved in a conspiracy to keep Nazism at bay by restoring the monarchy under Crown Prince Rupprecht, head of the House of Wittelsbach.

In November 1932 Hindenburg had rejected Hitler, saying that if he formed a cabinet it was 'bound to develop into a party dictatorship', but in January he appointed him Reich Chancellor.

What happened to make the eighty-four-year-old President change his mind? Schleicher wanted to split the Nazis by inviting Gregor Strasser into the government without Hitler. It was Schleicher who advised Hindenburg to replace Brüning with Papen in June 1932. He immediately dissolved the Reichstag, and in the new election, held at the end of July, the Nazis won 37 per cent of the vote – more than any other party. The new Reichstag passed a vote of no confidence in Papen, but instead of resigning, as he legally should have done, he dissolved the Reichstag.

In 1932 the Nazis were opportunistically swinging away from the Right towards the Left, and in November they sided with the Communists in the Berlin transport workers' strike. In one newspaper photograph Goebbels can be seen sharing a platform with Walter Ulbricht, the future East German leader who was largely responsible for the building of the Berlin Wall. In November, after persuading Hindenburg to dismiss Papen, Schleicher became Chancellor himself, but Papen, who believed that Hitler could be manipulated, succeeded in bringing Hindenburg round to this view. In January 1933, blamed for bringing Hitler to power, Papen retorted: 'You'll be surprised. We hired him.'⁹

Naturally, the Federal constitution was still in force after Hitler became Chancellor, and though he banned opposition newspapers in Bavaria, the state government overturned his ban on 23 February. Five days later, the burning of the Reichstag gave him a pretext for declaring a state of emergency, and the Nazis began to round up their political opponents.

Gerlich's monarchist plot was unrealistic, but he was by no means alone in thinking that Germany's only sane way out of the crisis was a return to monarchism. At the highest level, Hindenburg and Schleicher had been thinking along these lines, and Crown Prince Rupprecht would have been their candidate; but as a Wittelsbach he would have been less popular in Prussia than in Bavaria, while Hindenburg's age precluded the alternative possibility of making him regent for the Crown Prince's son.

In fact there was no realistic prospect of stopping the Nazis. Even the leader of the Bavarian social democrats, Erwin Auer, was inclining, desperately, towards monarchism.

Gerlich's principal colleague and collaborator was Georg Bell, an adventurous journalist with a flair for political intrigue. Remaining a member of the NSDAP until October 1932, he had been working for Ernst Röhm, who, as head of the SA, had been involved in an equally unrealistic conspiracy. Planning to make the police subordinate to the SA and the SS, to become commissar in charge of the whole German state, to get rid of Hitler and become leader of the party, Röhm had entered into a secret agreement with Sir Henry Deterding, an oil tycoon with a controlling interest in Royal Dutch Petroleum and the Shell group. Röhm was offering him a monopoly in return for his support.

Together with Bell and Fürst Waldburg, Gerlich arranged to meet Eugen Bolz, President of the State of Württemberg, on 8 March 1933. They wanted him to tell Hindenburg about Röhm's agreement with Deterding and Hitler's part in Geli's death. The Nazis would not get a parliamentary majority without support from two other right-wing parties, the *Stahlhelm* and the German National Unity party, who might withdraw their support if they knew about Röhm's plans.[10]

But when Gerlich, Bell and Waldburg met Bolz, it was already too late: swastika flags were flying from his ministry. Goering had ordered the Stuttgart Nazis to take control, and in Bavaria on 9 March the Nazis occupied the *Landtag*, the state Parliament, expelling the deputies. For the first time since Bismarck, the federal structure was broken by control from the centre. The South German state governments no longer had the power to govern. In Württemberg Bolz capitulated. He was appointed Minister of the Interior, only to be arrested in June and imprisoned till he was executed in 1944.

Ignoring both the ban on opposition papers and the friends who advised him to stay away from his office, Gerlich obstinately went on preparing an issue of the *Gerade Weg* for publication on 12 March. The leading article was to accuse the Nazis of starting the Reichstag fire, to expose their secret plans for the annihilation of the Churches, to reveal Röhm's secret agreement with Deterding and to expose the facts that Gerlich had unearthed about Geli's death.

But on 9 March Max Amann and Emil Maurice led a gang of stormtroopers into the offices, smashed all the machines and destroyed the contents of desks, files, cupboards and drawers, including the copy for the next issue of the *Gerade Weg*. Amann, who as editor of the *Völkischer Beobachter* had often been vilified by Gerlich, punched him hard in the face, smashing his spectacles and injuring both eyes. The man who had danced with Geli at the carnival was almost blinding the man who eighteen months after her death was trying to champion her. But the irony would not have occurred to either of them.

Gerlich was imprisoned and later sent to Dachau, where he was killed during the Night of the Long Knives in June 1934. Georg Bell, after hiding on a rooftop, escaped to Austria, but the Nazis pursued him across the border, and on 3 April he was shot in his hotel bedroom.

Gerlich's account of Geli's death tallies with that of Otto Strasser, who said he had learned the facts from his brother Paul, a Benedictine monk, and that Paul had learned them from their brother Gregor, who was killed, like Gerlich, during the Night of the Long Knives. Gregor Strasser said he had had to spend three days and three nights with Hitler to stop him killing himself after he shot Geli. (Presumably this was between Hitler's interview with Sauer and his departure for St Quirin.) According to the Strasser brothers, the public prosecutor, Glaser, had wanted to charge Hitler with murder, but Gürtner had not allowed him to, and Glaser escaped from Germany in 1933. All Gregor's papers were in the possession of his lawyer, Voss, but he too was murdered during the Night of the Long Knives, as was the owner of the Bratwurstglöckl, Herr Zehnter.[11]

According to Hanfstaengl, 'Not the least reason for Strasser's death at the same time was the too intimate knowledge he gained of Geli Raubal's death.'[12] This may be true, but Hitler had many grudges against Gregor Strasser, who, in spite of having been

– or because of having been – the most influential man in the party after Hitler, was hated by both Goering and Goebbels. In 1932, when he did not immediately rebuff Schleicher's attempt to entice him into the government, Strasser was accused of betraying the party and he resigned all his posts. When Hitler became Chancellor he was appointed as manager of a chemical factory, a job he kept till he was killed. And even if his death had nothing to do with Geli's, why would an innocuous restaurant proprietor have been killed if he had not known too much about what happened on the evening of Friday, 18 September?

The only survivor who could have provided more information was the priest, Father Johann Pant, who officiated at Geli's funeral. For nearly thirty years – until he died in 1959 – he was in a quandary about whether to speak out. In Paris during 1939, reading *Le Journal*, he found Geli's name in an article by Otto Strasser, revealing what he had learned from his two brothers. Father Pant then got in touch with the editor of the *Courier d'Autriche*:

> It was I who buried Angela Raubal, the little Geli of whom Otto Strasser wrote. They pretended that she committed suicide; I should never have allowed a suicide to be buried in consecrated ground. From the fact that I gave her Christian burial you can draw conclusions which I cannot communicate to you.[13]

This is not the only evidence that Father Pant believed Hitler killed her. While campaigning for the exhumation of her remains, the Viennese furniture restorer Hans Horváth contacted both Father Pant's nephew and an old man of seventy-five who had known him well. Both confirmed that he did not believe Geli had killed herself.[14]

It might look as if the speeding offence in Ebenhausen proves that Hitler was not in Munich at the time of the shooting, but the only indication of when the shot was fired is Dr Müller's certificate stating that it was during the evening of Friday the 18th. But since the failure to mention Frau Dachs in the police report suggests that some of the police officials were involved in the cover-up operation, we cannot be certain that Müller's

Hitler's dinner parties impressed such guests as Siegfried and
Winifred Wagner.

About a month before the twenty-one-year-old Geli moved
in, Hitler met a slim, fresh-faced, insecure, eighteen-year-old
shopgirl. Shy and apparently placid, she gave the impression
of being pliable. The daughter of a Munich schoolteacher,
Eva Braun was working for Heinrich Hoffmann, who sold
photographs (mainly of Hitler), photographic equipment and
miscellaneous paraphernalia from a shop in the same building
as his Schellingstrasse studio. Opportunistic, and aware of his
Führer's penchant for teenage blondes, he may have employed
Eva in the hope that Hitler would like her.

Their first meeting occurred late on a Friday afternoon in
early October 1929.

> I'd stayed on after closing time to file some papers and
> I'd climbed up a ladder to reach the files kept on the top
> shelves of the cupboard. At that moment the boss came
> in accompanied by a man of uncertain age with a funny
> moustache, a light-coloured, English style overcoat and a
> big felt hat in his hand. They both sat down on the other
> side of the room, opposite me. I tried to squint in their
> direction without appearing to turn round and sensed that
> this character was looking at my legs. That very day I'd
> shortened my skirt, and I felt slightly embarrassed because
> I wasn't sure I'd got the hem even. As you know, I don't like
> to ask Mother to help me. Hoffmann introduced us when I'd
> climbed down. 'Herr Wolf, our good little Fräulein Eva.'

After sending her out to buy beer and sausages, Hoffmann
invited her to sit down with them at the table.

> I was starving. I gobbled my sausage and had a sip of beer
> for the sake of politeness. The elderly gentleman was paying
> me compliments. We talked about music and a play at the
> Staatstheater, as I remember, with him devouring me with
> his eyes all the time. Then, as it was getting late, I rushed off.
> I refused his offer of a lift in his Mercedes. Just think what
> Papa's reaction would have been. But before I left, Hoffmann

written statements were an accurate reflection of what he believed. It is conceivable that Hitler and Geli were at the Bratwurstglöckl on the evening of Thursday the 18th and that the shooting took place some time between Thursday night and Friday evening, before Hitler and Hoffmann left to spend the night in Nuremberg. Since Hoffmann was less interested in telling the truth than in giving Hitler a convincing alibi, he could have been lying about the cheek-stroking on the landing and the tender whisper into Geli's ear. In which case Hitler and Hoffmann could have left Munich in time to spent the night in Nuremberg.

Alternatively, they could have spent the night in Munich and left early enough in the morning to drive southwards through Ebenhausen at 55 kilometres an hour, possibly in the hope of being stopped by the police and acquiring written evidence that would not quite provide an alibi but might come in useful when answering questions.

Wrong Side of the Footlights

We are now in a better position to analyse the explanations that have been put forward – or could have been – for Geli's death.

1. One is that she committed suicide, and
2. another is that Hitler murdered her.
3. But even if he pulled the trigger, the killing may have been more like manslaughter than premeditated murder.
4. She may have been killed by someone acting on his behalf of the party's, either with or
5. without his authority.
6. She may have died as the result of an accident that occurred when she was either alone with the pistol or
7. with someone else, possibly struggling to get hold of it.

Of the seven possibilities, the easiest to eliminate are 4, 5 and 6. There was no shortage of willing hit-men, but if she was going to be murdered in cold blood, she could have been taken to any convenient spot in Munich or outside. From the party's point of view, the worst possible place for her corpse to be found was Hitler's flat. Even if murder was going to be disguised as suicide, no one could have guaranteed that the press would not find out that she and Hitler had been living together.

Though the accident theory never caught on, it had its supporters, in spite of the fact that Geli had been taught how to use a pistol. According to Hitler's adviser on economics, Otto Wagener, the bullet's trajectory:

showed that she had the pistol in her left hand with the barrel towards her body. Since she was sitting at her desk and writing a totally innocent letter which was unfinished, we must assume that it came into her head to fetch the pistol and check whether it was loaded, at which point it went off and hit her in the heart – an unfortunate accident.[1]

The bullet did not hit her in the heart, and it would have been almost impossible for her to hold the pistol in her left hand with the barrel at such an angle that the bullet would lodge in the left side of her back; and though she broke off writing in the middle of a word, it does not follow that this happened immediately before her death. It may have been Hitler's return that interrupted her letter-writing, and once he had vetoed her trip to Vienna there would have been no point in going on with the letter.

Goering supported the accident theory – which does not mean that he believed it. Two weeks after Geli died, Hanfstaengl was present at a conversation between him and Hitler.

Hitler was apparently furious at [Gregor] Strasser for maintaining and publishing the fact that it was a suicide and had fallen on Goering's neck weeping with gratitude when Hermann suggested that it was just as likely to have been an accident. 'Now I know who is my real friend,' Hitler had sobbed. I think it was pure opportunism on Goering's part. He wanted to eliminate Strasser as a rival in Hitler's favour. Circumstances never healed these eternal jealousies in the party.[2]

There were other people who at one time or another said that it must have been an accident, as Angela did, though it seems unlikely that she believed this. In 1945 she testified: 'I can't understand why she did it. Perhaps it was an accident, and Angela [i.e. Geli] killed herself while she was playing with the pistol which she'd got from him.'[3]

It is not so easy to refute the suicide theory; though, apart from all the discrepancies in the stories put up by the Nazis to support it, there are two problems in the way of accepting it. One is that so long as Geli believed she was free to visit Vienna, she had no motive. While writing the letter about going to Semmering she was far from being in a state of suicidal depression, and though her spirits would have been dashed when she heard that Hitler had changed his mind about letting her go, she was so familiar with his vacillating that she is unlikely to have given up all hope so quickly or taken such a decision so precipitately.

The other problem is that the trajectory of the bullet seems inconsistent with the suicide theory. For a cartridge that enters above the heart to lodge just above the level of the hip, the barrel has to be pointing downwards and the hand holding the pistol has to be higher than the heart. Though it is not impossible to shoot oneself in this way, it is hard to imagine why she would have adopted such an awkward position.[4]

The strongest piece of evidence that seems to support the suicide theory is the police report on the speeding offence in Ebenhausen. This proves that Hitler was not in the Munich flat at 1.30 p.m. on Saturday the 19th, but does not prove that he was not there at the time of the shooting. It would be easier if we knew exactly when the shot was fired, but the only indication is Dr Müller's statement that she died during the evening of Friday the 18th, and he did not give any estimate of how long she had remained alive after the bullet had entered her body.

It is conceivable that Hitler and Geli were at the Bratwurstglöckl on the evening of Thursday the 18th, and that the shooting took place some time between Thursday night and Friday evening. One of Hitler's cooks, Therese Linke, said that Geli was lying in a pool of blood for three days before her body was found.[5] It is hard to see how Anni Winter and Maria Reichert could have been ignorant of her whereabouts for so long unless they had been given orders that prevented them from looking for her, but it is possible that Geli was shot before Hitler and Hoffmann left for Nuremberg. Wanting to provide an alibi, Hoffmann may have lied about the cheek-stroking on the landing and the tender whisper into Geli's ear, while the servants may have been ordered not to contradict this story.

If Hitler pulled the trigger, it was more likely to have been manslaughter than murder. Unaccustomed to alcohol, he might

have been out of control, and one of the questions we should
ask is what made him depart from his normal habits and start
drinking beer at the Bratwurstglöckl. Only a serious crisis would
have driven him to alcohol, but if Geli had become pregnant
when he was so close to taking power, the scandal could have
been devastating. Rumours about a pregnancy were circulating;
Hanfstaengl and Therese Linke were among those who believed
them. If she was pregnant, the Nazis would have had even
stronger reasons for wanting to get rid of her, and, once she
was dead, for avoiding an inquest, in which the pregnancy would
have been revealed. Any unbiased Minister of Justice would have
insisted on an inquest when there were so many grounds for
suspicion, but Gürtner promptly released the body.

We do not know how the *Münchener Post* reporter found
out about the 'violent quarrel between Herr Hitler and his niece'
on the Friday, but the violence may have been physical: it may
have been then that her nose was broken and her face bruised.
The trajectory of the bullet would be easier to explain if she
was on the floor when the shot was fired. At first, of course,
the violence would have been verbal. Nothing came to Hitler's
lips more easily than threats, and threats were more effective
when he had a pistol to wave about. The striving for effect was
usually theatrical, but the beer could have toppled him over to
the wrong side of the footlights.

Since we shall never know exactly what happened, we
have to speculate, but we can do that in the perspective of
his characteristic behaviour when he came up against major
obstacles. He was such a compulsive risk-taker that his life
was full of crises, but if Geli was pregnant, this one was
graver than most. He could have lost everything he wanted,
just when it seemed within reach. What he usually did when
confronted with a serious obstacle was threaten to kill himself
unless it was removed. All or nothing. When he was still in
his teens, despondency over Stefanie made him talk about
drowning himself. In 1923, before the putsch, he threatened
to shoot the triumvirate and himself unless the three of them
cooperated with him. Hiding in the Hanfstaengls' house, he
again threatened suicide till Helene managed to throw his
pistol into the flour barrel.

He said he neither expected nor wanted to reach 'the ripe old age of the ordinary citizen'.[6] Again, at the end of 1932, when Gregor Strasser did not immediately rebuff Schleicher's overtures, Hitler told Goebbels: 'If the Party falls apart, I'll put an end to it in five minutes with my pistol.'[7] He made a suicide pact with Eva Braun in 1945, and it is possible that on 18 September 1931 he was trying to make one with the pregnant Geli – or trying to intimidate her with the pistol. He may have shot her when he failed, or perhaps they were struggling for possession of it when it went off.

Seeing that she was dying, he may have intended to kill himself. If he changed his mind, it would not have been out of character. Even when he was sober, he was sometimes beside himself with rage. Things looked different when he calmed down, and in September 1931 he had good reasons for wanting to stay alive.

But even if he had killed her without intending to, or by some drunken mixture of accident and design, it would have been ruinous to let the truth come out. A cover-up operation would be essential.

If Hitler pulled the trigger, several people were involved as accessories after the fact. Gregor Strasser, Goering, Hess, Schwarz, Hoffmann, Baldur von Schirach, the Winters, Frau Reichert, Brückner and Schaub must all have known what had happened. Angela and Leo Raubal could hardly have failed to become suspicious.

The silence of the top Nazis needs no more explanation than Rauschning provided when he said that Hitler knew 'there is nothing more binding than crimes committed in company. . . . The "inner conspiracy" of the party *élite* was thus a circle of those who were all in the secret. Everyone was in the power of everyone else, and no one was any longer his own master.'[8] They were like members of a gang. Criminality was integral to the regime long before it became a regime.

Death threats could explain the silence of the others until 1945, but none of them spoke out after 1945 – not that they could have done without revealing that they had condoned a killing. The course of history could have been altered in 1931 if Glaser had been able to insist on holding an inquest, or in 1933 if Gerlich had managed to publish the evidence he had collected. But even before Hitler became Chancellor, anyone who accused him of murder or manslaughter would have been risking his life, and from 1933 onwards it was impossible to start legal proceedings against him.

Hanfstaengl says Anni Winter may have been given enough money to make it 'worth her while for the rest of her life to adhere to the official version of an inexplicable accident'.[9] The point about hush-money could apply to other members of Hitler's staff, but it is odd that he should talk about an 'accident'. He seems to have been ambivalent about Geli's death. In his book, which was not published till 1957, he does not contradict the suicide story, though he believed Geli's nose was broken and her face bruised. But the pamphlet that Gerlich was preparing is said to have contained evidence gleaned from 'E.H.', which may (or may not) mean that Hanfstaengl did not believe that Geli killed herself.[10] In 1957 it would have been almost impossible to overturn the suicide theory, and it would be understandable if he preferred not to try.

With the possible exception of Röhm, none of the more prominent Nazis would have betrayed their leader, though Schirach must have been in a quandary after he married Henny in March 1932. It is unlikely that he ever told her all he knew about Geli's death, though they named the first of their four children after her – Angela.

It is easy to explain Hoffmann's silence, and Henny's. His conscience never gave him much trouble, and he was Hitler's partner in a lucrative business: they shared the proceeds of Hoffmann's monopoly on photographs of the Führer.[11] Throughout the thirties, Hoffmann's publishing company produced books of photographs with such titles as *Hitler Conquers the German Heart, Germany's Awakening, Hitler Builds Greater Germany* and *Hitler Liberates Sudetenland*. Hoffmann's photographs had fulsome captions, and his son-in-law often contributed an adulatory preface. Hoffmann's well-endowed life continued until 1957, when he died at the age of seventy-two. He would have had less fun during his last twelve years if he had confessed his part in the cover-up.

Henny may have guessed that neither her father nor Baldur von Schirach was telling her all they knew, but in 1931 she was only eighteen and, as Hoffmann's daughter, she must have learnt not to ask questions. Later on she could hardly have denounced both her father and her husband as accomplices to murder.

The hardest silence to explain is Angela's. Having helped to bring Hitler up, she saw him in a different perspective from anyone else. In 1931, the forty-two-year-old Hitler was no longer the boy she remembered, but after working for him since 1927 she must have seen and overheard a great deal she would have preferred not to see or overhear. She may have thought that, for Geli, death was no worse than what had already happened. In theory Angela was free to leave; in practice she may, like his other servants, have been subject to intimidation. Without being able to count on their discretion, Hitler and the other Nazis could not have let them survive, and Geli's death would have reminded them that they were permanently in danger.

What about Leo Raubal? He possibly suffered more than the others at having to keep silent, but he could not have spoken out without revealing his mother to be an accessory after the fact.

Whether he pulled the trigger or not, Hitler was certainly close to killing himself after Geli's death. When he and Goering appeared at the Hamburg rally on 24 September, the day after the funeral, Hitler, according to one witness, 'looks very shaken but speaks very well'.[12] He and Goering were scheduled to speak the same evening at two other rallies in Hamburg, but Goering had to appear at these without him. Hitler was 'too ill and feverish'.[13]

Describing his state around this time as 'almost a nervous breakdown', Hans Frank said he had never seen Hitler looking so depressed. According to Rudolf Hess, Hitler was suicidal because of the rumours that he had shot Geli. He had been so 'fearfully vilified by this new campaign of lies that he wanted to make an end of everything. He could no longer look at a newspaper because this frightful filth was killing him. He wanted to give up politics and never again appear in public.'

It was characteristic of the Nazis to denounce the truth as

'lies', but the depression was probably genuine, though it is odd that he should have selected as his companion a man who described himself as a happy-go-lucky, bohemian *bon viveur*. Hoffmann writes that after leaving Hitler's flat on Saturday, 19 September, when Geli's body was found, he heard nothing from him till his telephone rang at midnight two days later. Hitler did not like being in the flat where she had died, and wanted Hoffmann to be with him until the funeral was over.

On the morning of Tuesday, 22 September he looked like a broken man. Schreck drove him and Hoffmann to Adolf Müller's house in St Quirin on the Tegernsee, south of Munich. Knowing that Hitler wanted to be left alone with Hoffmann, the Müllers had gone away and taken their staff. Schreck, who was dismissed, whispered to Hoffmann before leaving that he had taken Hitler's pistol away from him.

In the evening Hitler refused to eat, and, spending the night in the room underneath, Hoffmann heard him pacing up and down for hours. The following day, he resisted all Hoffmann's efforts to make him eat, and again spent most of the night pacing sleeplessly up and down. Perhaps he was thinking about whether to kill himself. He had run away again, as he had after the failure of the putsch eight years earlier. Once again he was in danger of being arrested, put on trial, imprisoned. He could kill himself now, as he had threatened to then. He could seize the initiative, sentence himself, shoot the Hitler he hated, or, having staked so much already, he could go on gambling, plotting, politicking and advancing the career of the Hitler he loved.

Suicide was a remedy he often prescribed for other people. One of Hess's friends, Karl Haushofer, had served in Japan as military attaché and had returned with an infectious respect for samurai values and ritual suicide. Both Gregor Strasser and Ernst Röhm were given chances to shoot themselves before being killed in the Night of the Long Knives.[14] In 1943 Hitler said that Field Marshal von Paulus should have shot himself instead of surrendering at Stalingrad. 'How can anyone be afraid of that second in which he can free himself from misery?' In July 1944, after the plot to assassinate him failed, Hitler said, almost regretfully, that it would have liberated him from anxiety, sleeplessness and nervous disease. 'It is only a fraction of a second, and then you are freed from all that, and you have quiet and eternal peace.'

But he had created something enormously powerful, a political machine that was carrying him towards total control over Germany. He had ruthless fellow-fighters who would do anything to help him, and already they were exerting their strength to stop him caving in. Perhaps the Leader, if he could not propel himself forwards, should let himself be led. Faltering and suicidal, he had never been less inspiring, but it did not matter, because he had generated enough momentum. By using violence and terrorism, by using the same methods and weapons as criminals, by collecting alienated, embittered, desperate men, human driftwood from a disintegrating society, he had surrounded himself with the right disciples – a gang that would help him to cover his tracks.

He pulled himself together. According to Hoffmann, he said: 'So now starts the battle, a battle that must lead to its objective.'[15] Toland elaborates the story, accepting the claim of Alfred Frauenfeld, the 'self-appointed National Socialist Gauleiter of Vienna', that he had waited for Hitler outside Vienna in a small car, since the Mercedes would have been too noticeable, and driven him to the cemetery. 'Once back in his own car, Hitler gazed fixedly ahead. Finally he said, as if thinking aloud, "So. Now let the struggle begin – the struggle which must and shall be crowned with success."'[16]

He may have said this, or something like it, but the rest of the story is untrue. According to Toland – and according to Hoffmann – he visited Geli's grave before he went to Hamburg. In fact he spoke in Hamburg on Thursday, 24 September, two days before his car was seen by the Austrian police crossing the border on Saturday, 26 September. At ten o'clock it drove up to the Central Cemetery in Vienna, where Schaub procured a permit for it to drive inside. It was seen driving away again at 10.30.[17]

Hoffmann says they were still in St Quirin when they were told over the telephone that the funeral had taken place, and that they left for Vienna the same evening. In fact, since St Quirin is over 500 miles from Hamburg, they were probably driving northwards while the funeral was in progress.

But the battle did start, and led quickly to its objective as Hitler fought with ferocious concentration. On Monday, 5 October 1931, less than two weeks after the funeral, he was received in Berlin by Heinrich Brüning, who was still Chancellor. Though Hitler was not yet a German citizen and could not stand for election, he was involved in preparations for the opening of the new Reichstag on 13 October, when the Nazi deputies appeared in brown shirts.

Five days after meeting Brüning, he had his first meeting with Hindenburg, who did not like him. During February 1932, in a complicated manoeuvre to achieve German citizenship, he got himself appointed as attaché to the Brunswick Legation in Berlin with responsibility for representing the agricultural interests of the province. In March, as a candidate for the presidency of the republic, he won over 30 per cent of the vote.

There were five election campaigns in 1932, and it became easier for people to unite behind him, believing in his belief in his mission. While the impoverished proletariat was still hoping for help from the Communists, the middle classes and the peasants were turning to the Nazis. The electorate was desperate enough for Hitler to cut a convincing figure as the man who could save Germany.

Between April and November the saviour image was promoted cleverly and energetically. Making his first appearance in a silvery aeroplane as he flew from one open-air rally to the next, he gave the impression of being a superman who could rescue Germany from hunger, poverty, unemployment and humiliation.[18]

In mid-June, after Papen created his 'cabinet of barons', the SA and the SS, which had been banned in April, were legalised again. In July the Nazis won 230 of the 608 seats in the Reichstag, but in August all that Hindenburg was prepared to offer Hitler was the position of Vice-Chancellor. In January 1933 a meeting between him, Hess, Himmler and Papen prepared the ground for the dismissal of Schleicher after a mere five weeks as Chancellor, and on 28 January 1933 his government resigned. Two days later – less than eighteen months after Geli's death – Hitler was invited to be Chancellor. If he had sacrificed Geli to make this possible, he had, from his point of view, done the right thing.

In the election held during March 1933, two weeks after the Reichstag fire, eighty-one seats went to the Communists, but by the first meeting of the new Reichstag, which was held three weeks later, the Communist delegates had all been sent to concentration camps or gone into hiding or emigrated.[19] Hitler had suspended civil rights and seized power in the states not previously under Nazi control, though their independent sovereignty was not legally overturned till the end of January 1934. On 23 March 1933 the Reichstag voted in favour of the 'Enabling Act' which gave his government emergency powers, and after Hindenburg died in August 1934, Hitler headed both the state and the government.

By the end of March 1935 he had reincorporated the Saarland into the Reich and introduced conscription to enlarge his army. In September the Nuremberg Laws stripped Jewish Germans of their civil rights and their right to take non-Jewish lovers or enter into mixed marriages. Gerlich had been right to predict 'enmity with neighbouring countries, internal totalitarianism, civil war, international war, lies, hatred, fratricide and infinite trouble'. Hindenburg had been right to predict, after their first meeting in November 1932, that if Hitler formed a cabinet it was 'bound to develop into a party dictatorship'. But neither the editor nor the President had stopped him from getting to the top.

No More Happy Picnics

After Geli's death, no one could fail to notice the difference in Hitler. He never again sat down to play the piano[1] and, as Henny observed, he took less trouble over his appearance and he was gloomier, mostly preserving a heavy silence about Geli.

A great deal changed in our lives. There were no more happy picnics. It was weird that nobody talked about Geli any more, as if she'd never existed. Her room was locked up, the clothes remained in the wardrobe, the pullovers, the pleated skirts, the hats she'd brought back from Vienna, the long evening dresses she'd worn at the Bayreuth Festival. The square blue gramophone, the many records of classical music and the first jazz records, everything remained in its old place. Only the blood was washed away, in so far as it's possible to get rid of bloodstains.[2]

Also kept in their old places were the sheet music she had used in her singing lessons and the librettos of the operas she had seen. Hitler had a bronze bust of her made by the sculptor Ferdinand Liebermann, who had to work from photographs. Later, after Hitler became Chancellor, he had a cast of it in the Chancellery. Anni Winter, the one person allowed inside Geli's room, had the job of keeping it clean and arranging fresh flowers once a week. The room was kept locked, and Hitler carried a key around with him.[3]

In the winter of 1931, visiting the Hoffmanns in their house, he looked through the loose photographs on the writing table and found one of three girls in dirndls lying next to the Alsatian on the grass in front of the Haus Wachenfeld – Geli, Elfriede and Henny. 'He gazed at the photograph, then pressed it to his lips and put it into his pocket.'[4]

If he was giving a performance, it was good enough for him to be taken in, along with everyone else. He continued the cult he had begun. Every Christmas Eve till 1939, he visited her room as if it were a shrine. Christmas was no longer an occasion for celebration. He still went to Obersalzberg, but neither enjoyed himself nor allowed his entourage to have fun. 'After the death of his niece Geli,' writes Christa Schroeder, 'Christmas was really a torture for him, and not pleasant for us either. It's true that he allowed a Christmas tree to be put in the corner of the hall, but Christmas carols were not sung.'[5]

In 1938, making a will, he stipulated that Angela should inherit all the furniture, clothes and personal effects in the room that was still known as Geli's room. Adolf Ziegler's portrait of Geli was hung in the main drawing room of the house in Obersalzberg. Hitler is said to have shed tears when he first saw the picture, and he thanked Ziegler by choosing him in preference to many better painters as president of the German Academy of Art.[6]

Apart from Anni Winter, the only person allowed inside the room – once – was Henny, on the day she married Baldur von Schirach in March 1932. The reception was held in Hitler's flat. When she wanted to change out of her wedding dress, he handed her a key. 'In Geli's room,' he said.

> Six months earlier we'd been listening to gramophone records in here. Now the blinds were half down, and I didn't want to make it any brighter. The air was perfumed with withered roses, with perfectly fresh early freesias, with dark cinnamon-like scents that had slowly dehydrated in their bottles. Here was Geli's still unused writing paper with the name Angela Raubal printed in English script in the top left corner. The photograph of Muck, her favourite dog, was still standing there, and though everything appeared unchanged, as if it had only just been abandoned, the room seemed to me like an Egyptian burial place.[7]

Geli was irreplaceable, and he had to find a replacement. That was the paradox. If Hitler had thought of Eva Braun as her natural successor, he would not have reacted as he did in 1932 when he met the woman later to be Frau Goebbels – Magda Quandt, a good-looking, elegant and intelligent woman of thirty-one, daughter of an engineer and a servant girl. She was having an affair with Goebbels, who introduced her as the divorced wife of the industrialist Günther Quandt.

Liking her and thinking she resembled Geli, Hitler confided in Otto Wagener. 'This woman could play a big role in my life without my being married to her. In my work she could be the female pole opposite to my one-sided masculine instincts. She could be a second Geli for me. It's a pity she's not married.'[8]

If Hitler was expecting Wagener to approach Magda on his behalf, he was not disappointed. After offering her a lift in his car to an SA rally in Brunswick, where Hitler and Goebbels were both going to speak, Wagener asked whether she would like a role in the Führer's life.

Neither accepting nor refusing what was unmistakeably an offer, she said he was right not to marry. 'His wife would sometimes – perhaps often – be just a piece of furniture, a cupboard that's liable to get in his way, or a microphone he speaks into, or a gramophone on which he wants to hear certain records he can put on or take off as he pleases.'[9]

She realised that, if she accepted the offer, she ought to be married to someone else. Wagener suggested Goebbels. She hesitated, but eventually agreed, and so did Goebbels, on condition she did not try to discourage extra-marital affairs. The master of propaganda needed constant reassurance from women that his diminutive body and his club foot did not make him unlovable.

He and Magda Quandt announced their engagement over lunch with Hitler, who attended the celebration afterwards at a hotel. Wagener remembered the mood as being 'so carefree that I had the feeling three people had at last found happiness'.[10] What Hitler now had was a variation – less satisfying for him – of the triangle he had once formed with Geli and Emil Maurice. Goebbels and Magda went on to produce a son and five daughters; rumours that Hitler had fathered the son turned out to be false,[11] but Hitler, who enjoyed being at the apex of sexual triangles with a narrow base and long sides, would not have been content with a purely passive role. He intervened after Goebbels, invited to stay at the Berghof, arrived with a pretty blonde starlet wearing a sable coat. She was given the bedroom next to Goebbels's, but at dinner Hitler ignored her. When he asked where Magda was, Goebbels said she was ill. Going to his study, Hitler telephoned her in Berlin, and, hearing that she was quite well, arranged for her to come in the morning on his private plane. The starlet had to leave after breakfast, shortly before Magda arrived. Later, Hitler intervened again to break up Goebbels's affair with a Czech film star, Lida Baarova, and, later still, while Magda was having an affair with Karl Hanke, the *Gauleiter* of Lower Silesia, Hitler made sure that she and Goebbels spent a night in the same bedroom.[12]

In 1945 all six Goebbels children were sacrificed on the altar of their parents' devotion to Hitler. Helga, the eldest, was twelve, and the youngest was four. Knowing that the parents intended to die in the bunker with their Führer, his cook, Konstanze Manzialy, offered to take the children to her home in the country and hide them till things were quieter. Magda refused, but it seems the decision had been taken by her husband. When Speer visited them for the last time, he was never left alone with Magda, who could say only that she was glad her eldest boy was not with them – Harald Quandt, the son of her first husband.[13] The children were wearing long white nightgowns when they were given drugged drinking chocolate before poison capsules were put into their mouths. Still in their nightgowns, the six little corpses were laid in a row.

Though Hitler thought she resembled Geli physically, Magda was too mature and sophisticated to succeed her. Eva Braun had neither of these faults, and there was nothing she would not do to occupy the space that was vacant.

True or false, the suicide story influenced their relationship. Eva made two suicide attempts, which may both have been intended to fail. The wound she inflicted by shooting herself in August 1932 was not too serious for her to telephone a doctor, but instead of ringing Dr Marx, the Jewish doctor who

was employing her older sister, Ilse, as a receptionist, she chose
Hoffmann's brother-in-law, Dr Plate. He could be counted on
to get in touch with Hitler, who arrived at the clinic with flowers
and said: 'She did it for love of me. Now I must look after her.
It mustn't happen again.'

The first phrase echoes what he had told her about Geli, but
the last phrase is more significant. Reichstag elections were to be
held early in November, and after the gossip about Geli's suicide,
voters would not have been favourably impressed if another
woman killed herself for him. Remembering the mistake over
the premature announcement that Geli had committed suicide,
he went back to Eva's bedside and advised her to say that it
had been an accident: she had been looking at the pistol when
it went off in her hands. This is what she told her parents.[14]

She may have been motivated more by intuition than calculation, but Christa Schroeder regarded her as a schemer:

> When he no longer had much time for her because of
> the electioneering, she pursued him cunningly with suicide
> attempts. And of course she succeeded, because as a politician
> Hitler couldn't have survived a second suicide from someone
> close to him. I say it again: the only woman he loved and
> would certainly have married later was his step-niece Geli
> Raubal.[15]

But he did not look after Eva, and it did happen again. She
made another suicide attempt in the spring of 1935, after he
had let three months go by without seeing her. She used sleeping
tablets, and this time succeeded in making him more attentive.
He arrived at the clinic with the gift she most wanted – a
basset hound puppy. Never again, he said, must she try to
kill herself. He had arranged for a monthly allowance to be
paid into a bank account he had opened in her name. He
had rented a flat for her, not far from his own, and in the
spring he would buy her a villa. Soon the builders would
have finished work on enlarging the Haus Wachenfeld, which
would be known from now on as the Berghof, and Angela,
who had always been hostile to Eva, had finally been sacked.
He subsequently treated Eva badly and neglected her for long

periods, but she never again tried to kill herself until they did it together in 1945.

Though she told her sisters that their sexual relationship was normal, she once confided to a close friend: '*Als Mann habe ich von ihm überhaupt nichts.*' This could be translated as 'I get nothing at all from him as a man', meaning she never got anything, but the present tense in German (unlike its English counterpart) does not have an alternative form to indicate continuous action, and the sentence could equally well mean 'I am getting nothing at all from him as a man', implying that she had not always been frustrated in the past and would not necessarily be in the future.

Several entries in her diary support this interpretation. On 16 March 1935 she wrote: 'He needs me for special reasons. It can't be otherwise (nonsense). When he says he loves me, he thinks it is only for the time being.' And on 10 May, 'The weather is magnificent and I, the mistress of the greatest man in Germany and in the whole world, I sit here waiting while the sun mocks me through the windowpanes.' It is sometimes said that the diary was faked, but that the faker was Eva herself.

They apparently became lovers at the beginning of 1932, about four months after Geli's death, and continued a desultory sexual relationship until 1943 when – possibly because the war was going so badly – he told her to expect nothing from him. What she confided to Speer was unambiguous: 'Hitler had told her that he was too busy, too immersed, too tired – he could no longer satisfy her as a man.' Speer, who had always liked her, described her as 'very feminine. A man's woman, incredibly undemanding for herself, helpful to many people behind the scenes – nobody ever knew that – and infinitely thoughtful of Hitler. She was a restful sort of girl. And her love for Hitler was beyond question'.[16]

It is revealing, though, that Christa Schroeder had the impression that they never made love. This tallies with claims that he was making about having overcome any need for a woman.[17] Nor should we take it for granted, even if they did sometimes make love, that her main function was to fulfil his sexual needs. There are, says Joachim Fest, grounds for supposing that the relationship, 'far from being a natural sexual bond, was intended solely to provide a strained confirmation of his manhood in his own eyes and those of his closest followers'.[18] Always highly conscious of the image he was projecting, he tried to impress the inner circle with his masculinity while wanting the rest of the world to believe he was too busy with public affairs to have time for private ones. Her presence in his life was a closely guarded secret. 'He hid her from everybody,' said Speer, 'except his most intimate circle.'[19] The German public knew nothing of her existence till the end of the war.

Epilogue: Mass Murderer

One killing might seem negligible in comparison with the extermination of over 6 million Jews, or with the worldwide cataclysm of the war. Without Hitler it would not have been fought – at least not in that way, not at that time. Over 40 million people were killed. If he ruined Geli's life and then shot her, deliberately or accidentally or half-accidentally, should it surprise us or make any difference to our view of him? Does the story of their relationship bring his sado-masochism into focus clearly enough for us to take new bearings on the Third Reich?

The historian Christopher R. Browning has warned us against what he calls 'an overly Hitlerocentric' interpretation of the Holocaust – 'one that focuses exclusively on the intentions and decisions of Hitler at the top while ignoring the attitudes and behaviour of those at the bottom'.[1] Another historian of the Third Reich, Tim Mason, coined the terms 'intentionalists' and 'functionalists' to differentiate between those who hold Hitler to be solely responsible for the atrocities and those who see what happened as 'an unplanned "cumulative rationalisation" produced by the chaotic decision-making process of a polycratic regime and the "negative selection" of destructive elements from the Nazis' ideological arsenal'.[2]

Writing from different viewpoints, several historians have tried either to exculpate Hitler or to shift the focus away from him. In a 1961 book, *The Destruction of the European Jews*, Raul Hilberg contended that 'German bureaucracy was so sensitive a mechanism that in the right climate it began to function almost by itself'. In 1977 David Irving published

Hitler's War, which argues that the Führer had forbidden mass murder of the Jews and knew nothing about the extermination until the autumn of 1943. A recent book, Daniel Jonah Goldhagen's *Hitler's Willing Executioners: Ordinary Germans and the Holocaust*, suggests that German anti-Semitism was 'the central causal agent . . . not only of Hitler's decision to annihilate European Jewry . . . but also of the perpetrators' willingness to kill and brutalise Jews'.[3]

More plausibly, Browning adopts a position between intentionalism and functionalism, arguing that until 1941 Hitler had wanted to expel Jews from Germany but not to massacre them. It was not Jews but Russians who were designated as the original victims of Nazi massacres. By the end of 1940 he had decided to attack Russia, and by March 1941 had announced it was to be a war of annihilation. In March 1941, before he had even started it, he warned senior officers against soldierly comradeship. 'The Communist is no comrade of ours either before or afterwards. . . . We are not waging war to preserve the enemy.' He gave orders for all captured commissars to be killed, and by the end of July 1941 the death squads had killed at least 62,805 civilians, most of them Jews.[4] The turning point came in July 1941, when Hitler decided to extend the massacre policy to Jews in the rest of Europe.

But while the functionalists have underestimated the part he played, they have also shown that previous historians had paid too little attention to initiatives taken by men who did the slaughtering. Some of the grisliest atrocities were perpetrated not by the SS, the SA or the Gestapo but by ordinary policemen who had not even joined the party. And they were not merely carrying out orders: they were given power of life or death over civilians in occupied territory. They could shoot innocent men, women and children with impunity, or allow them to escape. They could take part in genocidal massacres or abstain without being punished. (No one has been able to find any evidence that a soldier or policeman was ever punished with any severity for refusing to kill an unarmed civilian.)

Though it is hard to be precise about this, it would not be misleading to say that Hitler's sadism was leaking into the massive organisation around him. Whips were sometimes issued to police battalions for rounding up Jews. We do not know whether this was his idea, nor whether he issued instructions that soldiers and policemen should be allowed to use their own judgement when killing Jews and other civilians in occupied countries. Effectively his soldiers and policemen were being given the same godlike powers he had once enjoyed over rats, though this time the victims were human.

Not that he ever wanted to witness any of the killing, and he never visited a concentration camp. He had no desire to see Jews, Poles, gypsies or invalids starving to death or succumbing to the fumes of poison gas. It was enough to bask in the knowledge that his intentions were being fulfilled. In this way he could enjoy the reality as if it were a fantasy. He got pleasure from the idea of destruction on a massive scale, but did not want to confront men who were wounded or dying or dead. The closed curtains in his special train were in line with his refusal to visit the front or to go out, while living in the bunker, to look at the damage done to Berlin by shells and bombs. If he did not confront the reality, he did not have to admit responsibility.

His sado-masochistic impulses blended with his destructiveness and self-destructiveness. By killing the Jew outside himself, he thought he could eradicate the Jew inside; he was trying to overcome his sense of powerlessness by destroying. Anything was better than to be overwhelmed by other people. At the end, forced to give up all hope of winning the war, he wanted to bring down Germany and the world in ruins.

One of the ways that his sado-masochism leaked into the social structures of the Third Reich was in the denial of individual rights. Idealism, he maintained, 'leads men to voluntary acknowledgment of the privilege of force and strength and thus makes them become a dust particle of that order which forms and shapes the entire universe'. The individual must renounce his right to assert himself, express his opinions or search for happiness. Hitler's citizens, like his women, were required to subordinate themselves entirely to the will of their Leader.

While there is plentiful evidence of Hitler's ruthlessness towards Geli, Eva Braun and Renate Müller – he had little regard for their needs, feelings or rights – and of his masochistic sexual behaviour, there is little evidence that he enjoyed inflicting physical pain on women. But it seems that he did take vicarious pleasure in this, and, if we trust the testimony of the maid, Pauline Kohler, he may not always have remained a passive spectator.

The house in Obersalzberg went through several stages of enlargement, including the building of two new rooms. In one, which was fitted up like a gymnasium, the equipment included a vaulting horse, while the other room had a door with iron bars, like a prison cell. It was kept locked, and the maids were curious about what went on behind the door until an SS officer, Erich Keitner, explained. 'Sometimes girls are brought here for questioning if we have any reason to suspect their racial purity. After a few hours with us, they will usually talk very freely.' They were stripped, and made to stretch out on the vaulting horse, 'where the SS and possibly Hitler "inspected" and sometimes assaulted them'.[5]

Though we have no evidence that Hitler ever inflicted physical pain on Geli, Eva Braun or Renate Müller alongside the mental pain he made them suffer, the possibility cannot be ruled out. And if it is true that he gave twenty marks to each of the girls whom Emil Maurice found for him, he may have felt that he was paying for any form of pleasure he fancied.

The vaulting horse and the torture chamber in his house can be taken as representative of the way that his sado-masochism pollinated the brutality characteristic of the Third Reich. The hierarchy was based on sadistic cruelty. Terrorised by Hitler, Goering, Goebbels and Himmler terrorised subordinates in the same way. Commandants of concentration camps and high-ranking SS officers bullied their inferiors, who bullied theirs and tortured prisoners. At every level, the men who carried out orders were rewarded for their obedience with the pleasure of inflicting pain and humiliation on others lower down the scale.

When we think about the Third Reich, the first pictures that come to mind are images of mastery and slavery, domination and discipline – orderly rows of uniformed, well-drilled men goose-stepping in front of the solitary leader who acknowledges their dutiful exertion by extending one arm; narcissistic SS officers with whips and dogs herding terrified Jews into cattle trucks; helmeted, jackbooted soldiers with rifles and truncheons patrolling outside the broken windows of shops displaying Jewish stars; bare-chested athletes and brown-shirted soldiers parading at Nuremberg rallies; starving prisoners with hollow cheeks and protruding ribs staring out hopelessly from behind barbed wire; long lines of corpses laid out in rows; neat piles of soap made from human flesh.

Even in concentration camps, many prisoners had opportunities of bullying and humiliating those in weaker positions. Hitler's servile secretary, Martin Bormann, was dictatorial towards everyone else, including his wife and labourers employed on building projects. After Geli's death, when Bormann was making Obersalzberg into a Nazi encampment, he dispossessed farmers of their land by imposing compulsory purchase orders, demolished churches, and erected the spectacularly situated Eagle's Nest – a teahouse on the summit of the mountain. The builders, who had to construct a lift-shaft inside the mountain for the final part of the guests' upward journey, were bullied by foremen who were being bullied by Bormann. But masochistically submissive Germans were rewarded with sadistic mastery over racial and political minorities inside Germany and over everyone in occupied territories. By accepting the slavery that Hitler imposed, they could look forward to mastery over the world.

Like the history of the Third Reich, Hitler's rise to power can be viewed in this way. In *Mein Kampf* he wrote with surprising openness about the struggle between demagogue and audience at rallies and mass meetings. The speaker could please his public only by mastering it. Demoralised by defeat, inflation and unemployment, German audiences were susceptible to this form of bullying. Wage earners who had depended mainly on their work to give them their identity had forfeited not only their self-respect but the respect of their children.

In a period of prosperity they could have resisted Hitler's demand that they should dissolve their identity into that of the nation, but to their ears his hoarse harangues were siren songs. What he reiterated again and again was what he had written in *Mein Kampf*. The individual must subject his ego to the life of the community, must be prepared to sacrifice himself.

About ten years before Hitler was born, Dostoevsky had explained in *The Brothers Karamazov* why a demoralised people would rush at the opportunity to surrender its freedom to a charismatic leader. Ivan Karamazov makes up a prose poem which he sets in Spain during the Inquisition, when heretics were being burnt in the presence of the king, the court, the cardinals and the whole population of Seville. When Jesus appears in the city, people are irresistibly drawn to him, and when they implore him to bring a dead child back to life, he performs the miracle. But the Cardinal Inquisitor, a tall, ninety-year-old man with hollow cheeks and sunken eyes, orders the guards to arrest Jesus, who is shut in a gloomy prison where the Inquisitor visits him to insist that Jesus can add nothing to what he said fifteen centuries earlier and threatens to burn him like a heretic. Jesus had made a mistake in the wilderness, says the old man, when he refused to deprive people of their freedom. 'Men are tormented by no greater anxiety than to find someone speedily who will take over that gift of freedom with which the unfortunate creatures were born. But no one can take over their freedom without appeasing their conscience.'[6]

Dostoevsky's insight is basic to Erich Fromm's 1941 book *Escape from Freedom*, which devotes a chapter to the psychology of Nazism. Masochistic strivings, he argues, are aimed at losing oneself by submitting to a leader and getting rid of the freedom that is so burdensome. The masochist wants to surrender his independence, participating in a bigger and more powerful whole outside of himself.

> This power can be a person, an institution, God, the nation, conscience or a psychic compulsion. By becoming part of a power which is felt as unshakeably strong, eternal and glamorous, one participates in its strength and glory. One surrenders one's own self and renounces all strength and pride connected with it, one loses one's integrity as an individual and surrenders freedom, but one gains a new security and a new pride in the participation. . . .[7]

Though it might seem that pleasure in dominating another person is the opposite of pleasure in being dominated, sadism and masochism are almost invariably found together, as they were in Hitler. One of the reasons that Geli hated having to indulge his masochism was that she could no longer admire a man who begged her to abuse him, kick him and piss on him.

But in him the masochism existed alongside the cruelty that made him encourage SS officers to make women strip and lie back on a vaulting horse while they were 'inspected'. He sometimes punished himself, as when he used his whip on his own hand, and there was masochism in his willingness to commit suicide if his plans foundered. He too was willing to make himself into a speck of dust or dissolve himself into the greater entity.

If Hitler did shoot Geli, she was his first human victim. There is no evidence of his killing anyone during the First World War, in which his main job was to carry messages. But the boy who shot rats turned into the man who gassed Jews, and it looks as if Geli's death was a stepping stone in the development. At the Nuremberg trials, Goering said: 'Geli's death had such a devastating effect on Hitler that it . . . changed his relationship to everyone else.' Even Hoffmann said that 'At this time, the seed of inhumanity began to sprout in Hitler.' From now on, Henny observed, 'the tender element' was missing from his life. All three of them may have been overstating the point, but the change must have been substantial.

Hansfstaengl, who also noticed the difference in Hitler, uses the words 'narcissus' and 'demon'. The relationship

had provided him for the first and only time in his life with a release to his nervous energy which only too soon was to find its final expression in ruthlessness and savagery. . . . With her death the way was clear for his final development into a demon, with his sex life deteriorating again into a sort of bisexual narcissus-like vanity, with Eva Braun little more than a vague domestic adjunct.[8]

Another member of the inner circle to link his sexuality with *demonic* destructiveness was Baldur von Schirach. 'In relations with women he was erotically highly strung and at the same time sexually inhibited. And perhaps his power complex, his fanaticism and his demonic destructiveness are also the results of his inability to give happiness to a woman he really loved.'[9]

What seemed demonic was a manic appetite for human slaughter. Never his partner in the same sense as Geli, Eva could neither release his nervous energy nor restrain his destructiveness. Certain subjects had never been discussed with Geli, but at least there had been some human interaction. Eva's company never seemed to have much effect on him.

His appetite for carnage grew monstrously after Geli's death. In January 1945, making his last broadcast, he called himself a man 'who always knew only one thing – strike, strike and strike again'.[10] This may be a good precept for a boxer, but not for a statesman. In 1933, as soon as he was in power, he started preparing Germany for war. In March 1936 he reoccupied the demilitarised Rhineland, and in February 1938 appointed himself supreme commander of the armed forces. He annexed Austria in March, and in May announced that he was going to destroy Czechoslovakia.

His declared intention of occupying the Sudetenland was intended to precipitate war, but he pretended to be pleased when the British premier, Neville Chamberlain, gave in to his demands at the end of September. In mid-March 1939, after his troops marched into Czechoslovakia, war was again averted; but, having promised to support Poland, Britain and France finally declared war when his troops crossed the Polish border in September.

He immediately began to indulge his passion for mass slaughter by signing an order for the killing of invalids – 'useless eaters'. By August 1941, about 100,000 Germans had been executed – children who required special care, patients in hospitals and clinics, invalids and disabled people in nursing homes, psychiatric hospitals and concentration camps. About 20,000 gypsies had been slaughtered by the end of the war. In October 1939 he began liquidating what he termed the 'leading classes' in Poland – teachers, priests, intellectuals, entrepreneurs. About 70,000 Poles were killed in action, but by the end of the war about 6 million Poles were dead. Only half were Jewish.[11]

In April 1943 Hitler again came close to unveiling his solution to 'the Jewish problem' when the Hungarian regent, Admiral Miklós Horthy, argued that, having made it virtually impossible for Hungarian Jews to earn a living, he could not beat them to death. Hitler's Foreign Minister, Ribbentrop, explained that they must be either killed or sent to concentration camps; Hitler said that in Poland Jews who did not want to work were shot, and if they could not work 'they were treated like tuberculosis bacilli with which a healthy body may become infected. This is not cruel if one remembers that even innocent creatures of nature, such as hare and deer when infected, have to be killed so that they cannot damage others. Why should the beasts who brought us Bolshevism be spared more than those innocents?'[12]

But he did not talk like this in broadcast speeches or at dinner parties. In the Chancellery and on the terrace of the Berghof he impressed women such as Maria von Below and Margarete Speer as being fascinating and amiable, though there were certain topics, such as Geli and the Jews, that must never be broached. The one woman who dared to step across the threshold was Henny, in April 1943, after she had visited friends in occupied Amsterdam. Awakened by screams in the night and shouts of 'Aryans stand back', she had looked out of the window to see a crowd of scared women with bundles. The next day a school gymnasium was full of antique furniture, carpets, paintings and jewellery confiscated from families that had been rounded up. She talked to her husband, who could not stop her ringing Hitler and arranging to visit Obersalzberg.

Dinner was served shortly before midnight. 'He could no longer sleep at night, and did not want to be alone.' His eyesight was failing, and bulletins from the front were printed out in big letters so that he could read them without spectacles. From the way he kept pressing his handkerchief to his eyes, she knew the news was bad. He sat between her and Eva Braun, who finally got up to say goodnight. He kissed her hand. Turning to Henny, he asked: 'You've come from Holland?'

'Yes, that's why I'm here, I wanted to talk to you, I've seen frightful things, I can't believe that's what you want.'
He looked at me, astonished. 'It's war,' he said.
'But it was women I saw, how a crowd of women, poor,

helpless women were taken away, transported to a camp. I don't believe they'll come back, their property was taken away from them, their families no longer exist.'

'You're sentimental, Frau von Schirach.' Hitler stood up and drew me aside. 'What have Jews in Holland got to do with you?' Because I'd jumped to my feet, he grabbed my wrist and held it in both hands – as he always had when he wanted my full attention. Then he let go of me and formed with his hands two bowls which he moved up and down like scales as he said loudly and insistently: 'Look, every day, ten thousand of my most valuable men are killed, men who are irreplaceable, the best. The balance is wrong, the equilibrium in Europe has been upset. Because the others aren't being killed. They survive, the ones in camps, the inferior ones. So what's it going to look like in Europe in a hundred years? In a thousand? My responsibility is to my people, nobody else. I don't care about posterity. You must learn to hate. I had to.'

Twenty years earlier, in *Mein Kampf*, he had produced a similar argument in favour of human slaughter: 'If the best men were killed at the front, then at home one could at least exterminate the vermin.'

Henny retorted: 'I'm not here to take part in hatred but in love,' looking straight into his eyes, which was what he had taught her to do when she wanted to exert pressure. They were surrounded by seventeen men who could – the thought occurred to her – have stood up and said they were willing to die for him but not to be involved in slaughtering Jewish women.

But the men stared awkwardly into the fire or down on the floor. Under Hitler's cold gaze I took out my tortoiseshell casket. He knew this casket. It was a present from Mussolini, and he'd often played with it during our conversations, opening and closing it mechanically. 'I can no longer sit at your table,' I said softly, so that only he could understand me. Then I turned and went to the door. As I reached the three steps to the hall, I started to run.

One of Hitler's companions caught up with me. 'Why did

you do that? The Führer is furious. Go away, right now, tonight, immediately. He doesn't want to see you again.'[13]

Hitler had defeated France with astonishing speed – the armistice was signed in June 1940 – but by the end of the year he had decided to attack Russia. When the offensive started, on 22 June 1941, he was so confident that his army could take Moscow before the weather deteriorated that he did not equip it for a winter campaign, and when thousands of men were freezing to death he refused to authorise retreat or surrender. 'The army will hold its position to the last soldier and the last cartridge.'

Of the 91,000 Germans taken prisoner, only 5,000 returned, but instead of contrition Hitler expressed indignation that Field Marshal von Paulus had neither obeyed orders nor shot himself. 'What does "life" mean? Life is the nation: the individual must die. What remains alive beyond the individual is the nation.'[14]

By 6 December 1941, according to the war diary of his army operations staff, he realised that 'no victory could any longer be won'. Five days later he declared war on the United States.

From then on, fighting the two greatest world powers with no hope of winning, he was indulging his mania for mass slaughter. This point has been made by Sebastian Haffner, but it fails to emerge clearly in most accounts of the war. Had he brought the war to an end in the summer of 1941, he could have dominated Europe and kept the United States neutral, but he did not want an interval in the fighting which might have made it harder to galvanise Germany into a war with Russia.

Of the 5,160,000 Russians who had been taken prisoner by the beginning of May 1944, 473,000 had been 'executed', while about 3 million had starved to death in prison cages. Four 'special operations units' were sent to slaughter Russian civilians behind the lines, and by April 1942 they could report 560,000 deaths.[15]

Finally, Hitler's destructive genius was turned against Germany. On 22 August 1944, to paralyse the men most likely to press for early surrender, he ordered the arrest of about 5,000 former deputies, civil servants and local government officials. Anyone heard saying that Germany could not win the war was to be treated like a traitor – hanged or shot. Sixteen-year-old boys and sixty-year-old men were recruited to fight the advancing Allied armies, and in mid-December he launched a final offensive in the Ardennes, taking troops away from the Eastern Front in spite of warnings from his Chief of Staff that the Russians were massing forces for an attack.

By Christmas, anticipating defeat in the Ardennes, Hitler was desperate. Once again, according to Nicolaus von Below, 'he talked about killing himself; that the last chance had gone; that the Luftwaffe and Wehrmacht had betrayed him. I know the war is lost, he said. . . . A little later he made a 180 degree turn – it was frightening. We would never capitulate, he said. We might sink, but we'd take the world with us.'[16]

On 24 February, after Dresden and Potsdam had been annihilated by Allied bombing, Hitler said he was sorry Obersalzberg had been spared.[17] In March, when Russian and American armies were advancing into Germany, people were gladly surrendering to the Americans and trying to run away from the Russians. On the 18th he issued an order for all civilians to be evacuated from the war zones in the west; when a general at the staff conference objected that no trains were available, Hitler said they could walk.[18]

The following day he sent a teletype message to Speer, whom he had appointed as Minister of Armaments in 1942, ordering the destruction of 'all military, transportation, communications, industrial and supply facilities, as well as all resources within the Reich'. Speer realised:

> The message was the death sentence for the German people; it called for application of the scorched earth principle in its most sweeping form. . . . For an indefinite period there would have been no gas, no pure water, no coal, no transportation. All railroad facilities, canals, locks, ships and locomotives destroyed. Even where industry had not been demolished, it could not have produced anything for lack of electricity, gas and water . . . How was it possible, I thought, that one man wanted to transform this land into a desert?[19]

But Hitler refused to be dissuaded.

If the war is lost, the people will be lost also. It is not necessary to worry about what the German people will need for elemental survival. On the contrary, it is best for us to destroy even these things. For the nation has proved to be the weaker, and the future belongs solely to the stronger eastern nation. In any case, only those who are inferior will remain after this struggle, for the good have already been killed.[20]

This was consistent with what he had said in November 1942 when the army was encircled at Stalingrad: 'On this point too I am icily cold. If one day the German nation is no longer sufficiently strong or sufficiently ready for sacrifice to stake its own blood for its existence, then let it perish and be annihilated by some other stronger power. . . .[21] In that case I shall shed no tears for the German nation.' He had given it a chance to reflect his glory. Wanting to be Führer of a great nation, he felt entitled to destroy Germany if the Germans could not measure up to his standards of greatness. Nothing should be left but a wasteland.

In the Ruhr, *Gauleiters* made arrangements for mines to be demolished and canals to be blocked by sinking barges loaded with cement. The abandoned cities were to be burnt. Surrender was prohibited. From any house displaying a white flag, men and boys were to be taken into the street and shot. At the end of March, commanders were ordered to put up 'the most fanatical struggle against the now mobile enemy. No consideration for the population can be taken.'[22]

After twelve years of uncritical loyalty, Speer finally turned against Hitler. Given the task of destroying industry, he used his power against officials who were obeying their Führer, and plotted to kill everyone in the bunker by introducing poison gas into the ventilation system. Once again, Hitler was lucky. The plot was foiled by a last-minute reconstruction of the air shaft, but Speer arranged for most of Hitler's murderous orders to be disobeyed. Demolition squads were already at work, but Speer had machine guns issued for the defence of plants vital to the civilian economy, while the German commandant of Paris ignored Hitler's orders that the city should be destroyed. 'Within Hitler,' concludes Haffner, 'alongside the highly gifted politician there had always lurked a mass murderer. And though his lust for murder had originally seized only on Jews and Russians, wherever his intentions were crossed, that lust for murder overrode political reasoning.'[23]

Not that he was devoid of guilt feelings. In 1923, after several of his comrades had been killed in the abortive putsch, he developed a physical symptom – a twitching in his left arm – which returned towards the end of the war. He apparently made a quick recovery from the emotional strain of the purge on 30 June 1934. On 1 July, a Sunday, he made numerous appearances at the window of the Chancellery to greet the crowd that Goebbels had rounded up, and in the afternoon, while firing squads were still carrying out executions only a few miles away, in Lichterfelde, he was entertaining his guests at a garden party. But his sleep was disturbed for months afterwards, and he refused to take sleeping tablets in case they were poisoned. It was said that he woke up weeping from bouts of uneasy sleep and had fits of vomiting.[24]

There was nothing he would have enjoyed less than taking part in the slaughter. He may still have been at the garden party when he gave the order for Röhm to be executed, but Röhm understood him, as he showed when, about to be shot, he asked that Hitler should be the executioner.[25] Hitler never wanted to witness any of the executions he had ordered.

Hitler's sadism was fundamental, but sadists are rarely murderous, and Hitler had little in common with the Marquis de Sade, who was deeply shaken by the guillotining he saw during the French Revolution. Though de Sade's fiction shows how much he fantasised about torture and massacres, he was incapable of giving orders for someone else to be killed; and though he took pleasure in inflicting pain, he could have taken none in giving orders for it to be inflicted on his behalf in his absence.

What he and Hitler had in common was a lack of talent for ordinary relationships. But Hitler bore less resemblance to him than to the lethal libertines in his fiction, where women and boys were treated like horses or chairs – used as if they had no rights. Concentration camps constituted a real equivalent to the Gothic castles that de Sade imagined – fortified, inaccessible places where neither society nor scruple could restrain masters from using slaves sadistically. Bloodshed served as an appetiser. But even de Sade, excited though he was by the idea of cruelty and slaughter on a grand scale, never envisaged the scale that Hitler achieved.

In *Doktor Faustus* Thomas Mann made his Devil describe concentration camps and Gestapo torture chambers as if they were the closest modern equivalent to the medieval idea of hell.

> One must be satisfied with symbols, my good man, when speaking about hells, for there everything comes to an end – not just the descriptive word but absolutely everything – that is their main characteristic and that is what has to be said first, what strikes the newcomer, and what he cannot grasp and does not want to comprehend with his so-to-speak sound senses, because intelligence or some limitation of understanding prevents him, in short, because it is unbelievable, so unbelievable that one's face goes white, unbelievable, though it is immediately apparent on arrival that here everything comes to an end – mercy, grace, consideration, every last trace of regard for the reproachful, incredulous objection: 'This can simply not be done to a soul.' It is done, it happens, and without any words of reckoning, in inaccessible cellars, a long way out of God's earshot, and to all eternity.[26]

As Erich Fromm suggests, Hitler's awareness of his destructiveness was repressed. He rationalised all his acts of aggression as defensive: he was slaughtering Jews or Slavs or gypsies or invalids only in order to preserve the human species. He was cauterising diseased parts of the human race to stop infection from spreading.

Fromm calls Hitler's vegetarianism a 'reaction formation'. 'This is a clinically well-established form of dealing with repressed strivings; a person denies their existence by developing traits that are exactly the opposite. . . . His abstinence from meat was an atonement for his guilt and a proof of his incapacity to kill.'[27] Julius Schaub said that it was not until after Geli's death that he gave up eating meat,[28] though he had shown vegetarian tendencies before she arrived in Obersalzberg. In Munich during Easter 1926 he took a girl to a performance of Johann Strauss's *The Gypsy Baron* and, having dinner afterwards in a restaurant, he ordered liver of young venison. When a large portion arrived, he asked the waiter whether it was the whole liver of a kid. No, said the waiter, two kids. Which prompted Hitler to say: 'Man is an evil animal of prey. Two little innocent animals had to lose their lives just to tickle the palate of a glutton, I really think I'll become a vegetarian one day.' He pontificated about the cruel way that animals were butchered, and argued that meat-eating weakened the muscles. The strongest animals – the elephant, the bull and the horse – were all vegetarian.[29] The same pattern featured in the psychopathology of Himmler, who delivered long homilies about the viciousness of shooting from behind cover at innocent animals browsing on the edge of a wood, but prided himself on not caring about the number of Russian women who died while digging ditches.

The young Hitler, who shot rats, threw crusts of bread to mice. In later life he loved canaries, was moved to tears when one of them died, but admired the Roman Emperor Sulla, an early exponent of mass executions.[30] His desire to be worshipped as a hero had some of its roots in his capacity for hero-worship, and the greatest of all his heroes was Wagner, who, he said, had blamed decadence partly on meat-eating. 'So much of the decay of our civilisation had its origin in the abdomen – chronic constipation, poisoning of the juices, and the results of drinking to excess.' The real subject of *Parsifal*, he said, was how to protect the purity of noble blood. 'The eternal life granted by the grail is only for the truly pure and noble.'[31]

Straining after the heroic, Hitler had to go against his own nature. He killed 6 million Jews and made a fetish of racial purity without ever being able to find out whether his grandfather was Jewish. He made implicit and sometimes explicit claims to sexual adventures he had never had. He carried a whip and wore riding boots without ever having mounted a horse. 'But everything about him is jerky and abrupt. He is entirely without balance.'[32] The tantrums he threw showed how hard he was struggling to sustain the performance.

What was constantly being denied was his background, his family, his childhood experience. People must at all costs be prevented from finding out who he was. The one person who could not be prevented was Geli, who came from the same family. That was why she could give him something that no other man or woman could ever offer – the opportunity to relax. She was his only friend.

Notes

Prologue: Hitler in Love

1. Hanfstaengl, p.47.
2. H. von Schirach, p.241.
3. Wagener, p.358.
4. Wagener, p.102.
5. H. von Schirach.
6. Bullock, *Hitler*, p.394.
7. Fest, *Hitler*, p.322.
8. Hanfstaengl, pp.168–9.
9. Bullock, *Hitler*, pp.393–4.
10. Fest, *Hitler*, pp.321–3.

Chapter 1: The Boy Who Shot Rats

1. Article by Patrick Hitler in *Paris Soir*, 5 August 1939, and OSS interview HSB 926–7, quoted in Toland, p.246.
2. Frank, pp.330–1.
3. Correspondence between Rittmeister von Schuh and Dr Hans Dietrich Röhrs, and between Dr Röhrs and John Toland, quoted in Toland, pp.247 and 952.
4. *Table Talk*, pp.143 and 721.
5. Steinert, p.16.
6. Fest, *Hitler*, p.15.
7. Maser, pp.2–19.
8. Maser, pp.14–19.
9. Shirer, p.21.
10. Maser, pp.19–21.
11. *Mein Kampf*, pp.29–30.
12. Stierlin, p.34.
13. Margarete Roloefs, quoted in Knopp, p.137.
14. *Table Talk*, p.413.
15. Interview with Patrick Hitler, 10 September 1943. Hitler Source Book, National Archive, Washington DC.
16. Schroeder, p.63.
17. Maser, p.28.
18. Schroeder, p.64.

Chapter 2: Sit Down, Hitler

1. Jetzinger, pp.85–6.
2. Haffner, *Ailing Empire*, p.30.
3. *Mein Kampf*, p.114.
4. *Mein Kampf*, p.12.
5. *Mein Kampf*, p.14.
6. Hamann, pp.27 and 37.
7. *Monologe*, p.185, 8–9 January 1942.

8. *Table Talk*, p.641.
9. Heiden, p.303.
10. Paula Hitler, interview in *New York Times*, 5 March 1959, quoted in Waite, p.51.
11. Gun, pp.45–6.
12. Hamann, p.515.
13. Jetzinger, p.71.
14. *Table Talk*, p.316, and Fromm *Anatomy*, p.383.
15. Kubizek, p.38.
16. Kubizek, pp.63–4.
17. Kubizek, p.44.
18. Jetzinger, p.107.
19. Hamann, p.517.
20. Kubizek, pp.55–62.

Chapter 3: Doss House

1. Maser, p.38.
2. Edward Bloch in *Collier's Magazine*, 15 and 22 March 1941, quoted in Hamann, p.54.
3. Thomas Mann, 'A Brother', in *The Order of the Day: Political Essays and Speeches of Two Decades*, New York, 1943.
4. Zweig, pp.84–6.
5. Hamann, p.519.
6. Kubizek, p.190.
7. Kubizek, p.177.
8. Hamann, p.250.
9. Kubizek, pp.175–6.
10. Kubizek, p.174.
11. *Mein Kampf*, p.19.
12. Rauschning, p.262.
13. Gun, p.21.
14. Joachimstaler, p.41.
15. Jenks, p.27.
16. Testimony of Reinhold Hanisch, quoted in Heiden.
17. Joseph Greiner, *Das Ende des Hitler-Mythes*, Zurich, 1947, p.16.
18. Jetzinger, pp.140–2, and Jones, pp.214–15.
19. Joachimstaler, pp.67–9.
20. Joachimstaler, p.39.
21. Joachimstaler, p.43.
22. Schorske, p.130.
23. Hamann, pp.337–63.
24. Knopp, p.120.

Chapter 4: Playing on the Black Notes

1. Dr Morell's deposition to the United States Commission, 1945.
2. H. von Schirach, pp.152–3.
3. Schroeder, p.363.
4. Heinz Linge, ed. Werner Maser, *Bis zum Untergang, Als Chef des Persönlichen Dienstes bei Hitler*, Munich, 1980.
5. Sereny, p.398.
6. H. von Schirach, pp.53–4.
7. Hanfstaengl, pp.137–8.
8. Letter to the author from Dr William Dorrell, 15 December 1996.
9. Waite, pp.152–3.
10. Hanfstaengl, pp.123–4.
11. Bullock, *Hitler and Stalin*, p.403.
12. Hanfstaengl, p.124.
13. Felix Kersten, *Totenkopf und Treue. Heinrich Himmler ohne Uniform. Aus den Tagebüchern des finnischen Medizinalrates*, quoted in Maser p.218.
14. Wiesenthal, pp.130–3.
15. *Table Talk*, pp.43–4.
16. Herbert Lüthy, 'Der Führer persönlich' in *Der Monat*, November 1953, quoted in Fest, *Face*, pp.30–1.
17. Hamann, pp.515–18.
18. Schroeder, p.155.

Chapter 5: The Good Soldier

1. Maser, p.76.
2. *Table Talk*, p.14.
3. Toland, p.63.
4. Letters from Hitler to Joseph Popp and Ernst Hepp, 22 and 26 January 1915, quoted in Joachimstaler, p.125.
5. Letter to the Popps, quoted in Joachimstaler, p.116.
6. *Table Talk*, p.609.
7. Fest, *Hitler*, p.72.
8. William L. Shirer, *Berlin Diary*, New York, 1941, p.137.
9. Harold Nicolson, *Diaries and Letters Vol.2: The War Years 1939–45*, New York, 1967, p.39.
10. Rauschning, p.85.
11. Kershaw, *Myth*, p.33.
12. Rauschning, p.89.
13. Hoffmann, *Friend*, pp.51–2.
14. Sereny, p.13.
15. Sereny, pp.156–7.
16. Sereny, p.237.
17. Richard Grunberger, *The Twelve-Year Reich: A Social History of Nazi Germany 1933–1945*, New York, 1971, p.121.
18. Pauline Kohler in *OSS Source Book*, p.677, quoted in Waite, p.49.
19. Thomas, p.36.
20. Fritz Wiedemann, *Der Mann der Feldherr werden wollte, Erlebnisse und Erfahrungen des Vorgesetzten Hitlers im I. Weltkreig und seines späteren Persönlichen Adjutanten*, Munich, 1964, pp.25–7.
21. Schroeder, pp.152 and 158.
22. Joachimstaler, pp.161–2.
23. Joachimstaler, p.141.
24. *Monologe*, p.77.
25. Friedrich Wiedemann, *Der Mann der Feldherr werden wollte*.
26. Irving, *Goebbels*, between pp.204 and 205.
27. *Monologe*, p.71.
28. *Table Talk*, p.44.
29. Fest, *Hitler*, p.14

Chapter 6: Thundering Demon

1. Haffner, *Ailing Empire*, pp.107–19.
2. Karl Mayr, 'I was Hitler's Boss', *Current History*, November 1941, quoted in Joachimstaler, p.186, and Knopp, p.134.
3. Knopp, pp.132–3.
4. Joachimstaler, pp.216–218.
5. Craig, pp.411–12.
6. Klaus Mann, *The Turning Point*, New York, 1942, p.44.
7. *Mein Kampf*, pp.190–1.
8. Karl Alexander von Müller, *Im Wandel einer Welt: Erinnerungen 1919–32*, Munich, 1966.
9. *Süddeutche Arbeiterzeitung*, Stuttgart, 5 October 1931, and *Pfälzische Post*, Ludwigshafen, 28 October 1931.
10. Report by Oberleutnant Bendt to Gruppenkommando 4, 25 August 1919, quoted in Joachimstaler, p.247.
11. Letter from Karl Mayr to Wolfgang Kapp, 24 September 1919, quoted in Joachimstaler, p.229.
12. *Mein Kampf*, p.323.
13. *Völkischer Beobachter*, 14 August 1921.
14. Bracher, p.128.
15. Fest, *Hitler*, p.146.
16. Hitler, quoted in Rauschning, p.89, and in Fest, *Hitler*, p.144.
17. de Jonge, p.93.
18. Zweig, p.237.
19. Heiden, p.377.
20. Strasser, p.74.
21. Rauschning, p.68.

Chapter 7: Mothers and Daughters

1. *Mein Kampf*, p.56.
2. Rauschning, pp.258–9.
3. Lutz Becker, conversation with the author, 15 September 1996.
4. Herbert Blank in *Adolf Hitler Wilhelm III*, quoted in *Zwischenspiel Hitler: Ziele und Wirklichkeit des Nazionalsozialismus*, Vienna, 1932.
5. Hanfstaengl, p.89.
6. Eva G. Reichmann, *Hostages of Civilisation: The Sources of National Socialist Anti-Semitism*, London, 1950, quoted in Fest, *Face*, p.567.
7. Adolf Hitler file in Franklin Delano Roosevelt Library, Washington DC.
8. Knopp, p.40.
9. Maser, pp.192–3.
10. Hanfstaengl, p.80.
11. Hanfstaengl, p.43.
12. Görlitz and Quint, p.145.
13. Friedelind Wagner, *The Royal Family of Bayreuth*, London, 1948, quoted in Bullock, *Hitler*, p.80.
14. Rauschning, p.30.
15. Eitner, pp.89–90.
16. *Table Talk*, p.212.
17. Sereny, p.119.
18. *Table Talk*, pp.212–13.
19. Karl and Jeanetta Lyle Menninger, *Love against Hate*, New York, 1942, p.57, quoted in Waite, p.143.
20. Hanfstaengl, p.52.
21. David Pryce Jones, *Unity Mitford: A Quest*, London, 1976, p.168.
22. Gun, p.125.
23. Eitner, p.232.
24. Hanfstaengl, pp.60–1.
25. *Der Spiegel*, 1965, No.19, p.122.
26. Gun, p.77.
27. Irving, *War Path*, p.108.
28. Hoffmann, *Friend*, p.42.
29. Hoffmann, *Friend*, pp.43–5.
30. Hoffmann, *Friend*, pp.44–9.
31. Hoffmann, *Friend*, pp.15–16.

Chapter 8: Putsch

1. Letter from Thomas Mann to his brother Heinrich, 17 February 1923, *Thomas Mann–Heinrich Mann Briefwechsel 1900–1949*, Frankfurt, 1975.
2. Bullock, *Hitler and Stalin*, p.92.
3. Bracher, p.144.
4. Fest, *Hitler*, p.172.
5. Bracher, pp.142–6.
6. Quoted in Fest, *Hitler*, p.184.
7. Fest, *Face*, p.187.
8. Hanfstaengl, pp.107–8.
9. Hanfstaengl, pp.110–12.
10. Heinrich Bennecke, *Hitler und die SA*, Munich, 1962, pp.103–4, quoted in Bracher, p.157.
11. Lothar Gruchmann, *Justiz im Dritten Reich 1933–40*, Munich, 1988, p. 50.
12. Kershaw, *Hitler*, p.42.
13. Fest, *Hitler*, p.193.
14. Fest, *Hitler*, p.193.
15. Hanfstaengl, p.114.

Chapter 9: Reaching My Peak

1. Haffner, *Ailing State*, p.150.
2. Rauschning, p.165.
3. Sereny, p.119.
4. *Table Talk*, pp.283–4.
5. *Table Talk*, p.629.

6. *Table Talk*, p.717.
7. *Table Talk*, p.294.
8. *Table Talk*, p.294.
9. Julius Schaub, unpublished memoirs, Institut für Zeitgeschichte, Munich, Irving Collection ED 100/202.
10. *Table Talk*, p.215.
11. Letter from Hitler to Maria Reiter, 8 February 1927, quoted in Knopp, p.135.
12. Speer, p.46.
13. Rauschning, p.22.
14. Schwarzwalder, p.141.
15. H. von Schirach, p.49.
16. Schroeder, p.172.
17. Fest, *Hitler*, p.236.
18. Fest, *Hitler*, p.254.
19. Peter D. Stachura, 'Der Fall Strasser: Gregor Strasser, Hitler and National Socialism 1930–32' in Peter D. Stachura (ed.), *The Shaping of the Nazi State*, London, 1978.
20. Bullock, *Hitler*, p.134.
21. Friedrich Nietzsche, *Also Sprach Zarathustra*, Part III, *The Wanderer*.
22. Speer, p.46.
23. Rauschning, p.22.
24. Arthur Koestler, 'Hitler and His Godfathers', *Observer*, 30 January 1983.
25. Interview with Ignatius Phayre, *Current History*, July 1936, quoted in Toland, p.394.

Chapter 10: A Darling Thing

1. Rosenbaum, *Vanity Fair*.
2. H. von Schirach, pp.46–7.
3. Toland, p.229.
4. Quoted in Waite, p.226.
5. H. von Schirach, p.50.
6. Schroeder, p.235.
7. Bridget Hitler, p.59.
8. Bridget Hitler, p.351.
9. B. von Schirach, p.104.
10. Gun, p.20.
11. Toland, p.229.
12. Görlitz and Quint, p.299.
13. Julius Schaub, unpublished memoirs, Institut für Zeitgeschichte, Munich, Irving Collection, ED 100/202.
14. Gun, p.25.
15. Rolf Rietzler, 'Das Grab von Onkel Adolfs Nichte', *Der Spiegel*, 1987, No.24, pp.83–97.
16. Rosenbaum, *Vanity Fair*.
17. Pätzold and Weissbecker, p.123.
18. H. von Schirach, pp.239–40.
19. Egon Hanfstaengl, quoted in Knopp, p.147.
20. Hanfstaengl, p.162.
21. B. von Schirach, quoted in Waite, p.226.
22. Julius Schaub, unpublished memoirs.
23. Hoffmann, *Friend*, p.124.
24. H. von Schirach, p.49.
25. H. von Schirach, p.51.
26. Gun, p.21.
27. Schroeder, p.61.
28. Gun, p.21.
29. Hanfstaengl, pp.66–7.
30. H. von Schirach, p.55.
31. Schroeder, p.296.
32. Julius Schaub, unpublished memoirs.
33. H. von Schirach, p.65.
34. B. von Schirach, pp.104–5.
35. Josef Goebbels, unpublished diary for 30 March 1928, quoted in Irving, *Goebbels*, p.552.
36. Gun, pp.20–1.
37. Toland, p.252.
38. Hanfstaengl, p.161.
39. H. von Schirach, p.62.

40. Gun, p.14.
41. Heiden, p.306, Gun, pp.92 and 183, and Friedelind Wagner, *Nacht über Bayreuth*, Cologne, 1994.
42. Hanfstaengl, German edition, p.232.
43. Unpublished letter from Geli to Emil Maurice, 24 December 1927, quoted by permission of the Munich auctioneers Hermann Historica, who sold it in 1993.
44. Josef Goebbels, unpublished diary for 19 October 1928.
45. Sereny, pp.192–3.
46. Knopp, p.160.
47. Traudl Junge, quoted in Sereny, pp.249–50.

Chapter 11: The Forest Glade

1. H. von Schirach, pp.55–9.
2. Knopp, p.131.
3. H. von Schirach, p.70.
4. B. von Schirach, pp.105–6.
5. B. von Schirach, p.106.
6. H. von Schirach, pp.59–60.
7. Hanfstaengl, German edition, p.232.
8. Hanfstaengl, pp.161–2.
9. Strasser, p.84.
10. Rolf Rietzler, 'Das Grab von Onkel Adolfs Nichte', *Der Spiegel*, 1987, No.24, pp.83–97.
11. Sereny, p.106.
12. Hanfstaengl, p.156.
13. Friedrich Nietzsche, *The Genealogy of Morals*, Second Essay, Section 17, quoted in Stern, p.43.
14. H. von Schirach, pp.51–4.
15. Waite, p.9.
16. H. von Schirach, pp.51–4.
17. Josef Goebbels, unpublished diary for 2 August 1929, quoted in Irving, *Goebbels*, p.84.
18. Schroeder, pp.153–4.
19. H. von Schirach, p.48.
20. David Irving, unpublished interview with Adolf Vogl and his wife, Institut für Zeitgeschichte, Munich.
21. David Irving, unpublished interview with Henriette von Schirach, Institut für Zeitgeschichte, Munich.
22. Hanfstaengl, pp.163–4.
23. Schroeder, pp.213 and 235–6.
24. Fromm, *Anatomy*, pp.409–11.
25. Friedrich Nietzsche, *Also Sprach Zarathustra*, Part I, *On Old Women and Young Ones*.
26. *Quick*, 3 May 1964, quoted in Waite, p.51.
27. H. von Schirach, p.243.
28. *Table Talk*, pp.352–3.
29. Jetzinger, p.130.
30. Sereny, pp.113–14.
31. Sereny, pp.287 and 136–7.
32. Gun, p.100, and Infield, *Eva and Adolf*, p.76.
33. Albert Speer, conversation with Erich Fromm, quoted in Fromm, *Anatomy*, p.411.

Chapter 12: Luxury and Terrorism

1. Schroeder, p.234.
2. Gun, pp.16–17.
3. Eva Braun's account to her sister, quoted in Gun, pp.57–9.
4. Toland, p.253.
5. H. von Schirach, p.62.
6. Gun, p.22.
7. Gun, p.23.
8. Toland, p.229.
9. Infield, *Eva and Adolf*, p.43.
10. Infield, *Eva and Adolf*, p.44.
11. H. von Schirach, p.64.
12. Clive James, 'Blaming the Germans', *New Yorker*, 22 April 1996.
13. Hans Kallenbach, *Mit Adolf Hitler auf der Festung Landsberg*, Munich, 4th edn, 1943.

Chapter 13: Things He Makes Me Do

1. Irving, *Goebbels*, pp.91–6.
2. Irving, *Goebbels*, p.96.
3. Hoffmann, *Hitler wie ich ihn sah*, pp.125–6.
4. Ilse Hess, interview with John Toland, quoted in Toland, pp.229–30.
5. H. von Schirach, pp.63–4, and Hoffmann, *Hitler wie ich ihn sah*, pp.125–6.
6. Hoffmann, *Friend*, p.151.
7. Hoffmann, *Hitler wie ich ihn sah*, p.126.
8. Waite, p.238.
9. Hanfstaengl, p.162.
10. Heiden, pp.303–4.
11. Schwarzwalder, p.155.
12. Hanfstaengl, pp.164–5.
13. Toland, p.252.
14. Schwarzwalder, p.154.
15. *OSS Source Book* 919.
16. *Liberty*, 20 December 1941, quoted in Infield, *Hitler's Secret Life*.
17. *OSS Source Book* 22, quoted in Waite, p.241, and Schwarzwalder, p. 156.
18. *Völkischer Beobachter*, 8 October 1937.
19. Hanfstaengl, pp.162–3.
20. Hanfstaengl, p.162.
21. Langer, p.134.
22. H.R. Trevor-Roper in *Book World*, 10 September 1972, quoted in Waite, p.237.

Chapter 14: Like Characters in a Western

1. H. von Schirach, p.64.
2. Heiden, p.351.
3. B. von Schirach, p.114.
4. Josef Goebbels, unpublished diaries, 16 September 1930.
5. Kershaw, *Myth*, p.31.
6. Kershaw, *Myth*, pp.31–2.
7. Hanfstaengl, p.167.
8. Julius Schaub, unpublished memoirs, Institut für Zeitgeschichte, Munich, Irving Collection, ED 100/202.
9. B. von Schirach, p.116.
10. Gun, pp.55–6.
11. Gun, pp.55–6.
12. H. von Schirach, pp.244–5.
13. B. von Schirach, p.138.
14. Julius Schaub, unpublished memoirs.
15. Julius Schaub, unpublished memoirs.
16. Gun, p.18.
17. H. von Schirach, p.67.

Chapter 15: Island of Liars

1. Police report from the Polizeidirektion München to the Staatsministerium des Innern, 28 September 1931, Bayerisches Hauptstaatsarchiv, Munich.
2. H. von Schirach, p.68.
3. Police report.
4. Waite, p.227.
5. Bridget Hitler, pp.71–5.
6. Hanfstaengl, pp.167–8.
7. Hanfstaengl, p.165.
8. Police report.
9. Police report.
10. *Volksbote*, 23 September 1931.
11. H. von Schirach, p.68.
12. Interview with Maria Reichert in Schulze-Wilde collection, quoted in Toland, pp.253–4.
13. Toland, p.953.
14. Gun, pp.17–18.
15. Toland, p.253.

16. Gun, p.67.
17. Toland, p.953.
18. Friedelind Wagner in *OSS Source Book* 938.

Chapter 16: Gentlemen from the Brown House

1. Görlitz and Quint, p.322.
2. Fest, *Face*, p.321.
3. Toland, p.255.
4. Steinert, p.252.
5. Bullock, *Hitler and Stalin*, p.251.
6. Gun, p.16.
7. Hoffmann, *Hitler wie ich ihn sah*, p.129, and H. von Schirach, p.67.
8. Hoffmann, *Friend*, p.153.
9. Hoffman, *Friend*, p.153.
10. Report found by Anton Joachimstaler, and quoted by Rolf Rietzler in *Der Spiegel*, 1987, No.24, pp.83–97.
11. Hoffmann, *Friend*, p.154.
12. Hoffmann, *Hitler wie ich ihn sah*, p.130.
13. Gun, pp.17–18.
14. Hoffmann, *Hitler wie ich ihn sah*, p.130, and H. von Schirach, p.68.
15. Fest, *Hitler*, p.784.
16. H. von Schirach, p.68.
17. Hanfstaengl, p.166.

Chapter 17: Members of a Gang

1. Bridget Hitler, pp.102–3.
2. Hanfstaengl, p.168.
3. H. von Schirach, pp.79–80.
4. David Irving, unpublished interview with Leo Raubal, Institut für Zeitgeschichte, Munich.
5. David Irving, unpublished interview with Adolf Vogl, Institut für Zeitgeschichte, Munich.
6. David Irving, unpublished interview with Henriette von Schirach, Institut für Zeitgeschichte, Munich.
7. Schroeder, pp.42–3.
8. Joachimstaler, p.103.
9. Haffner, *Ailing Empire*, pp.178–9.
10. Hans-Günter Richardi and Klaus Schumann, *Geheimakte Gerlich/Bell: Röhms Pläne für ein Reich ohne Hitler*, Munich, 1993.
11. Irving, *Goebbels*.
12. Hanfstaengl, p.168.
13. Strasser, pp.210–13.
14. Rolf Rietzler in *Der Spiegel*, 1987, No.24, pp.83–97.

Chapter 18: Wrong Side of the Footlights

1. Wagener, p.357.
2. Hanfstaengl, p.167.
3. Schroeder, p.297.
4. I am indebted to Dr William Dorrell and Mrs Jane Dorrell, who discussed the trajectory with me.
5. David Irving, unpublished interview with Therese Linke, Institut für Zeitgeschichte, Munich.
6. *Table Talk*, p.681.
7. Haffner, *Meaning*, p.20.
8. Rauschning, p.99.
9. Hanfstaengl, p.167.
10. Conversation on 21 October 1996 with Michael Schäfer, who is writing a dissertation on Gerlich.
11. Hanfstaengl, p.176.
12. N.L. Krebs, diary entry for 24 September 1931, quoted in Hitler, *Reden, Schriften, Anordnungen Februar 1925 bis Januar 1933*, vol. 4, part 2, ed. Christian Hartmann, Munich, 1996.
13. N.L. Krebs, diary entry for 24 September 1931.
14. Hanfstaengl, p.168.
15. Hoffmann, *Hitler wie ich ihn sah*, pp.130–1.

16. Toland, pp.255–6.
17. Hoffmann, *Hitler wie ich ihn sah*, p.111.
18. Fest, *Face*, pp.35–9.
19. Haffner, *Ailing Empire*, p.183.

Chapter 19: No More Happy Picnics

1. Irving, *War Path*, p.110.
2. H. von Schirach, p.73.
3. H. von Schirach, p.68, and Gun, p.25.
4. H. von Schirach, p.74.
5. Schroeder, p.175.
6. Gun, pp.25–6.
7. H. von Schirach, pp.74–5.
8. H. von Schirach, p.179.
9. H. von Schirach, p.181.
10. Irving, *Goebbels*, pp.130–1.
11. Irving, *Goebbels*, pp.204 and 590.
12. Kohler, pp.131–2.
13. Albert Speer, conversation with Erich Fromm, quoted in Fromm, *Anatomy*, p.400.
14. Gun, pp.69–71.
15. Schroeder, p.156.
16. Sereny, p.193.
17. Wagener, p.358.
18. Fest, *Face*, p.399.
19. Sereny, p.109.

Epilogue: Mass Murderer

1. Browning, *Fateful Months*, p.4.
2. Browning, *Path to Genocide*, p.86.
3. Goldhagen, p.9.
4. Browning, *Path to Genocide*, p.100.
5. Kohler, p.72.
6. Dostoevsky, *The Brothers Karazamov*, Book 5, Chapter 5.
7. Fromm, *Escape from Freedom*, p.154.
8. Hanfstaengl, pp.168–9.
9. B. von Schirach, p.110.
10. Haffner, *Meaning*, p.111.
11. Communication to the author from Professor Ian Kershaw, 17 February 1997.
12. Sereny, p.420.
13. H. von Schirach, *Der Preis der Herrlichkeit – Erlebte Zeitgeschichte*, Munich, 1975, pp.5–10.
14. Helmut Heiber (ed.), *Hitlers Lagerbesprechungen*, Stuttgart, 1962, pp.779–80.
15. Haffner, *Meaning*, pp.136–7.
16. Sereny, p.474.
17. Fest, *Hitler*, pp.731–2.
18. Speer, p.439.
19. Speer, p.442.
20. Speer, p.440.
21. Haffner, *Meaning*, p.120.
22. Fest, *Hitler*, p.731.
23. Haffner, *Meaning*, p.162.
24. Rauschning, p.171, and Fest, *Hitler*, pp.466–7.
25. Fromm, *Anatomy*, p.404.
26. Thomas Mann, *Doktor Faustus*, Ch.25.
27. Fromm, *Anatomy*, p.404.
28. Schroeder, p.180.
29. Schroeder, p.180.
30. Rauschning, p.257.
31. Rauschning, pp.226–7.
32. Rauschning, p.256.

Bibliography

Bezymenski, Lev, *The Death of Adolf Hitler: Unknown Documents from Soviet Archives*, London, 1968

Bracher, Karl Dietrich, *The German Dictatorship: The Origins, Structure and Consequences of National Socialism*, trans. Jean Steinberg, New York, 1970

Browning, Christopher R., *Fateful Months: Essays on the Emergence of the Final Solution*, London, 1985

——*Ordinary Men: Reserve Police Battalion 101 and the Final Solution in Poland*, New York, 1992

——*The Path to Genocide: Essays on Launching the Final Solution*, Cambridge, 1992

Bullock, Alan, *Hitler: A Study in Tyranny*, London, 1952

——*Hitler and Stalin: Parallel Lives*, London, 1991, new ed. 1993

Carr, William H., *Hitler: A Study in Personality and Politics*, London, 1978

Craig, Gordon A., *Germany 1866–1945*, Oxford, 1978

de Jonge, Alex, *The Weimar Chronicle: Prelude to Hitler*, London, 1979

Eitner, Hans-Jürgen, *Der Führer*, Munich, 1981

Frank, Hans, *Im Angesicht des Galgens*, Munich, 1953

Fromm, Erich, *The Anatomy of Human Destructiveness*, London, 1974

——*Escape from Freedom*, New York, 1941

Goldhagen, Daniel Jonah, *Hitler's Willing Executioners: Ordinary Germans and the Holocaust*, New York, 1996

Görlitz, Walter and Quint, Herbert, *Adolf Hitler: Eine Biographie*, Stuttgart, 1952

Gun, Nerin E., *Eva Braun: Hitler's Mistress*, London, 1969

Haffner, Sebastian, *The Ailing Empire: Germany from Bismarck to Hitler*, trans. Jean Steinberg, New York, 1989

——*The Meaning of Hitler*, trans. Ewald Mosers, London, 1979

Hamann, Brigitte, *Hitlers Wien: Lehrjahre eines Diktators*, Munich, 1996

Hanfstaengl, Ernst, *Hitler: The Missing Years*, London, 1957

Heiden, Konrad, *Hitler*, authorised trans. (anon), Toronto, 1936

Hilberg, Raul, *The Destruction of the European Jews*, Chicago, 1961

Hitler, Adolf, *Hitler's Secret Book*, trans. Salvator Attanasio, New York, 1961

——*Mein Kampf*, trans. Ralph Manheim, London, 1969

——*Monologe im Führerhauptquartier 1941–44, Die Aufzeichnungen Heinrich Heims*, ed. Werner Jochmann, Hamburg, 1980

——*Table Talk 1941–1944*, trans. Norman Cameron and R. H. Stevens, London, 1953

Hitler, Bridget, *The Memoirs of Bridget Hitler*, ed. Michael Unger, London, 1979

Hoffmann, Heinrich, *Hitler Was My Friend*, London, 1955

——*Hitler wie ich ihn sah*, Munich, 1974

Infield, Glenn B., *Eva and Adolf*, New York, 1974

——*Hitler's Secret Life*, New York, 1979

Irving, David, *Goebbels: Mastermind of the Third Reich*, London, 1996

——*The War Path: Hitler's Germany 1933–39*, New York, 1978

Jenks, William A., *Vienna and the Young Hitler*, New York, 1960

Jetzinger, Fritz, *Hitler's Youth*, trans. Lawrence Wilson, London, 1958

Joachimstaler, Anton, *Korrektur einer Biographie: Adolf Hitler 1908–1920*, Munich, 1989

Jones, J. Sydney, *Hitler in Vienna 1907–13*, London, 1983

Kershaw, Ian, *Hitler*, London, 1991

——*The Hitler Myth: Image and Reality in the Third Reich*, Oxford, 1987

Kohler, Pauline, *The Woman Who Lived in Hitler's House*, New York, 1972

Knopp, Guido, *Hitler: Eine Bilanz*, Berlin, 1995

Kubizek, August, *Young Hitler: The Story of Our Friendship*, trans. E. V. Anderson, London, 1954, new ed. 1973

Langer, Walter, *The Mind of Adolf Hitler: The Secret Wartime Report*, New York, 1972

Maser, Werner, *Hitler: Legend, Myth and Reality*, trans. Peter and Betty Ross, London, 1973

Matcham, Samuel W., Jr., *Why Hitler?: The Genesis of the Nazi Reich*, Westport, Connecticut, 1996

Olden, Rudolf, *Hitler*, trans. Walter Ettinghausen, New York, 1936

Pätzold, Kurt and Weissbecker, Manfred, *Adolf Hitler: Eine Politische Biographie*, Leipzig, 1995

Petrova, Ada and Watson, Peter, *The Death of Hitler*,

Rauschning, Hermann, *Hitler Speaks: A Series of Political Conversations with Adolf Hitler on his Real Aims*, London, 1940

Rietzler, Rolf, 'Das Grab von Onkel Adolfs Nichte', *Der Spiegel*, 1987, no. 24, pp. 83–99

Rosenbaum, Ron, 'Explaining Hitler', *New Yorker*, 1 May 1995

——'Hitler's Doomed Angel', *Vanity Fair*, April 1992

von Schirach, Baldur, *Ich glaubte an Hitler*

von Schirach, Henriette, *Frauen um Hitler. Nach Materialen von Henriette von Schirach*, Munich, 1983

Schorske, Carl, *Fin-de-Siècle Vienna: Politics and Culture*, London, 1980

Schroeder, Christa, *Er war mein Chef: Aus dem Nachlass der Sekretärin von Adolf Hitler*, ed. Anton Joachimstaler, Munich, 1985

Schwarzwalder, Willi, *Hitlers Geld*, Munich, 1995

Sereny, Gitta, *Albert Speer: His Battle with Truth*, London, 1995

Shirer, William L., *The Rise and Fall of the Third Reich*, London, 1960

Speer, Albert, *Inside the Third Reich*, trans. Richard and Clara Winston, London, 1970

Steinert, Marlis, *Hitler*, trans. from French into German Guy Montag and Volker Wieland, Munich, 1994

Stern, J. P., *The Führer and the People*, London, 1975

Stierlin, Helm, *Adolf Hitler: Familienperspektiven*, Frankfurt, 1975, new ed. 1995

Stone, Norman, *Hitler*, London, 1980

Strasser, Otto, *Hitler and I*, trans. Gwenda David and Eric Mosbacher, London, 1940

Thomas, Hugh, *Doppelgängers: The Truth about the Bodies in the Berlin Bunker*, London, 1995

Toland, John, *Adolf Hitler*, New York, 1976

Trevor-Roper, Hugh, *The Last Days of Hitler*, London, 1947

Tyrell, Albrecht, *Vom Trommler zum Führer: Der Wandel von Hitlers Selbstverständnis 1919–24*, Munich, 1975

Wagener, Otto, *Hitler aus nächster Nähe: Aufzeichnungen eines Vertrauten 1929–32*, ed H. A. Turner, Berlin, 1978

Waite, Robert G. L., *The Psychopathic God Adolf Hitler*, New York, 1977

Wiesenthal, Simon, *Justice Not Vengeance*, trans. Ewald Osers, London, 1989

Zweig, Stefan, *The World of Yesterday*, London, 1953

Index